CREDIT RATING AGENCY REFORM

CREDIT RATING AGENCY REFORM

JOHN DE LUCA
AND
PAUL RUSSO
EDITORS

Nova Science Publishers, Inc.
New York

LIBRARY OF CONGRESS CATALOGING-IN-PUBLICATION DATA
Available upon request

ISBN: 978-1-60692-192-0

Published by Nova Science Publishers, Inc. ✤ New York

CONTENTS

PREFACE

This book discusses the three amendments that the SEC Commission is proposing that would impose additional requirements on nationally recognized statistical rating organizations ("NRSROs") in order to address concerns about the integrity of their credit rating procedures in the light of the role they played in determining credit ratings for securities collateralized by or linked to subprime residential mortgages. The Commission today makes a proposal related to structured finance products rating symbology. Thirdly, this book discusses the rule amendments that the Commission intends to propose that would be intended to reduce undue reliance in the Commission's rules on NRSRO ratings.

In August 2007, the Securities and Exchange Commission's Staff initiated examinations of three credit rating agencies, to review their role in the recent turmoil in the subprime mortgage-related securities markets. The purpose of the examinations was to develop an understanding of the practices of the rating agencies surrounding the rating of RMBS and CDOs. This book includes a summary report by the Commission's Staff of the issues identified in those examinations.

Finally, an overview of the subprime mortgage securitization process is provided as well as the seven key informational frictions that arise. Ways that market participants work to minimize these frictions is discussed and how this process broke down is speculated. Key structural features of a typical subprime securitization is presented, and how rating agencies assign credit ratings to mortgage-backed securities is documented. How these agencies monitor the performance of mortgage pools over time is also outlined.

Chapter 1 - Today, in the first of three related actions the Commission is proposing rule amendments that would impose additional requirements on nationally recognized statistical rating organizations ("NRSROs") in order to address concerns about the integrity of their credit rating procedures and methodologies in the light of the role they played in determining credit ratings for securities collateralized by or linked to subprime residential mortgages. Second, the Commission also today makes a proposal related to structured finance products rating symbology. And third, two weeks from today, the Commission intends to propose rule amendments that would be intended to reduce undue reliance in the Commission's rules on NRSRO ratings.

Chapter 2 - In August 2007, the Securities and Exchange Commission's Staff initiated examinations of three credit rating agencies -- Fitch Ratings, Ltd. ("Fitch"), Moody's Investor Services, Inc. ("Moody's") and Standard & Poor's Ratings Services ("S&P") -- to review their role in the recent turmoil in the subprime mortgage-related securities markets.

These firms registered with the Commission as nationally recognized statistical rating organizations in September 2007 (collectively, the examined firms are referred to in this report as the “rating agencies” or “NRSROs”). These firms were not subject to the Credit Rating Agency Reform Act of 2006 or Commission regulations for credit rating agencies until September 2007. The focus of the examinations was the rating agencies’ activities in rating subprime residential mortgage-backed securities (“RMBS”) and collateralized debt obligations (“CDOs”) linked to subprime residential mortgage-backed securities. The purpose of the examinations was to develop an understanding of the practices of the rating agencies surrounding the rating of RMBS and CDOs. This is a summary report by the Commission’s Staff of the issues identified in those examinations.

Chapter 3 - In this paper, we provide an overview of the subprime mortgage securitization process and the seven key informational frictions that arise. We discuss the ways that market participants work to minimize these frictions and speculate on how this process broke down. We continue with a complete picture of the subprime borrower and the subprime loan, discussing both predatory borrowing and predatory lending. We present the key structural features of a typical subprime securitization, document how rating agencies assign credit ratings to mortgage-backed securities, and outline how these agencies monitor the performance of mortgage pools over time. Throughout the paper, we draw upon the example of a mortgage pool securitized by New Century Financial during 2006.

In: Credit Rating Agency Reform
Editors: John De Luca and Paul Russo, pp. 1-93
ISBN: 978-1-60692-192-0

Chapter 1

CREDIT RATING AGENCY BACKGROUND

Securities and Exchange Commission

I. BACKGROUND

A. Introduction

Beginning in the early 2000s, originators started to increasingly make residential mortgage loans based on lower underwriting standards ("subprime loans").[1] For the first few years there did not appear to be any negative repercussions from this lending practice. However, beginning in mid-2006, home values leveled off and soon began to decline, which, in turn, led to a corresponding increase in delinquencies and, ultimately, defaults in subprime loans.[2] This marked increase in subprime loan delinquencies and, ultimately, in defaults has had substantial adverse effects on the markets for, and market values and liquidity of, residential mortgage-backed securities ("RMBS") backed by subprime loans and on collateralized debt obligations ("CDOs") linked to such loans (collectively "subprime RMBS and CDOs").[3]

Moreover, the impacts from the troubles experienced by subprime loans extended beyond subprime RMBS and CDOs to the broader credit markets and the economy as a whole.[4] As a result, the parties that participated in various parts of the process of making subprime loans, packaging them into subprime RMBS and CDOs, and selling these debt instruments, including mortgage brokers, loan originators, securities sponsors and underwriters, and NRSROs have come under intense scrutiny. Today, the Commission is proposing a series of new requirements that are designed to address concerns that have been raised about NRSROs in light of the role they played in this process. Additionally, two weeks from today, the Commission will complete its proposal of this series of rule changes. These changes would be intended to reduce undue reliance in the Commission's rules on NRSRO ratings, thereby promoting increased investor due diligence.

B. The Credit Rating Agency Reform Act of 2006

The purpose of the Credit Rating Agency Reform Act of 2006 (the "Rating Agency Act"), enacted on September 29, 2006, is to "improve ratings quality for the protection of investors and in the public interest by fostering accountability, transparency, and competition in the credit rating industry."[5] The operative provisions of the Rating Agency Act became applicable upon the Commission's adoption in June 2007 of a series of rules implementing a registration and oversight program for credit rating agencies that register as NRSROs.[6]

To date, a total of nine credit rating agencies have been granted registration with the Commission as NRSROs pursuant to the Rating Agency Act and the rules thereunder.[7[7] These registrants include the credit rating agencies most active in rating subprime RMBS and CDOs: Fitch Ratings, Inc. ("Fitch"), Moody's Investors Service ("Moody's"), and Standard and Poor's Rating Services ("S&P").[8] In the fall of 2007, the Commission, exercising the new authority conferred by the Rating Agency Act, began a staff examination of the NRSROs' activities in rating subprime RMBS and CDOs in order to review whether they adhered to their stated and documented procedures and methodologies for rating these debt instruments and the extent, if any, to which their ratings may have been impaired by conflicts of interest.[9]

In addition to the examination, the Commission has worked closely with other regulators and supervisors of the financial markets in analyzing the credit market turmoil and in developing recommendations and principles for market participants, including NRSROs.[10] For example, the President's Working Group on Financial Markets issued a Policy Statement on Financial Market Developments in March 2008.[11] Further, as a member of the International Organization of Securities Commissions ("IOSCO"), the Commission played a substantial role in drafting The Role of Credit Rating Agencies in Structured Finance Markets, which was issued for consultation by IOSCO in March 2008.[12] Also, the Commission, as part of its participation in the Financial Stability Forum, worked with its counterparts in the US and abroad on The Report of the Financial Stability Forum on Enhancing Market and Institutional Resilience released in April 2008, which discussed credit rating agencies.[13]

These and other efforts have assisted the Commission in identifying a number of areas in which its current NRSRO rules could be augmented to address concerns about the role NRSROs played in the credit market turmoil.[14] As a result, the Commission is proposing amendments to its existing NRSRO rules and a new rule with the goal of improving the quality of credit ratings determined by NRSROs generally and, in particular, for structured finance products such as RMBS and CDOs.[15] These proposals and the proposals to be considered in two weeks are designed to:

- Enhance the disclosure and comparability of credit ratings performance statistics;
- Increase the disclosure of information about structured finance products;
- Require more information about the procedures and methodologies used to determine credit ratings for structured finance products;
- Strengthen internal control processes through reporting requirements; and
- Address conflicts of interest arising from the process of rating structured finance products; and

- Reduce undue reliance in the Commission's rules on NRSRO ratings, thereby promoting increased investor due diligence.

The Commission believes these proposals would further the purpose of the Rating Agency Act to improve the quality of NRSRO credit ratings by fostering accountability, transparency, and competition in the credit rating industry.[16]

C. The Role of Credit Ratings in the Credit Market Turmoil

The growth in the origination of subprime loans began in the early 2000s.[17] For example, Moody's reports that subprime loans amounted to $421 billion of the $3.03 8 trillion in mortgages originated in 2002 (14%) and $640 billion of the $2.886 trillion in mortgages originated in 2006 (22%).[18] This growth was facilitated by steadily rising home values and a low interest rate environment.[19] In addition, increases in the breadth of the credit risk transfer markets as a result of new investors willing to purchase credit based structured finance products provided an opportunity for lenders to originate subprime loans and then move them off their balance sheets by packaging and selling them through the securitization process to investors as subprime RMBS and CDOs.[20] The investors in subprime RMBS and CDOs included domestic and foreign mutual funds, pension funds, hedge funds, banks, insurance companies, special investment vehicles, and state government operated funds.

This "originate to distribute" business model created demand for residential mortgage loans, including subprime loans. For example, according to Moody's, of the approximately $2.5 trillion worth of mortgage loans originated in 2006, $1.9 trillion were securitized into RMBS and approximately 25%, or $520 billion worth, of these loans were categorized as subprime.[21] The demands of the loan securitization markets encouraged lenders to lower underwriting standards to maintain a steady volume of loans and to use less traditional products such as adjustable rate, negative amortization, and closed-end second lien mortgages.[22]

1. The Creation of Subprime RMBS and CDOs

The creation of an RMBS begins by packaging a pool of mortgage loans, usually numbering in the thousands, and transferring them to a bankruptcy remote trust. The trust purchases the loan pool and becomes entitled to the interest and principal payments made by the borrowers. The trust finances the purchase of the loan pool through the issuance of RMBS. The monthly interest and principal payments from the loan pool are used to make monthly interest and principal payments to the investors in the RMBS.

The trust typically issues different classes of RMBS (known as "tranches") offering a sliding scale of coupon rates based on the level of credit protection afforded to the security. Credit protection is designed to shield the tranche securities from loss of interest and principal arising from defaults of the loans backing the RMBS. The degree of credit protection afforded a tranche security is known as its "credit enhancement" and is provided through several means. The primary source of credit enhancement is subordination, which creates a hierarchy of loss absorption among the tranche securities. For example, if a trust issued securities in 10 different tranches of securities, the first (or senior) tranche would have nine subordinate tranches, the next highest tranche would have eight subordinate tranches and so on down the capital structure. Losses of interest and principal experienced by the trust from delinquencies and defaults among loans in the pool are allocated first to the lowest tranche until its principal amount is exhausted and then to the next lowest tranche and so on up the capital structure. Consequently, the senior tranche would not incur any loss until the principal amounts from all the lower tranches have been exhausted through the absorption of losses from the underlying loans.

A second form of credit enhancement is over-collateralization, which is the amount that the principal balance of the mortgage pool underlying the trust exceeds the principal balance of the tranche securities issued by the trust. This excess principal creates an additional "equity" tranche below the lowest tranche security to absorb losses. In the example above, the equity tranche would sit below the 10th tranche security and protect it from the first losses experienced as a result of defaulting loans.

A third form of credit enhancement is excess spread, which consists of the amount by which the interest derived from the underlying loans in the aggregate exceeds interest payments due to investors in the tranche securities in the aggregate plus the administrative expenses of the trust such as fees due the loan servicer as well as premiums due on derivatives contracts and bond insurance. In other words, the excess spread is the amount that the monthly interest income from the pool of loans exceeds the weighted average interest due to the RMBS bondholders. This excess spread can be used to build up loss reserves or pay off delinquent interest payments due to a tranche security.

A fourth form of credit enhancement sometimes employed is bond insurance. When used, bond insurance is typically purchased only for the senior RMBS tranche.

The creation of a typical CDO is similar to that of an RMBS. A bankruptcy remote trust is created to hold the CDO's assets and issue its securities. The underlying assets, however, are generally debt securities rather than mortgage loans. The CDO trust uses the interest and principal payments from the approximately 200 underlying debt securities to make interest and principal payments to investors in the securities issued by the trust. The trust is structured to provide differing levels of credit enhancement to the securities it issues. Similar to RMBS, credit enhancement is provided through subordination, over-collateralization, excess spread, and bond insurance. In addition to the underlying assets, one significant difference between a CDO and an RMBS is that the CDO may be actively managed such that its underlying assets change over time, whereas the mortgage loan pool underlying an RMBS remains static for the most part.

In recent years, CDOs have been some of the largest purchasers of subprime RMBS and the drivers of demand for those securities. For example, according to Fitch, the average percentage of subprime RMB S in the collateral pools of CDOs it rated grew from 43.3% in 2003 to 71.3% in 2006.[23] Generally, the CDOs holding subprime RMBS issued fell into one of two categories: high grade and mezzanine. High grade CDOs are generally defined as those that hold RMBS tranches with AAA, AA, or A credit ratings, whereas mezzanine CDOs are those that hold RMBS tranches rated predominantly BBB. Securities issued by mezzanine CDOs pay higher yields than those issued by high grade CDOs since the BBB-rated RMBS underlying the mezzanine CDOs pay higher yields than the AAA to A rated RMBS underlying high grade CDOs. In addition to CDOs holding subprime RMBS, a market for CDOs holding other CDOs that held subprime RMBS developed in recent years. These debt instruments are known as "CDOssquared."

As the market for mortgage related CDOs grew, CDO issuers began to use credit default swaps to replicate the performance of subprime RMBS and CDOs. In this case, rather than purchasing subprime RMBS or CDOs, the CDO entered into credit default swaps referencing subprime RMBS or CDOs, or indexes on RMBS. These CDOs, in some cases, are composed entirely of credit default swaps ("synthetic CDOs") or a combination of credit default swaps and cash RMBS ("hybrid CDOs"). The use of credit default swaps allowed the CDO securities to be issued more quickly, since the issuer did not have to wait to accumulate actual RMBS for the underlying collateral pool.

2. Determining Credit Ratings for Subprime RMBS and CDOs

A key step in the process of creating and ultimately selling a subprime RMBS and CDO is the issuance of a credit rating for each of the tranches issued by the trust (with the exception of the most junior "equity" tranche). The credit rating for each rated tranche indicated the credit rating agency's view as to the creditworthiness of the debt instrument in terms of the likelihood that the issuer would default on its obligations to make interest and principal payments on the debt instrument.[24] To varying degrees, many investors rely on credit ratings in making the decision to purchase subprime RMBS or CDOs, particularly with respect to the senior AAA rated tranches. Some investors use the credit ratings to assess the risk of the debt instruments. In part, this may be due to the large number of debt instruments in the market and their complexity. Other investors use credit ratings to satisfy client investment mandates regarding the types of securities they can invest in or to satisfy regulatory requirements based on certain levels of credit ratings, or a combination of these conditions. Moreover, investors typically only have looked to ratings issued by Fitch, Moody's, and S&P, which causes the arrangers[25] of the subprime RMBS and CDOs to use these three NRSROs to obtain credit ratings for the tranche securities they brought to market.

The procedures followed by these three NRSROs in developing ratings for subprime RMBS are generally similar. The arranger of the RMBS initiates the rating process by sending the credit rating agency a range of data on each of the subprime loans to be held by the trust (e.g., principal amount, geographic location of the property, credit history and FICO score of the borrower, ratio of the loan amount to the value of the property, and type of loan: first lien, second lien, primary residence, secondary residence), the proposed capital structure of the trust, and the proposed levels of credit enhancement to be provided to each RMBS tranche issued by the trust. Upon receipt of the information, the NRSRO assigns a lead analyst who is responsible for analyzing the loan pool, proposed capital structure, and proposed credit enhancement levels and, ultimately, for formulating a ratings recommendation for a rating committee composed of analysts and/or senior-level personnel not involved in the analytic process.

The next step in the ratings process is the development of predictions, based on a quantitative expected loss model and other qualitative factors, as to how many of the loans in the collateral pool would default under stresses of varying severity. This analysis also includes assumptions as to how much principal would be recovered after a defaulted loan is foreclosed. Each NRSRO generally uses between 40 and 60 specific credit characteristics to analyze each loan in the collateral pool of an RMBS in order to assess the potential future performance of the loan under various possible scenarios. These characteristics include the loan information described above as well as the amount of equity that the borrowers have in their homes, the amount of documentation provided by borrowers to verify their assets and/or income levels, and whether the borrowers intend to rent or occupy the homes.[26]

The purpose of this loss analysis is to determine how much credit enhancement a given tranche security would need for a particular category of credit rating. The severest stress test (i.e., the one that would result in the greatest number of defaults among the underlying loans) is run to determine the amount of credit enhancement required for an RMBS tranche issued by the trust to receive an AAA rating. For example, this test might result in an output that predicted that under the "worst case" scenario, 40 percent of the loans in the underlying pool would default and that after default the trust would recover only 50 percent of the principal amount of each loan in foreclosure. Consequently, to get an AAA rating, an RMBS tranche security issued by the trust would need credit enhancement sufficient to cover at least 20 percent of the principal amount of all the RMBS tranches issued by the trust. In other words, absent other forms of credit enhancement such as excess spread, at least 20 percent of the principal amount of the RMBS tranches issued by the trust, including the equity tranche, would have to be subordinate to the senior tranche and, therefore, obligated to absorb the losses resulting from 40% of the underlying loans defaulting.[27] The next severest stress test is run to determine the amount of credit enhancement required of the AA tranche and so on down the capital structure. The lowest rated tranche (typically BB or B) is analyzed under a more benign market scenario. Consequently, its required level of credit enhancement – typically provided primarily or exclusively by a subordinate equity tranche – is based on the number of loans expected to default in the normal course given the lowest possible level of macroeconomic stress.

Following the determination of the level of credit enhancement required for each credit rating category, the next step in the ratings process is to check the proposed capital structure of the RMBS against these requirements. For example, if the proposed structure would create a senior RMBS tranche that had 18 percent of the capital structure subordinate to it (the other RMBS tranches, including, as applicable, an equity tranche), the analyst reviewing the transaction might conclude that based on the output of the loss model the senior tranche should be rated AA since it would need 20 percent subordination to receive an AAA credit rating. Additionally, the analyst could take other factors into consideration such as the quality of the loan servicer or the actual performance of similar pools of loans underlying other RMBS trusts to determine that in this case 18 percent subordination would be sufficient to support an AAA rating (to the extent these factors were not covered by the model).

Typically, if the analyst concludes that the capital structure of the RMBS did not support the desired ratings – in the example above, if it determined that 18 percent credit enhancement is insufficient for the desired AAA rating – this preliminary conclusion would be conveyed to the arranger. The arranger could accept that determination and have the trust issue the securities with the proposed capital structure and the lower rating or adjust the structure to provide the requisite credit enhancement for the senior tranche to get the desired AAA rating (e.g., shift 2 percent of the principal amount of the senior tranche to a lower tranche or add or remove certain mortgages from the proposed asset pool). Generally, arrangers aim for the largest possible senior tranche, i.e., to provide the least amount of credit enhancement possible, since the senior tranche – as the highest rated tranche – pays the lowest coupon rate of the RMBS' tranches and, therefore, costs the arranger the least to fund.

The next step in the process is a cash flow analysis on the interest and principal expected to be received by the trust from the pool of subprime loans to determine whether it will be sufficient to pay the interest and principal due on each RMBS tranche issued by the trust. The NRSROs use quantitative cash flow models that analyze the amount of principal and interest payments expected to be generated from the loan pool each month over the terms of the RMBS tranche securities under various stress scenarios. The outputs of this model are compared against the priority of payments (the "waterfall") to the RMBS tranches specified in the trust legal documents. The waterfall documentation could specify over-collateralization and excess spread triggers that, if breached, would reallocate principal and interest payments from lower tranches to higher tranches until the minimum levels of over-collateralization and excess spread were reestablished. Ultimately, the monthly principal and interest payments derived from the loan pool need to be enough to satisfy the monthly payments of principal and interest due by the trust to the investors in the RMBS tranches as well as to cover the administrative expenses of the trust.

In addition to expected loss and cash flow analysis, the analysts review the legal documentation of the trust to evaluate whether it is bankruptcy remote, i.e., isolated from the effects of any potential bankruptcy or insolvency of the arranger. They also review operational and administrative risk associated with the trust, using the results of periodic examinations of the principal parties involved in the issuance of the security, including the mortgage originators, the issuer of the security, the servicer of the mortgages in the loan pool, and the trustee.[28] In assessing the servicer, for example, an NRSRO might review its past performance with respect to loan collection, billing, recordkeeping, and the treatment of delinquent loans.

Following these steps, the analyst develops a rating recommendation for each RMBS tranche, which then is presented to a rating committee composed of analysts and/or senior-level personnel not involved in the analytic process. The rating committee votes on the ratings for each tranche and usually approaches the arranger privately to notify it of the ratings decisions. In most cases, an arranger can appeal a rating decision, although the appeal is not always granted (and, if granted, may not necessarily result in any change in the rating decision). Final ratings decisions are published and subsequently monitored through surveillance processes. The NRSRO typically is paid only if the credit rating is issued, though sometimes it receives a breakup fee for the analytic work undertaken even if the credit rating is not issued.

The process for assigning ratings to subprime CDOs also involves a review of the creditworthiness of each tranche of the CDO. As with RMBS, the process centers on an examination of the pool of assets held by the trust and analysis of how they would perform individually and in correlation during various stress scenarios. However, this analysis is based primarily on the credit rating of each RMBS or CDO in the underlying pool or referenced through a credit default swap entered into by the CDO. In other words, the credit rating is the primary characteristic of the underlying debt instruments that the

NRSROs take into consideration when performing their loss analysis. Hence, this review of the debt instruments in the collateral pool and the potential correlations among those securities does not "look through" those securities to their underlying asset pools. The analysis, consequently, generally only goes one level down to the credit ratings of the underlying instruments or reference securities.

CDOs collateralized by RMBS or by other CDOs often are actively managed. Consequently, there can be frequent changes to the composition of the cash assets (RMBS or CDOs), synthetic assets (credit default swaps), or combinations of cash and synthetic assets in the underlying pool. As a result, NRSRO ratings for managed CDOs are based not on the closing date composition of the pool but instead on covenanted limits for each potential type of asset that could be put in the pool. Typically, following a post-closing period in which no adjustments can be made to a CDO's collateral pool, the CDO's manager has a predetermined period of several years in which to adjust that asset pool through various sales and purchases pursuant to covenants set forth in the CDO's indenture. These covenants set limitations and requirements for the collateral pools of CDOs, often by establishing minimum and maximum concentrations for certain types of securities or certain ratings.

NRSROs use a CDO's indenture guidelines to run "worst-case" scenarios based on the various permutations of collateral permitted under the indenture. For example, an indenture might specify that a CDO's collateral pool must include between 10 and 20 percent AAA-rated subprime RMBS, with the remaining 80 to 90 percent composed of investment-grade, but not AAA, subprime RMBS. In preparing a rating for that CDO, an NRSRO will run its models based on all possible collateral pools permissible under the indenture guidelines, placing the most weight on the results from the weakest potential pools (i.e., the minimum permissible amount, 10 percent, of AAA-rated securities and the lowest-rated investment grade securities for the remaining 90 percent). As with RMBS ratings, the model results are then compared against the capital structure of the proposed CDO to confirm that the level of subordination, over-collateralization and excess spread available to each tranche provides the necessary amount of credit enhancement to sustain a particular rating.

3. The Downgrades in Credit Ratings of Subprime RMBS and CDOs

As noted above, the development of the credit risk transfer markets gave rise to an "originate to distribute" model whereby mortgage loans are originated with the intent to securitize them. Under this model, arrangers earn fees from originating, structuring, and underwriting RMBS and servicing the loans underlying the RMBS, as well as frequently a third set of fees from structuring, underwriting, and managing CDOs composed of RMBS. Moreover, the yields offered by subprime RMBS and CDO tranches (as compared to other types of similarly rated debt instruments) led to increased investor demand for these debt instruments. The originate to distribute model creates incentives for originating high volumes of mortgage loans while simultaneously reducing the incentives to maintain high underwriting standards for making such loans. The continued growth of the housing market through 2006, which led to increased competition among lenders, also contributed to looser subprime loan underwriting standards.[29]

By mid-2006, however, the steady rise in home prices that had fueled this growth in subprime lending came to an end as prices began to decline.[30] Moreover, widespread areas of the country began to experience declines whereas, in the past, poor housing markets generally had been confined to distinct geographic areas.[31] The downturn in the housing market has been accompanied by a marked increase in delinquencies and defaults of subprime loans.[32]

The increases in delinquency and default rates have been concentrated in loans made in 2006 and 2007, which indicates that borrowers have been falling behind within months of the loans being made.[33] For example, by the fourth quarter of 2006, the percentage of subprime loans underlying RMBS rated by Moody's that were in default within six months of the loans being made stood at 3.54 percent, nearly four times the average six month default rate of 0.90 percent between the first quarter of 2002 and the second quarter of 2005. Similarly, default rates for subprime loans within 12 months of the loans being made rose to 7.39 percent as compared to 2.00 percent for the period from the first quarter of 2002 through the second quarter of 2005.[34] Figures released by S&P show similar deterioration in the performance of recent subprime loans.[35] According to S&P, the serious delinquency rate[36] for subprime loans underlying RMBS rated by S&P within twelve months of the initial rating was 4.97 percent of the current aggregate pool balance for subprime RMBS issued in 2005, 10.55 percent for subprime RMBS issued in 2006, and 15.19 percent for subprime RMBS issued in 2007.[37]

Along with the deterioration in the performance of subprime loans, there has been an increase in the losses incurred after the loans are foreclosed. According to S&P, the actual realized losses on loans underlying 2007 subprime RMBS after 12 months of seasoning were 65 percent higher than the losses recorded for RMBS issued in 2006 at the same level of seasoning.[38]

The rising delinquencies and defaults in subprime loans backing the RMBS rated by the NRSROs has exceeded the projections on which they based their initial ratings. Furthermore, the defaults and foreclosures on subprime loans have resulted in realizable losses to the lower RMBS tranches backed by the loans and, correspondingly, to the lower CDO tranches backed by those RMBS. As discussed above, the reduction in the amount of monthly principal and interest payments coming from the underlying pool of subprime loans or, in the case of a CDO, RMBS tranches or other CDO tranches is allocated to the tranches in ascending order. In addition to directly impairing the affected tranche, the losses – by reducing the principal amount of these tranches – decreased the level of subordination protecting the more senior tranches. In other words, losses suffered by the junior tranches of an RMBS or CDO directly reduced the level of credit enhancement – the primary factor considered by NRSROs in rating tranched securities – protecting the senior tranches of the instrument. These factors have caused the NRSROs to reevaluate, and in many cases downgrade, their ratings for these instruments.

- As of February 2008, Moody's had downgraded at least one tranche of 94.2 percent of the subprime RMBS deals it rated in 2006 (including 100 percent of 2006 RMBS deals backed by subprime second-lien mortgage loans) and 76.9 percent of all subprime RMBS deals it rated in 2007. Overall, 53.7 percent and 39.2 percent of 2006 and 2007 tranches, respectively, had been downgraded by that time. RMBS tranches backed by first lien loans issued in 2006 were downgraded an average of 6.0 notches from their original ratings, while RMBS tranches backed by second-lien loans issued that year were downgraded 9.7 notches on average. The respective figures for 2007 first- and second-lien backed tranches were 5.6 and 7.8 notches.[39]

- As of March 2008, S&P had downgraded 44.3 percent of the subprime RMBS tranches it had rated between the first quarter of 2005 and the third quarter of 2007, including 87.2 percent of second-lien backed securities. Downgrades to subprime RMBS issued in 2005 averaged four to six notches, while the average for those issued in 2006 and 2007 was 6.0 to 11 notches.[40]
- As of December 7, 2007, Fitch had issued downgrades to 1,229 of the 3,666 tranches of subprime RMBS issued in 2006 and the first quarter of 2007, representing a par value of $23.8 billion out of a total of $193 billion.[41] Subsequently, on February 1, 2008, Fitch placed all subprime first-lien RMBS issued in 2006 and the first half of 2007, representing a total outstanding balance of approximately $139 billion, on Rating Watch Negative.[42]

The extensive use of subprime RMB S in the collateral pools of CDOs has led to similar levels of downgrade rates for those securities as well. Moreover, the use of subprime RMB S as reference securities for synthetic CDOs magnified the effect of RMBS downgrades on CDO ratings. Surveillance of CDO credit ratings has been complicated by the fact that the methodologies used by the NRSROs to rate them relied heavily on the credit rating of the underlying RMBS or CDOs. Consequently, to adjust the CDO rating, the NRSROs first have needed to complete their reviews of the ratings for the underlying RMBS or adjust their methodologies to sufficiently account for the anticipated poor performance of the RMB S.[43] Ultimately, the NRSROs have downgraded a substantial number of CDO ratings.

- Over the course of 2007, Moody's issued 1,655 discrete downgrade actions (including multiple rating actions on the same tranche), which constituted roughly ten times the number of downgrade actions in 2006 and twice as many as in 2002, previously the most volatile year for CDOs. Further, the magnitude of the downgrades (number of notches) was striking. The average downgrade was roughly seven notches as compared to a previous average of three to four notches prior to 2007. In the words of a March 2008 report by Moody's, "[T]he scope and degree of CDO downgrades in 2007 was unprecedented."[44]
- As of April 1, 2008, S&P had downgraded 3,068 tranches from 705 CDO transactions, totaling $321.9 billion in issuance, and placed 443 ratings from 119 transactions, with a value of $33.8 billion, on CreditWatch negative, "as a result of stress in the U.S. residential mortgage market and credit deterioration of U.S. RMBS."[45]
- By mid-December, 2007, Fitch had issued downgrades to 158 of the 431 CDOs it had rated with exposure to RMBS.[46] Among the 30 CDOs with exposure to the subprime RMBS which "suffered the greatest extent and magnitude of negative rating migration," all but $82.7 million of the $20.7 billion in balance was downgraded.[47]

The scope and magnitude of these downgrades has caused a loss of confidence among investors in the reliability of RMBS and CDO credit ratings issued by the NRSROs.[48] This lack of confidence in the accuracy of NRSRO ratings has been a factor in the broader dislocation in the credit markets.[49] For example, the complexity of assessing the risk of structured finance products and the lack of commonly accepted methods for measuring the risk has caused investors to leave the market, including the market for AAA instruments, particularly investors that had relied primarily on NRSRO credit ratings in assessing whether to purchase these instruments.[50] This has had a significant impact on the liquidity of the market for these instruments.[51]

In the wake of these events, the NRSROs that rated subprime RMBS and CDOs have come under intense criticism and scrutiny. It has been suggested that changes may be needed to address the conflicts of interest inherent in the process of rating RMBS and CDOs.[52] The NRSROs that have been the primary ratings providers for subprime RMBS and related CDOs each operate under an "issuer-pays" model in which they are paid by the arranger to rate a proposed RMBS or CDO. The arranger has an economic interest in obtaining the highest credit rating possible for each security issued by the trust and the NRSRO has an economic interest in having the arranger select it to rate the next RMBS or CDO brought by the arranger to market. Observers have questioned whether, given the incentives created by this arrangement, the NRSROs are able to issue unbiased ratings, particularly as the volume of deals brought by certain arrangers increased in the mid-2000s.[53] The above concerns are compounded by the arrangers' ability to "ratings shop." Ratings shopping is the process by which an arranger will bring its proposed RMBS and CDO transaction to multiple NRSROs and choose, on a deal-wide or trancheby-tranche basis, which two (or in some cases one) to use based on the preliminary ratings of the NRSROs.

In addition, the interaction between the NRSRO and the arranger during the RMBS and CDO rating process has raised concerns that the NRSROs are rating products they designed (i.e., evaluating their own work).[54] A corporate issuer is more constrained in how it can adjust in response to an NRSRO to improve its creditworthiness in order to obtain a higher rating. In the context of structured finance products, the arranger has much more flexibility to make adjustments to obtain a desired credit rating by, for example, changing the composition of the assets in the pool held by the trust or the subordination levels of the tranche securities issued by the trust. In fact, an arranger frequently will inform the NRSRO of the rating it wishes to obtain for each tranche and will choose an asset pool, trust structure, and credit enhancement levels based on its understanding of the NRSROs' quantitative and qualitative models. The credit analyst will use the expected loss and cash flow models to, in effect, check whether the proposed assets, trust structure and credit enhancement levels are sufficient to support the credit ratings desired by the arranger.

The NRSRO rules adopted by the Commission in June of 2007 preceded the full emergence of the credit market turmoil. The Commission, in light of its experience since the final rules became effective, is proposing amendments to those rules and a new rule with the goal of further enhancing the utility of NRSRO disclosure to investors, strengthening the integrity of the ratings process, and more effectively addressing the potential for conflicts of interest inherent in the ratings process for structured finance products.

II. Proposed Amendments

A. Amendments to Rule 17g-5

The Commission adopted Rule 17g-5, in part, pursuant to authority "to prohibit, or require the management and disclosure of, any conflicts of interest relating to the issuance of credit ratings by an [NRSRO]."[55] The rule identifies a series of conflicts arising from the business of determining credit ratings. Under the rule, some of these conflicts must be disclosed and managed, while other specified conflicts are prohibited outright.

Paragraph (a) of Rule 17g-5 prohibits an NRSRO from having a conflict identified in paragraph (b) of the rule unless the NRSRO discloses the type of conflict on Form NRSRO and establishes, maintains, and enforces procedures to manage it.[56] Paragraph (b) identifies eight types of conflicts, which include being paid by issuers or underwriters to determine credit ratings with respect to securities or money market instruments they issue or underwrite[57] or being paid by persons for subscriptions to receive or access credit ratings where such persons also may own investments or have entered into transactions that could be favorably or adversely impacted by a credit rating.[58]

Paragraph (c) of Rule 17g-5 prohibits outright four types of conflicts of interest. Consequently, an NRSRO would violate the rule if it has the type of conflict described in paragraph (c) even if it disclosed the conflict and established procedures to manage it. In the Adopting Release, the Commission explained that these conflicts were prohibited because they would be difficult to manage given their potential to cause undue influence.[59]

The Commission is proposing to amend Rule 17g-5 to require the disclosure and establishment of procedures to manage an additional conflict and to prohibit certain other conflicts outright, as described below.

1. Addressing the Particular Conflict Arising from Rating Structured Finance Products by Enhancing the Disclosure of Information Used in the Rating Process

a. The Proposed Amendment

The Commission is proposing to amend Rule 17g-5[60] to add to the list of conflicts that must be disclosed and managed the additional conflict of repeatedly being paid by certain arrangers to rate structured finance products. This conflict is a subset of the broader conflict already identified in paragraph (b)(1) of Rule 17g-5; namely, "being paid by issuers and underwriters to determine credit ratings with respect to securities or money market instruments they issue or underwrite."[61] In the case of structured finance products, the Commission preliminarily believes this "issuer/underwriter-pay" conflict is particularly acute because certain arrangers of structured finance products repeatedly bring ratings business to the NRSROs.[62] As sources of constant deal based revenue, some arrangers have the potential to exert greater undue influence on an NRSRO than, for example, a corporate issuer that may bring far less ratings business to the NRSRO.[63]

Consequently, the Commission is proposing amendments to Rule 17g-5 that would require additional measures to address this particular type of "issuer/underwriter-pay" conflict.

Specifically, the proposed amendment would re-designate paragraph (b)(9) of Rule 17g-5 as paragraph (b)(10) and in new paragraph (b)(9) identify the following conflict: issuing or maintaining a credit rating for a security or money market instrument issued by an asset pool or as part of any asset-backed or mortgage-backed securities transaction that was paid for by the issuer, sponsor, or underwriter of the security or money market instrument. To address this conflict, proposed new paragraph (a)(3) would require that as a condition to the NRSRO rating a structured finance product the information provided to the NRSRO and used by the NRSRO in determining the credit rating would need to be disclosed through a means designed to provide reasonably broad dissemination of the information.[64] The intent behind this disclosure is to create the opportunity for other NRSROs to use the information to rate the instrument as well. Any resulting "unsolicited ratings" could be used by market participants to evaluate the ratings issued by the NRSRO hired to rate the product and, in turn, potentially expose an NRSRO whose ratings were influenced by the desire to gain favor with the arranger in order to obtain more business.[65]

The proposed amendment would require the disclosure of information provided to an NRSRO by the "issuer, underwriter, sponsor, depositor, or trustee." The Commission preliminarily believes that, taken together, these are the parties that provide all relevant information to the NRSRO to be used in the initial rating and rating monitoring processes. The Commission is not proposing to specify the party – NRSRO, arranger, issuer, depositor, or trustee – that would need to disclose the information. It may be that the issuer through the arranger and trustee would be in the best positions to disclose the information. In this case, in contracting with these parties to provide a rating for a structured finance product, the NRSRO could require a representation from them that the necessary information would be disclosed as required by the proposed rule. The Commission notes, however, that the proposed rule does not provide a safe harbor for an NRSRO arising from such a representation. Consequently, an NRSRO would violate the proposed rule if it issued a credit rating for a structured finance product where the information is not disclosed notwithstanding any representations from the arranger.

The goal of this proposed amendment is to promote the effective management of this conflict of interest, increase the transparency of the process for rating structured finance products, and foster competition by making it feasible for more market participants, in particular NRSROs that are not contracted by the arranger to issue a rating but still wish to do so, to perform credit analysis on the instrument and to monitor the instrument's creditworthiness. As noted above, by providing the opportunity for more NRSROs to determine credit ratings for structured finance products, this proposal is designed to increase the number of ratings extant for a given instrument and, in particular, promote the issuance of ratings by NRSROs that are not hired by the arranger. The goal would be to expose an NRSRO that was unduly influenced by the "arranger- pay" conflict into issuing higher than warranted ratings.[66] An ancillary benefit would be that the proposal could make it easier for users of credit ratings to identify potentially inaccurate credit ratings and incompetent NRSROs. The proposal also is designed to make it more difficult for arrangers to exert influence on the NRSROs that they hire to determine ratings for structured finance products. Specifically, by opening up the rating process to greater scrutiny, the proposal is designed to make it easier for the hired NRSRO to resist pressure from the arranger by increasing the likelihood that any steps taken to inappropriately favor the arranger could be exposed to the market. Further, as noted above, an ancillary benefit of the proposal is that it could operate as a check on inaccuracy and incompetence.

To further these goals, the proposal would require the disclosure of the following information:

- All information provided to the nationally recognized statistical rating organization by the issuer, underwriter, sponsor, depositor, or trustee that is used in determining the initial credit rating for the security or money market instrument, including information about the characteristics of the assets underlying or referenced by the security or money market instrument, and the legal structure of the security or money market instrument;[67]
- All information provided to the nationally recognized statistical rating organization by the issuer, underwriter, sponsor, depositor, or trustee that is used by the nationally recognized statistical rating organization in undertaking credit rating surveillance on the security or money market instrument, including information about the characteristics and performance of the assets underlying or referenced by the security or money market instrument.[68]

For the purposes of the proposed amendment, the Commission would consider only information that is taken into account in generating the credit rating or in performing surveillance to be "used" by the NRSRO in those contexts. This would exclude information about collateral pools (i.e., "loan tapes") provided by the arranger containing a mix of assets that is different than the composition of the final collateral pool upon which the credit rating is based. The proposed rule also would exclude from disclosure most, if not all, communications between the NRSRO and the issuer, underwriter, sponsor, depositor, or trustee to the extent the communications do not contain information necessary for the NRSRO to determine an initial credit rating or perform surveillance on an existing credit rating.

The Commission recognizes that the NRSRO would define the information that it uses for purposes of generating credit ratings and, likely, would obtain representations from the arranger that the information is being disclosed as required under the rule. There is a potential that an NRSRO that uses relatively little information to generate credit ratings would be favored by arrangers to minimize the amount of information subject to the disclosure requirement. The Commission preliminarily believes that there is some degree of standardization as to the information used by NRSROs to rate structured finance products (e.g., loan level information, payment priorities among the issued tranched securities, and legal structure of the issuer). An NRSRO that requires less than the standard level of information would need to convince users of credit ratings, most notably investors, that its ratings process was credible. Otherwise, arrangers ultimately would not use the NRSRO since it would be more difficult to sell the structured finance products if they carried ratings that were not accepted by the marketplace. Nonetheless, the Commission, if this proposal is adopted, intends to monitor whether it results in a significant reduction in the information provided to NRSROs.

The timing and scope of the disclosures of the first set information described above – information used in determining the initial credit rating – would depend on the nature of the offering: public, private, or offshore.[69] In an offering registered under the Securities Act of

1933 (15 U.S.C. 77a et seq.), the information would need to be disclosed on the date the underwriter and the issuer or depositor set the offering price of the securities being rated (the "pricing date").[70] In offerings that are not registered under the Securities Act of 1933 (15 U.S.C. 77a et seq.), the information would need to be disclosed to investors in the offering and entities meeting the definition of "credit rating agency" in Section 3 (a)(6 1) of the Exchange Act (which would include credit rating agencies registered, and not registered, as NRSROs)[71] and on the pricing date and disclosed publicly on the first business day after the transaction closes.

The Commission is proposing the pricing date as the time of the first disclosures because it preliminarily believes that this is the earliest date upon which the asset pool and legal structure of the trust are settled on. Thus, the information that would be disclosed would reflect the actual characteristics of the securities to be issued and not, for example, preliminary assets pools with different compositions of loans. At the same time, the disclosure of the information before the securities are sold is designed to provide the opportunity for other credit rating agencies to use the information to develop "unsolicited ratings" for the tranche securities before they are purchased by investors. To the extent unsolicited ratings are issued, they would provide investors with a greater range of credit assessments and, in particular, assessments from credit rating agencies that are not subject to the "arranger-pay" conflict.

The Commission anticipates that the information that would need to be disclosed (i.e., the information used by the hired NRSRO to determine the initial rating) generally would include the characteristics of the assets in the pool underlying the structured finance product and the legal documentation setting forth the capital structure of the trust, payment priorities with respect to the tranche securities issued by the trust (the waterfall), and all applicable covenants regarding the activities of the trust. For example, for an initial rating for an RMBS, this information generally would include the "loan tape" (frequently a spreadsheet) that identifies each loan in the pool and its characteristics such as type of loan, principal amount, loan-to-value ratio, borrower's FICO score, and geographic location of the property. In addition, the disclosed information also would include a description of the structure of the trust, the credit enhancement levels for the tranche securities to be issued by the trust, and the waterfall cash flow priorities. With respect to the loan pool information, the Commission does not intend that the proposed disclosure would include any personal identifying information on individual borrowers or properties (such as names, phone numbers, addresses or tax identification numbers).

After the disclosure of the information used by the NRSRO to perform the initial rating, the proposed amendment would require the disclosure of information about the underlying assets that is provided to, and used by, the NRSRO to perform any ratings surveillance.[72] The Commission anticipates that generally this information would consist of reports from the trustee describing how the assets in the pool underlying the structured finance product are performing. For an RMBS credit rating, this information likely would include the "trustee report" customarily generated to reflect the performance of the loans constituting the collateral pool. For example, an RMBS trustee may generate reports describing the percentage of loans that are 30, 60, and 90 days in arrears, the percentage that have defaulted, the recovery of principal from defaulted loans, and information regarding any modifications to the loans in the asset pool. The disclosure of this information would allow NRSROs that were not hired to rate the deal, including ones that determined unsolicited initial ratings, to monitor on a continuing basis the creditworthiness of the tranche securities issued by the trust. The proposed amendment provides that this information would need to be disclosed at the time it is provided to the NRSRO. This is designed to put other NRSROs and other interested parties on an equal footing with the NRSRO hired by the arranger insomuch as they would all obtain the information at the same time. Consequently, they all could begin any surveillance processes simultaneously.

The goal of this aspect of the proposal again would be to expose an NRSRO that was allowing business considerations to impact its judgment. For example, in order to maintain favor with a particular arranger, an NRSRO may be reluctant to downgrade a credit rating for a structured finance product to its appropriate category even where a downgrade is implied by its surveillance procedures and methodologies. Increasing the number of credit ratings extant for the instrument, including ratings not paid for by the arranger, would make it more difficult to conceal the fact that a particular NRSRO was being unduly influenced by an arranger as to its surveillance process.

As discussed below, the manner and breadth of the disclosures, including how widely the information could be disseminated, would depend on the nature of the offering for the rated structured finance product: public, private, or offshore. The proposed amendment's requirement that the information be "disclosed through a means designed to provide reasonably broad dissemination" would be interpreted by the Commission to mean in the manner described in sections II.A. 1 .b.i – iii below that discuss the proposed amendment in the context of public, private, and offshore offerings.

The Commission is proposing these amendments to Rule 17g-5, in part, pursuant to the authority in Section 15E(h)(2) of the Exchange Act.[73] The provisions in this section of the statute provide the Commission with authority to prohibit, or require the management and disclosure of, any potential conflict of interest relating to the issuance of credit ratings by an NRSRO.[74] The Commission preliminarily believes the proposed amendments are necessary and appropriate in the public interest and for the protection of investors because they are designed to address conflicts of interest and improve the quality of credit ratings for structured finance products by: (1) increasing the transparency of the ratings process and thereby making it more apparent when an NRSRO may be allowing business considerations to impair its objectivity and (2) enhancing competition by creating the opportunity for NRSROs that are not hired to rate structured products to nonetheless determine credit ratings and establish track records for rating these products.

The Commission preliminarily believes that it is appropriate to require an NRSRO to address and manage the conflict of interest raised by the NRSRO's recurring relationships with structured finance product arrangers by making the rating process more transparent in terms of the information used to determine the ratings. This would create an opportunity for other NRSROs (including subscriber based NRSROs), unregistered credit rating agencies, and other interested parties to assess the creditworthiness of these products and issue their own credit ratings or credit assessments.[75] Market participants and observers would be able to compare the ratings of the NRSROs hired by the arrangers against the ratings of NRSROs and others not hired by the arrangers. As discussed above, the Commission preliminarily believes that this would enhance the integrity of the ratings process by making it easier for users of credit ratings to compare NRSROs and evaluate whether an NRSRO's objectivity had been compromised by the undue influence of an arranger. It also could make it easier for the NRSROs hired to determine credit ratings for structured finance products to resist pressure from arrangers insomuch as the parties would be aware that the potential for exposing a compromised NRSRO had been increased through the proposed amendment's disclosure requirements.

The Commission generally requests comment on all aspects of this proposed amendment. In addition, the Commission requests comment on the following questions related to the proposal.

- Would the information proposed to be required to be disclosed sufficient to permit the determination of an unsolicited credit rating? Conversely, would the proposed amendment require the disclosure of more information than would be necessary to permit the determination of an unsolicited credit rating? Commenters believing more information should be disclosed should specifically describe the additional information and the practicality of requiring its disclosure, while commenters believing that less information should be disclosed should specifically describe what information would be unnecessary and explain why it would be unnecessary to disclose.
- The proposed amendment would require the disclosure of information provided to an NRSRO by the "issuer, underwriter, sponsor, depositor, or trustee" based on the Commission's preliminary belief that these would be the parties relevant to an NRSRO's performance of the ratings process, i.e., that taken together, these are the parties that would provide all relevant information to the NRSRO. Are there other entities that should be included in this category?
- Should the Commission provide a "safe harbor" so that an NRSRO that obtained a representation from one or more parties to a transaction to disclose the required information would not be held in violation of the rule if the party did not fulfill its disclosure obligations under the representation?
- Should the Commission also require the disclosure of information about the steps, if any, that were taken by the NRSRO, issuer, underwriter, sponsor, depositor, or trustee to verify information about the assets underlying or referenced by the security or money market instrument, or, if no such steps were taken, a disclosure of that fact?
- Would the disclosure of the initial information on the pricing date provide enough time for other NRSROs to determine unsolicited ratings before the securities were sold to investors? If not, would it be appropriate to require that this information be disclosed prior to the pricing date? Alternatively, would it be more appropriate to require NRSROs hired by the arranger to wait a period of calendar or business days (e.g., 2, 4, 10 days) after the asset pool is settled upon by the arranger before issuing the initial credit rating in order to provide other NRSROs with sufficient time to determine an unsolicited rating?
- Should the Commission also require the disclosure of the results of any steps taken by the NRSRO, issuer, underwriter, sponsor, depositor, or trustee to verify information about the assets underlying or referenced by a structured finance product? Alternatively, should the Commission require a general disclosure of whether any steps were taken to verify the information and, if so, a description of those steps?

- Do NRSROs obtain information about the underlying assets of structured products – particularly in the surveillance process – from third-parties such as vendors rather than from issuers, underwriters, sponsors, or trustees? If so, would it be necessary to require the disclosure of this information as proposed or can the goals of the proposed amendments in promoting unsolicited ratings be achieved under current practices insomuch as the information necessary for surveillance can be obtained from third-party vendors, albeit for a fee?
- Does the information provided to NRSROs by issuers, underwriters, sponsors, depositors, or trustees about assets underlying structured products (e.g., mortgage loans, home equity loans, consumer loans, credit card receivables) commonly include personal identifying information about individuals such as names, social security numbers, addresses, and telephone numbers? If so, are there practical ways to ensure that this information is not disclosed?
- Does any of the information provided to NRSROs by issuers, underwriters, sponsors, depositors, or trustees about assets underlying structured products contain proprietary information? Commenters that believe this is the case should specifically identify any such information.

b. Proposed Guidance for Compliance with Provisions of the Securities Act of 1933

As noted above, the proposed amendments to Rule 17g-5 that would require the disclosure of information about the underlying assets of a structured finance product implicate the Securities Act.[76] As explained below, the means by which information would be disclosed for the purposes of the proposed amendments to Rule 17g-5 would be governed by the nature of the offering. The Securities Act restricts the types of offering communications that issuers or other parties subject to the Securities Act's provisions (such as underwriters) may use during a registered public offering and, for private offerings, restricts the methods by which communications may be made so as to avoid general solicitation or general advertising of the private offering to potential purchasers. Communications that may be considered offers[77] are subject to these restrictions.[78] Likewise, with respect to unregistered offshore offerings that are intended to comply with the safe harbor provisions of Regulation S, communications that are deemed to be offers in the United States or directed selling efforts in the United States are prohibited. Information about securities that are the subject of an offering that has been provided to NRSROs and is required to be disclosed pursuant to the proposed rules would be considered offers or directed selling efforts and therefore subject to these restrictions relating to offering communications.[79]

In the following three sections, the Commission provides guidance on how the information that would be required to be disclosed under proposed new paragraph (a)(3) of Rule 17g-5 ("Paragraph (a)(3) Information") would need to be disclosed under the proposed amendment and consistent with the Securities Act. As discussed below, the manner and breadth of the disclosures under the proposed amendment would depend on whether the structured finance product was issued under a public, private, or offshore offering.

I. Public Offerings

With respect to registered offerings at the time the Paragraph (a)(3) Information would be required to be disclosed (the pricing date), the information would be written communications and the issuer, underwriter, or other offering participant also would have to comply with the Securities Act with regard to the disclosure of such written communications.[80] In addition, such written communications would be subject to the civil liability and antifraud provisions of the Securities Act.[81]

As discussed in the Commission's Securities Offering Reform Release adopting several reforms to the securities offering process,[82] issuers of structured finance products have potentially two sets of rules under the Securities Act on which they may rely in using written offering materials. If the offering is registered on Securities Act Form S3,[83] then the written materials may constitute ABS informational and computational materials, as defined in Item 1101 of Regulation AB,[84] and should be filed on Exchange Act Form 8-K[85] in accordance with Rules 167 and 426 of the Securities Act.[86] The written materials may constitute a free writing prospectus, as defined in Rule 405 of the Securities Act.[87] In that case, the information that is disclosed must be filed in accordance with Rules 164 and 433 of the Securities Act.[88] Given that the Paragraph (a)(3) Information could constitute offering materials, the Commission believes it is important to explain how the rules under the Securities Act may be relied upon when Paragraph (a)(3) Information is made publicly available.[89]

Most elements of the Paragraph (a)(3) Information would need to be filed in accordance with the rules governing free writing prospectuses or ABS informational and computational materials pursuant to Rules 433 and 426.[90] Currently, the timing or filing requirements under these rules is tied to when the information is provided to specific investors. However, unlike other free writing prospectuses and ABS informational and computational materials that may be provided to specific investors, in a public offering, the Paragraph (a)(3) Information would be required to be disclosed publicly. Therefore, the Commission believes that it is appropriate to clarify when the materials should be filed with the Commission.

Under Rule 426, ABS informational and computational materials are required to be filed by the later of the due date for filing the final prospectus under Rule 424(b) or two days after the date of first use. Under Rule 433, a free writing prospectus must be filed with the Commission no later than the date of first use. However, in order to conform certain asset-backed free writing prospectuses with the filing requirements for ABS informational and computational materials in Rule 426, Rule 433(d)(6) provides that a free writing prospectus containing only ABS information and computational materials may be filed in the time provided by Rule 426(b). Thus, under both rules the information must be filed by the later of the due date for filing the final prospectus under Rule 424(b) or two days after the date of first use.

In addition, Rule 433 requires filing by issuers of free writing prospectuses prepared by or on behalf of, or used or referred to by, issuers or, depositors, sponsors, servicers, or affiliated depositors, whether or not the issuer, but not by underwriters or dealers, unless they contain issuer information or are distributed in a manner reasonably designed to lead to its broad dissemination. The Paragraph (a)(3) Information that would be required to be disclosed would not be considered underwriter or dealer information, even if prepared by the underwriter or dealer, given the broad dissemination and thus would need to be filed.

Rules 164 and 167 provide the exemption from Section 5(b)(1) of the Securities Act for the use of free writing prospectuses and ABS informational and computational materials, respectively. For the most part, Rule 164 should be available for the use of the Paragraph (a)(3) Information, even where the issuer is an ineligible issuer,[91] given that the rule provides that ineligible issuers that are asset-backed issuers may use a free writing prospectus as long as the free writing prospectus contains only specified information.[92] Much of the Paragraph (a)(3) Information should contain information that can be included in a free writing prospectus used by an asset-backed issuer pursuant to Rule 164. To the extent that Rule 167 is not available because the offering is registered on Form S-1 rather than Form S-3, and Rule 164 is not available, the information should be filed in an amendment to the registration statement.

In addition, the Commission understands that currently at least some of the information that would constitute Paragraph (a)(3) Information, if not included in a free writing prospectus, is often included as a schedule to pooling and servicing agreements. Those agreements, along with their schedules and exhibits, should be filed by the time of the offering of securities. Therefore they should be filed at the time of the takedown as exhibits to a Form 8-K incorporating them by reference into the Form S-3 registration statement.[93]

The Commission generally requests comment on all aspects of this proposed guidance. In addition, the Commission requests comment on the following questions related to the proposal.

- Do we need to give more guidance on the relationship between the proposed disclosure requirements regarding information about the underlying assets provided to, and used by, the NRSRO to perform ratings surveillance and the requirements of Regulation FD?[94] If commenters believe that the proposed requirements are not consistent with Regulation FD, they should provide a detailed explanation as to why not.
- The proposed disclosure requirements regarding information about the underlying assets provided to, and used by, the NRSRO to perform ratings surveillance may be the same as the information required to be disclosed on Form 10-D for so long as the issuer has an Exchange Act reporting obligation. Given that the Form 10-D reporting obligation is typically suspended for most asset-backed issuers after the first year of reporting, does the proposed disclosure requirement raise any issues regarding Exchange Act reporting?
- ABS informational and computation materials, as defined in Item 1101 of Regulation AB, can include, among other things, factual information regarding the pool assets underlying the asset-backed securities, including origination, acquisition and pool selection criteria, information regarding any prefunding or revolving period applicable to the offering, information regarding significant obligors, data regarding the contractual and related characteristics of the underlying pool assets (e.g., weighted average coupon, weighted average maturity, delinquency and loss information and geographic distribution) and other factual information concerning the parameters of the asset pool appropriate to the nature of the underlying assets, such as the type of assets comprising the pool and the programs under which the loans were originated.[95] As noted above, the Commission believes that at least some of the proposed Paragraph (a)(3) Information could fall within this category

and therefore constitute ABS informational and computational materials. Since there may be a wide variety of information that is provided to an NRSRO, it is not clear that all information provided would fit within the definition of ABS informational and computation materials, or in the various categories of free writing prospectus. Should the Commission provide additional interpretation regarding what types of material that could be provided and would be required to be disclosed to fit within this category? Is there information that is likely to be provided and disclosed that does not appear to fit within these definitions? Should the Commission instead revise the definitions to specifically include the information required to be disclosed?

- Is there any need for the Commission to revise Securities Act Rules 426 or 433 to clarify when the materials need to be filed?
- Are there any additional requirements in Regulation AB or under the Securities Act that are implicated by the proposed amendments? Is there any information that would typically need to be disclosed under this proposed amendment that is not already generally disclosed in filings with the Commission?
- Should the Commission amend Regulation AB to require that the Paragraph (a)(3) Information be disclosed?

II. Private Offerings

The proposed amendments also would implicate the Securities Act restrictions affecting private offerings. Offerings of securities made in reliance on an exemption from registration contained in Securities Act Section 4(2),[96] the rules promulgated thereunder or pursuant to Regulation D,[97] are offerings that are not made to the public. As a result, general solicitation or advertising is prohibited in these offerings under Securities Act Section 4(2) and the applicable Securities Act rules.[98] As a result of the application of the general solicitation and advertising restrictions, public disclosure of offering or security information pursuant to the proposed rules could cause the private offering exemptions to be unavailable to securities offerings to which the proposed rules apply.

As discussed above, the Commission believes it is likely that much of the information that would need to be disclosed under the proposed amendment would contain extensive loan level data, and thus anticipates that a common medium for disclosure of this information would be an Internet Web site. The Commission has indicated that the placement of private offering materials on an Internet Web site, without sufficient procedures to limit access only to accredited investors, is inconsistent with the prohibition against general solicitation or advertising in Securities Act Rule 502(c).[99] However, as discussed above, the Commission also believes that to address the conflict of interest inherent in the structured finance product arranger-pay business model it would be beneficial to make this information available to investors and entities meeting the definition of "credit rating agency" in Section 3(a)(61) of the Exchange Act (which would include NRSROs)[100] on the date the placement agent and the issuer or depositor set the offering price of the securities being rated, and to the general public on the first business day after the offering closes.

The Commission believes, therefore, that in a private offering, Paragraph (a)(3) Information would need to be provided to investors, NRSROs, and credit rating agencies by posting the information on a password-protected Internet Web site.[101] On the first business day after the offering closes, however, the Paragraph (a)(3) Information would need to be disclosed publicly. The Commission believes that removing the password protection from the Internet Web site where the Paragraph (a)(3) Information is posted after the offering closes is consistent with the Securities Act restrictions on private offerings while satisfying the requirements of proposed Rule 1 7g-5(a)(3).

As discussed above, the Commission believes it would be appropriate to allow early access to credit rating agencies other than those hired to issue a rating to provide them with an opportunity to perform independent assessments of the validity of ratings and identify flaws, opportunities for improvement, or compromised procedures in the hired NRSRO's approach. While permitting access to this information to credit rating agencies in addition to accredited investors extends beyond the Commission's previous interpretations on what constitutes a general solicitation or advertising, the Commission believes it balances those issues with the benefits of having other credit rating agencies able to assess the quality of, or provide additional, ratings.[102] This approach is designed to promote competition among NRSROs by providing credit ratings agencies that were not paid by the issuer to rate the issuer's products with information they need to issue unsolicited ratings and allowing other market participants to also have access to the information to allow them to evaluate the ratings. In a private offering, disclosure of this information is undertaken in two steps in order to avoid issues of general solicitation. The Commission is providing the above guidance only in the context of the proposed amendments. Moreover, the guidance expressed in this release is applicable only if the proposed amendments are adopted.

The Commission generally requests comment on all aspects of this proposed guidance. In addition, the Commission requests comment on the following questions related to the proposal.

- Are there other parties besides credit rating agencies and investors that should be eligible to access Paragraph (a)(3) Information in the context of a private offering without raising issues of general solicitation?
- Should any of the foregoing guidance regarding the use of Paragraph (a)(3) Information be codified?
- Is expanding the categories of parties who can access the information that would be contained in the proposed Paragraph (a)(3) Information consistent with the purposes of the Securities Act?
- Is there any Paragraph (a)(3) Information that should remain accessible only to credit rating agencies and investors, rather than, as proposed, disclosed to the public on the business day after the offering has closed?
- Should the requirement to publicly disclose the Paragraph (a)(3) Information on the first business day after the offering has closed also permit the NRSRO, depositor, etc. to omit deal-specific information relating to the transaction such that only "generic" information is provided to the public?
- Does disclosure of information provided for purposes of credit rating surveillance raise issues of general solicitation in the context of subsequent offerings of the same asset class? If so, does this vary by asset class?

III. Offshore Offerings

Similar to private offerings, the proposed amendments would implicate restrictions under Regulation S. Under the General Statement of Regulation S,[103] the provisions of Section 5 of the Securities Act apply to offers and sales of securities that occur in the United States and do not apply to those that occur outside the United States. Regulation S contains various safe harbor procedures that issuers, offering participants and others can follow for unregistered offerings outside the United States. These procedures include restrictions against offers being made to persons in the United States[104] and restrictions against directed selling efforts in the United States by the issuer, distributor, any of their respective affiliates, or persons acting on their behalf.[105]

As noted above, the Commission believes that it is likely that much of the information that would be required to be disclosed would contain extensive loan level data and thus anticipates that a common medium for disclosure of this information would be an Internet Web site. The Commission has provided guidance with respect to the use of Internet Web sites for securities offerings outside the United States.[106] This guidance sets out a general approach that when adequate measures are implemented to prevent U.S. persons from participating in an offshore offer, the Commission would not view the offer as occurring in the United States for registration purposes. The Commission believes that this guidance can be equally applied to the proposed disclosure of the proposed Paragraph (a)(3) Information.

Under this guidance, what constitutes adequate measures would depend on all of the facts and circumstances of a particular transaction. As the Commission noted previously:

> "We generally would not consider an offshore Internet offer made by a non-U.S. offeror as targeted at the United States, however, if: (1) the Web site contains a prominent disclaimer making it clear that the offer is directed only to countries other than the United States; . . . and (2) the Web site offeror implements procedures that are reasonably designed to guard against sales to U.S. persons in the offshore offering."[107]

These procedures are not exclusive.

The Commission's prior guidance distinguishes among foreign issuers and U.S. issuers each conducting offshore offerings under Regulation S and U.S. offerings conducted on an exempt basis. The Commission believes it is appropriate to continue this treatment with respect to the proposed disclosure of the Paragraph (a)(3) Information. Under this guidance, a foreign issuer making an offshore offering with no concurrent U.S. private offering is not required to password-protect Internet-based offering communications so long as adequate measures are put in place. Thus, credit rating agencies and other market participants should be able to have ready access to any Paragraph (a)(3) Information that is posted by a foreign issuer. A foreign issuer making an offshore offering concurrently with private offerings in the United States could implement additional other procedures to prevent its offshore Internet communications from being used to solicit participants for its U.S.-based exempt offering, and U.S. issuers conducting an offshore offering should implement procedures similar to those for private placements, such as password-type procedures, under which only non-U.S. persons can obtain access to the materials. Consistent with the procedures for private offerings, there could be pricing date disclosure to credit rating agencies that are not purchasers in the offering through a password-protected Internet Web site. As a result, when a foreign issuer is conducting a U.S. private offering under Section 4(2), and when a U.S. issuer is conducting an offshore offering under Regulation S or a private offering under Section 4(2), it would follow the procedures outlined in Section II.A.1.b.ii above with respect to private offerings, including procedures calling for public disclosure of Paragraph (a)(3) Information on the business day after the closing date.

The Commission generally requests comment on all aspects of this proposed guidance. In addition, the Commission requests comment on the following questions related to the proposal.

- Are there other parties besides credit rating agencies that should be eligible to access Paragraph (a)(3) Information in the context of an offshore offering without raising issues of directed selling efforts or offers of securities in the Unites States?
- Should any of the foregoing guidance regarding the use of Paragraph (a)(3) Information be codified?
- Is expanding the categories of parties who can access the information that would be contained in the proposed Paragraph (a)(3) Information consistent with the purposes of the Securities Act?
- Is there any Paragraph (a)(3) Information that should remain accessible only to credit rating agencies and investors, rather than, as proposed, be disclosed to the public on the business day after the offering has closed?
- Should the requirement to publicly disclose the Paragraph (a)(3) Information on the first business day after the offering has closed also permit the NRSRO, depositor, etc. to omit deal-specific information relating to the transaction such that only "generic" information is provided to the public?

2. Rule 17g-5 Prohibition on Conflict of Interest Related to Rating an Obligor or Debt Security where Obligor or Issuer Received Ratings Recommendations from the NRSRO or Person Associated with the NRSRO

The Commission is proposing to amend Rule 17g-5(c) to add a new paragraph (5) that would prohibit an NRSRO from issuing a credit rating with respect to an obligor or security where the NRSRO or a person associated with the NRSRO, as defined in Section 3 (a)(63) of the Exchange Act,[108] made recommendations to the obligor or the issuer, underwriter, or sponsor of the security (that is, the parties responsible for structuring the security) about the corporate or legal structure, assets, liabilities, or activities of the obligor or issuer of the security. This proposal would prohibit the NRSRO and, in particular, its credit analysts from making recommendations to obligors, issuers, underwriters, and sponsors such as arrangers of structured finance products about how to obtain a desired credit rating during the rating process. It also would prohibit an NRSRO from issuing a credit rating where a person associated with the NRSRO, such as an affiliate, made such recommendations.

The Commission is proposing this amendment to Rule 17g-5, in part, pursuant to the authority in Section 15E(h)(2) of the Exchange Act.[109] The provisions of this section of the statute provide the Commission with authority to prohibit, or require the management and disclosure of, any potential conflict of interest relating to the issuance of credit ratings by an NRSRO.[110] The Commission preliminarily believes the proposed amendment is necessary and appropriate in the public interest and for the protection of investors because it would address a potential practice that could impair the objectivity, and, correspondingly, the quality, of a credit rating. It has been suggested that during the process of rating structured finance products the NRSROs have recommended to arrangers how to structure a trust or complete an asset pool to receive a desired credit rating and then rated the securities issued by the trust – in effect, rating their own work.[111] This proposal would prohibit this conduct based on the Commission's preliminary belief that it creates a conflict that cannot be effectively managed insomuch as it would be very difficult for an NRSRO to remain objective when assessing the creditworthiness of an obligor or debt security where the NRSRO or person associated with the NRSRO made recommendations about steps the obligor or issuer of the security could take to obtain a desired credit rating.

The proposal is not intended to prohibit all interaction between the NRSRO and the obligor, issuer, underwriter, or sponsor during the rating process. The Commission preliminarily believes that the transparency of an NRSRO's procedures and methodologies for determining credit ratings is enhanced when the NRSRO explains to obligors and issuers the bases, assumptions, and rationales behind rating decisions. For example, the Commission understands that in the structured finance area, NRSROs may provide information to arrangers about the output of expected loss and cash flow models. The information provided by the NRSRO during the rating process allows the arranger to better understand the relationship between model outputs and the NRSRO's decisions with respect to necessary credit enhancement levels to support a particular rating. The arranger then can consider the feedback and determine independently the steps it will take, if any, to adjust the structure, credit enhancement levels, or asset pool. However, if the feedback process turns into recommendations by the NRSRO about changes the arranger could make to the structure or asset pool that would result in a desired credit rating, the NRSRO's role would transition from an objective credit analyst to subjective consultant. In this case, the Commission believes it would be difficult for the NRSRO to remain impartial since the expectation would be that the changes suggested by the NRSRO would result in the credit ratings sought by the arranger.

The prohibition would extend to recommendations by persons associated with the NRSRO to address affiliates. For example, an NRSRO's holding company could establish an affiliate to provide consulting services to issuers about how to obtain desired credit ratings from the NRSRO subsidiary. The Commission believes it would be difficult for the NRSRO to remain objective in this situation since the financial success of the affiliate would depend on issuers getting the ratings they desired after taking any steps recommended by the affiliate. This would create undue pressure on the NRSRO's credit analysts to determine credit ratings that favored the affiliate.

The Commission generally requests comment on all aspects of this proposed amendment. In addition, the Commission requests comment on the following questions related to the proposal.

- Is this type of conflict one that could be addressed through disclosure and procedures to manage it instead of prohibiting it? Should the Commission, rather than prohibiting it, add this type of conflict to the list of conflicts in paragraph (b) of Rule 17g-5, which, under paragraph (a) of the rule, must be addressed through disclosure and procedures to manage them?
- Would there be practical difficulties for an NRSRO that is part of a large conglomerate in monitoring the business activities of persons associated with the NRSRO such as affiliates located in other countries to comply with the proposed requirement? If so, given the greater separation between the NRSRO and these types of persons associated with the NRSRO, should the Commission require instead that, for these types of persons associated with the NRSRO only, the NRSRO disclose this conflict and manage it through information barriers rather than prohibit it?
- The Commission recognizes that the line between providing feedback during the rating process and making recommendations about how to obtain a desired rating may be hard to draw in some cases. Consequently, should the Commission specify the type of interactions between an NRSRO and the person seeking the rating that would and would not constitute recommendations for the purposes of this rule? Commenters that believe the Commission should provide more guidance on this issue should provide suggested definitions.

3.Rule 17g-5 Prohibition on Conflict of Interest Related to the Participation of Certain Personnel in Fee Discussions

The Commission is proposing to amend Rule 17g-5[112] by adding a new paragraph (c)(6) of Rule 1 7g-5 to address the conflict of interest that arises when a fee paid for a rating is discussed or arranged by a person within the NRSRO who has responsibility for participating in determining credit ratings (including analysts and rating committee members) or for developing or approving procedures or methodologies used for determining credit ratings, including qualitative and quantitative models.

The Commission is proposing this amendment to Rule 17g-5, in part, pursuant to the authority in Section 15E(h)(2) of the Exchange Act.[113] The provisions of this section of the statute provide the Commission with authority to prohibit, or require the management and disclosure of, any potential conflict of interest relating to the issuance of credit ratings by an NRSRO.[114] The Commission preliminarily believes the proposed amendment is necessary and appropriate in the public interest or for the protection of investors because it would address a potential practice that could impair the objectivity, and, correspondingly, the quality, of a credit rating. This amendment is designed to effectuate the separation within the NRSRO of persons involved in fee discussions from persons involved in the credit rating analytical process. While the incentives of the persons discussing fees could be based primarily on generating revenues for the NRSRO; the incentives of the persons involved in the analytical process should be based on determining accurate credit ratings. There is a significant potential for these distinct incentive structures to conflict with one another where persons within the NRSRO are engaged in both activities.

The potential consequences are that a credit analyst or person responsible for approving credit ratings or credit rating methodologies could, in the context of negotiating fees, let business considerations undermine the objectivity of rating process. For example, an individual involved in a fee negotiation with an issuer might not be impartial when it comes to rating the issuer's securities. In addition, persons involved in approving the methodologies and processes used to determine credit ratings could be reluctant to adjust a model to make it more conservative if doing so would make it more difficult to negotiate fees with issuers. For these reasons, the Commission preliminarily believes that this conflict should be prohibited.

The Commission generally requests comment on all aspects of this proposed amendment. In addition, the Commission requests comment on the following items related to the proposal.

- Should the proposed prohibition also be extended to cover participation in fee negotiations by NRSRO personnel with supervisory authority over the NRSRO personnel participating in determining credit ratings or developing or approving procedures or methodologies used for determining credit ratings?
- Instead of prohibiting this conflict outright, would disclosure and procedures to manage the conflict adequately address the conflict? If so, what specific disclosures should be required? What other measures should be required in addition to disclosures?
- Would there be practical difficulties in separating analytic and fee discussions for a small NRSRO, including one that has limited staff, that are significant enough that the Commission should consider a different mechanism to address the conflict? If so, what sort of mechanism and with what conditions? Should the Commission adopt an exemption from the prohibition for small NRSROs and, instead, require them to disclose the conflict and establish procedures to manage it? For example, the exemption could apply to NRSROs that have less than 10, 20, or 50 associated persons. Commenters that endorse an exemption for small NRSROs should provide specific details as to how the Commission should define an NRSRO as "small" for purposes of the exemption. For example, for purposes of the Final Regulatory Flexibility Analysis for the Adopting Release the Commission concluded that an NRSRO with total assets of $5 million or less was a "small" entity for purposes of the Regulatory Flexibility Act.[115] Would that be an appropriate way to define a small NRSRO for purposes of this exemption?

4. Rule 17g-5 Prohibition of Conflict of Interest Related to Receipt of Gifts

The Commission is proposing to amend Rule 17g-5[116] by adding a new paragraph (c)(7) that would prohibit an NRSRO from having a conflict of interest relating to the issuance or maintenance of a credit rating where a credit analyst who participated in determining or monitoring the credit rating, or a person responsible for approving the credit rating, received gifts, including entertainment, from the obligor being rated, or from the issuer, underwriter, or sponsor of the securities being rated, other than items provided in the context of normal business activities such as meetings that have an aggregate value of no more than $25. Thus, this proposed prohibition would prohibit any gifts to credit analysts and persons on credit rating committees from the obligors, issuers, underwriters, or sponsors with respect to whom they had determined, monitored or approved credit ratings. It also would create an exception for items provided during normal business activities such as meetings to the extent they do not in the aggregate exceed $25 per meeting. For example, the provision of pens, notepads, or minor refreshments, such as soft drinks or coffee, generally are incidental to meetings and other normal course business interactions and not treated as gifts per se. The proposed $25 exception is designed to be high enough to permit these types of exchanges without implicating the prohibition.

The Commission is proposing these amendments to Rule 17g-5, in part, pursuant to the authority in Section 15E(h)(2) of the Exchange Act.[117] The provisions in this section of the statute provide the Commission with authority to prohibit, or require the management and disclosure of, any potential conflict of interest relating to the issuance of credit ratings by an NRSRO as the Commission deems necessary or appropriate in the public interest or for the protection of investors.[118] The Commission preliminarily believes the proposed amendment is necessary and appropriate in the public interest or for the protection of investors because it would address a potential practice that could impair the objectivity, and, correspondingly, the quality, of a credit rating.

Persons seeking credit ratings for an obligor or debt security could use gifts to gain favor with the analyst responsible for determining the credit ratings and cause the analyst to be less objective during the rating process. In the case of a substantial gift, the potential to impact the analyst's objectivity could be immediate. With smaller gifts, the danger is that over time the cumulative effect of repeated gifts can impact the analyst's objectivity. Therefore, the proposal would establish an absolute prohibition on gifts with the exception of minor incidentals provided in business meetings.

The Commission generally requests comment on all aspects of this proposed amendment. In addition, the Commission request comment on the following questions related to the proposal.

- Instead of prohibiting this conflict outright, should the Commission require that NRSROs disclose it and establish procedures to manage it? If so, what specific disclosures should be required?
- Instead of prohibiting gifts outright, should the Commission establish a yearly limit on the aggregate value of gifts that would be permitted under the prohibition? For example, the Commission could provide in the rule that the prohibition would not be triggered until the aggregate value of all gifts received from a particular person in a twelve month period exceeded $100, $500 or $1,000 or some other amount.
- Is the proposed $25 aggregate value an appropriate threshold for incidentals provided at meetings, or should a higher or lower threshold be applied?
- Should the Commission adopt a recordkeeping requirement with respect to the receipt of gifts by analysts and persons responsible for approving credit ratings in addition to the prohibition? For example, the Commission could require an NRSRO to

document for each gift the identity of the person providing the gift, the recipient, and the nature of the gift.

B. Amendments to Rule 17g-2

The Commission adopted Rule 17g-2, in part, pursuant to authority in Section 17(a)(1) of the Exchange Act requiring NRSROs to make and keep such records, and make and disseminate such reports, as the Commission prescribes by rule as necessary or appropriate in the public interest, for the protection of investors, or otherwise in furtherance of the Exchange Act.[119] Rule 17g-2 requires an NRSRO to make and retain certain records relating to its business and to retain certain other business records made in the normal course of business operations. The rule also prescribes the time periods and manner in which all these records are required to be retained. The Commission is proposing to amend this rule to require NRSROs to make and retain certain additional records and to require that some of these proposed new records be made publicly available.

1. A Record of Rating Actions and the Requirement that they be made Publicly Available

The Commission is proposing to amend Exchange Act Rule 17g-2[120] to add a new paragraph (8) to Rule 1 7g-2 that would require a registered NRSRO to make and retain a record showing all rating actions (initial rating, upgrades, downgrades, and placements on watch for upgrade or downgrade) and the date of such actions identified by the name of the security or obligor and, if applicable, the CUSIP for the rated security or the Central Index Key (CIK) number for the rated obligor. Furthermore, the Commission is proposing to amend Rule 17g-2(d) to require that this record be made publicly available on the NRSRO's corporate Internet Web site in an interactive data file that uses a machine-readable computer code that presents information in eXtensible Business Reporting Language ("XBRL") in electronic format ("XBRL Interactive Data File"). The purpose of this disclosure is to provide users of credit ratings, investors, and other market participants and observers the raw data with which to compare how the NRSROs initially rated an obligor or security and, subsequently, adjusted those ratings, including the timing of the adjustments. In order to expedite the establishment of a pool of data sufficient to provide a useful basis of comparison, this requirement would apply to all currently rated securities or obligors as well as to all future credit ratings.

The goal of this proposal is to foster greater accountability of the NRSROs with respect to their credit ratings as well as competition among the NRSROs by making it easier for persons to analyze the actual performance of the credit ratings the NRSROs issue in terms of accuracy in assessing creditworthiness. The disclosure of this information on the history of each credit rating would create the opportunity for the marketplace to use the information to develop performance measurement statistics that would supplement those required to be published by the NRSROs themselves in Exhibit 1 to Form NRSRO. The intent is to tap into the expertise and flexibility of credit market observers and participants to create better and more useful means to compare credit ratings. This goal is to make NRSROs more accountable for their ratings by enhancing the transparency of the results of their rating processes for particular securities and obligors and classes of securities and obligors and encourage competition within the industry by making it easier for users of credit ratings to judge the output of the NRSROs.

As noted above, the proposed amendments would require that the record be made publicly available on the NRSRO's corporate Internet Web site in an XBRL Interactive Data File that uses a machine-readable computer code that presents information in XBRL. The Commission is proposing to require that an NRSRO use this format to publicly disclose the ratings action data because it would allow users to dynamically search and analyze the information, thereby facilitating the comparison of information across different NRSROs. In addition, an XBRL Interactive Data File would enable investors, analysts, and the Commission staff to capture and analyze the ratings action data more quickly and at less of a cost than is possible using another format. The Commission further believes that the XBRL Interactive Data File would be compatible with a wide range of open source and proprietary XBRL software applications and that as the ratings action data becomes more widely available, advances in interactive data software, online viewers, search engines, and other Web-based tools may further enhance the accessibility and usability of the data.

The Commission's experience in having certain issuers use XBRL for EDGAR filings has demonstrated the benefits of this format to investors, filers, and Commission staff.[121] Expanding its use to NRSRO ratings history data would be consistent with Commission policy to utilize this format where practical.

The proposed amendment to Rule 17g-2(d) also would provide that the records be made publicly available no later than six months after the date of the rating action. The Commission anticipates that the record required under this amendment would need to be updated frequently as new credit ratings are issued and existing credit ratings are upgraded, downgraded and put on ratings watch. For purposes of the internal record, the NRSRO would need to keep the record current to reflect the complete ratings history of each extant credit rating. However, for purposes of the requirement to make the record publicly available, the NRSRO would be permitted to disclose the record on its Internet Web site six months after the record is updated to reflect a new ratings action. The proposed six-month time lag for publicly disclosing the updated record is designed to accommodate NRSROs that operate using the subscriber-pay model because they are paid for access to their current credit ratings. It also is designed to preserve the revenues that NRSROs operating using the issuer-pay model derive from selling download access to their current credit ratings.[122] The Commission preliminarily believes the six-month time lag would not have any negative effect on the goal of this proposed amendment because the information on credit ratings actions that would be disclosed – perhaps many years worth for some credit ratings – should be sufficient to develop meaningful performance metrics for comparing NRSROs.

Finally, the proposed amendments also would amend the instructions to Exhibit 1 to Form NRSRO to require the disclosure of the Web address where the XBRL Interactive Data File could be accessed. This is designed to inform persons who use credit ratings where the ratings histories can be obtained.

The Commission is proposing these amendments, in part, under authority to require NRSROs to make and keep for prescribed periods such records as the Commission prescribes as necessary or appropriate in the public interest, for the protection of investors, or otherwise in furtherance of the purposes of the Exchange Act.[123] The Commission preliminarily believes the proposed new recordkeeping and disclosure requirements are necessary and appropriate in the public interest and for the protection of investors, or otherwise in furtherance of the purposes of the Exchange Act. Specifically, by proposing to require NRSROs to make ratings actions publicly available in an XBRL Interactive Data File, market participants would be able to create their own performance measurement metrics, including default and transition matrices, by which to judge the accuracy of NRSRO ratings. In addition, users of credit ratings would be able to compare side-by-side how each NRSRO initially rated a particular security, when the NRSRO took actions to adjust the rating upward or downward, and the degree of those adjustments. Furthermore, users of credit ratings, academics and information venders could use the raw data to perform analyses comparing how the NRSROs differ in their initial ratings and their monitoring for different types of asset classes. This could identify an NRSRO that is an outlier in terms of issuing high or low credit ratings or consistently reassesses ratings on a delayed basis for some or all asset classes when compared to other NRSROs. It also could help identify NRSROs that are consistently more or less accurate than others. This information also may identify NRSROs whose objectivity may be impaired because of conflicts of interest.

The Commission generally requests comment on all aspects of this proposed amendment. In addition, the Commission requests comment on the following questions related to the proposal.

- Is the six-month delay before publicly disclosing a rating action sufficiently long to address the business concerns of the subscriber-based NRSROs and the issuer-paid NRSROs? Should the delay be for a longer period such as one or two years or even longer? Alternatively, is six months too long and should it be a shorter period of time such as three months or even shorter?
- Should the rule require that a notice be published along with the XBRL Interactive Data File warning that because of the permitted delay in updating the record some of the credit ratings in the record may no longer reflect the NRSRO's current assessment of the creditworthiness of the obligor or debt security? For example, the notice could explain that the information in the record is sixth months old and state that the credit ratings contained in record may not be up-to-date.
- Are there ways in which the NRSROs should be required to sort the credit ratings contained on the record such as by asset class or type of ratings?
- What mechanisms are appropriate for identifying rated securities? Are there other identifiers in addition, or as an alternative, to CUSIP or CIK number that could be used in the rule?
- Should the Commission allow the ratings action data to be provided in a format other than XBRL, such as pipe delimited text data ("PDTD") or eXtensible Markup Language ("XML")? Is there another format that is more widely used or would be more appropriate than XBRL for NRSRO data? What are the advantages/disadvantages of requiring the XBRL format?
- Should the Commission require that the information on the assets underlying a structured finance products discussed in Section II.A. 1.a above be provided in a specific format such as PDTD, XML, or XBRL? Again, is there another format that is more widely used or would be more appropriate for such data? What are the advantages/disadvantages of requiring a specific format?

- Should the Commission take the lead in creating the new tags that are needed for the XBRL format or should it allow the tags to be created by another group and then review the tags? How long would it take to create new tags?
- The Commission anticipates that the data provided by NRSROs would be simple and repetitive (i.e., the data would be name, CUSIP, date, rating, date, rating, etc.). Is there a need for more detailed categories of data?
- What would be the costs to an NRSRO to provide data in the XBRL format? Would there be a cost burden on smaller NRSROs? Is there another format that would cost less but still allow investors and analysts to easily download and analyze the data?
- Should the Commission institute a test phase for providing this information in an XBRL format (such as a voluntary pilot program, similar to what it is currently doing for EDGAR filings)? How long should this test phase last?
- Where is the best place to store the data provided by NRSROs? Currently, information that needs to be made publicly available is stored on each NRSRO's Web site. Should the Commission create a central database to store the information? If so, should it use the EDGAR database or should it create a new database?

2. A Record of Material Deviation from Model Output

The Commission is proposing to amend paragraph (a)(2) of Rule 17g-2 to add an additional record that would be required to be made for each current credit rating, namely, if a quantitative model is a substantial component in the process of determining the credit rating, a record of the rationale for any material difference between the credit rating implied by the model and the final credit rating issued. The NRSRO issuing the rating would be responsible for making the determination of what constituted a "substantial component" of the rating process as well as what constituted a "material" difference between the rating issued and the rating implied by the model.[124] This proposal is designed to enhance the recordkeeping processes of the NRSROs so that Commission examiners (and any internal auditors of the NRSRO) could reconstruct the analytical process by which a credit rating was determined. This would facilitate their review of whether the NRSRO followed its disclosed and internally documented procedures for determining credit ratings.

The requirement to make the record would be triggered in cases where a quantitative model is a substantial component of the credit ratings process for the type of obligor or security being rated and the output of the model would result in a materially different conclusion if the NRSRO relied on it without making an out-of-model adjustment. For example, the Commission preliminarily believes the expected loss and cash flow models used by the NRSROs to rate RMBS and CDOs are substantial components of the rating process. The following hypothetical scenario is intended as an illustrative example of an instance when an out-of-model adjustment would be material to the RMBS rating process thereby triggering the requirement to document the rationale for the adjustment under the proposed rule. A credit analyst uses the NRSRO's expected loss model to analyze a $1 billion (aggregate principal amount) loan pool received from an arranger that is proposed to collateralize an RMBS. The results of the model imply that the senior RMBS tranche would need to have at least 20% subordination in order to receive an AAA rating. However, the NRSRO's methodologies and procedures for rating RMBS allow for the subordination level suggested by the model output to be adjusted based on certain qualitative factors such as the experience and competence of the loan servicer or the recent performance of similar loan pools. Based on the superior competence of the loan servicer, the analyst concludes that the senior tranche only needs 19% subordination and, ultimately, the ratings committee agrees. Consequently, the RMBS is issued with a senior tranche having 19% subordination and receiving an AAA rating from the NRSRO. In this case, under the proposed amendment, the NRSRO would be required to make a record that identified the rationale – the servicer's superior competence – for determining a credit rating that was different from the rating implied by the model.

As the above scenario demonstrates, the failure to make such a record could hamper the ability of the Commission to review whether an NRSRO was following its stated procedures for determining credit ratings. In the above scenario, the analyst could adjust the rating requirements implied by the model by applying qualitative factors with respect to the loan servicer or the performance of similar pools. A record indicating which rationale was applied would make it easier for the Commission to review whether the procedures were followed.

The Commission is proposing this amendment, in part, under authority to require NRSROs to make and keep for prescribed periods such records as the Commission prescribes as necessary or appropriate in the public interest, for the protection of investors, or otherwise in furtherance of the purposes of the Exchange Act.[125] The Commission preliminarily believes this proposed new recordkeeping requirement is necessary and appropriate in the public interest and for the protection of investors, or otherwise in furtherance of the purposes of the Exchange Act. Specifically, as explained above, the Commission preliminarily believes that maintaining records identifying the rationale for material divergences from the ratings implied by qualitative models used as a substantial component in the ratings process would assist the Commission in evaluating whether an NRSRO is adhering to its disclosed procedures for determining ratings. Further, as the Commission noted in the Adopting Release, "books and records rules have proven integral to the Commission's investor protection function because the preserved records are the primary means of monitoring compliance with applicable securities laws." In the absence of such a recordkeeping requirement, there may be no way to determine whether an analyst modified the requirements for obtaining a certain category of credit rating (e.g. AAA) as indicated by the model results by applying appropriate qualitative factors permitted under the NRSRO's documented procedures or because of undue influence from the person seeking the credit rating or other inappropriate reasons such as those prohibited by Rule 17g-6.[126]

The Commission generally requests comment on all aspects of this proposed amendment. In addition, the Commission requests comment on the following questions related to the proposal.

- Would this proposal have the impermissible effect of regulating the substance of credit ratings in any way?
- Should the Commission define in the rule when the use of a model would be a "substantial component" in the process of determining a credit rating? Commenters endorsing the adoption of such a definition should provide specific proposals.

- Are there certain types of rated products (e.g., corporate debt, municipal bonds) which generally employ a quantitative model as a substantial component of the ratings process? Commenters should identify the types of bonds and a general description of the models used to rate them.
- Should the Commission define in the rule when the divergence from a model would be "material"? Commenters endorsing the adoption of such a definition should provide specific proposals.
- Is the hypothetical scenario of the RMB S rating process used to illustrate when a divergence would be material for purposes of the proposed amendment reasonable? For example, is the adjustment of the subordination level from 20% to 19% for a $1 billion loan pool a material divergence? Would a lesser adjustment of the subordination level (e.g., 20% to 19.5%) also be material?
- Are there alternative types of records that may be created or retained by an NRSRO that would allow the Commission to understand when and why an NRSRO's final rating differed materially from the rating implied by the model?
- Should the Commission require that the information about material deviations from the rating implied by the model be publicly disclosed by the NRSRO in the presale report or when the rating is issued?

3. Records Concerning Third-Party Analyst Complaints

The Commission is proposing an amendment to Exchange Act Rule 17g-2[127] to add a requirement that an NRSRO retain records of any complaints regarding the performance of a credit analyst in determining credit ratings. Specifically, the proposed amendment would add a new paragraph (b)(8) to Rule 17g-2 to require an NRSRO to retain any communications that contain complaints about the performance of a credit analyst in initiating, determining, maintaining, monitoring, changing, or withdrawing a credit rating.

The Commission is proposing these amendments, in part, under authority to require NRSROs to make and keep for prescribed periods such records as the Commission prescribes as necessary or appropriate in the public interest, for the protection of investors, or otherwise in the furtherance of the Exchange Act.[128] The Commission preliminarily believes the proposed new recordkeeping requirements are necessary and appropriate in the public interest and for the protection of investors, or otherwise in furtherance of the Exchange Act, because they would assist the Commission in reviewing how NRSROs address conflicts interest that could impair the integrity of their credit rating processes. For example, an NRSRO might respond to complaints from issuers that an analyst is too conservative by removing the analyst from the responsibility of rating the securities of those issuers and assigning a new analyst that is more willing to determine credit ratings desired by the issuers. As discussed above with respect to the proposed amendments to Rule 17g-5, the potential for this type of response to complaints about analysts is particularly acute in the structured finance area given that certain arrangers of structured finance products repeatedly bring ratings business to the NRSROs.[129] The pressure to maintain the business relationship with these arrangers could cause an NRSRO to remove an analyst responsible for rating the structured finance products these arrangers bring to market if they complained about how the analyst was determining credit ratings and implied that they might take their business to other NRSROs.

The records proposed under these amendments would allow the Commission, in evaluating the integrity of the NRSRO's ratings process, to better assess whether analyst reassignments or terminations were for reasons unconnected to a conflict of interest (e.g., the analyst's poor performance) or as a result of the "arranger-pay" conflict of interest described above. For example, the examiners could review the complaint file that would be established by this proposed amendment and follow-up with the relevant persons within the NRSRO as to how the complaint was addressed. The potential for such a review by Commission examiners could reduce the willingness of an NRSRO to reassign or terminate a credit analyst for inappropriate business considerations.

The Commission generally requests comment on all aspects of this proposed amendment. In addition, the Commission requests comment on the following questions related to the proposal.

- In addition to the proposed recordkeeping requirement, should the Commission require the NRSROs to publicly disclose when an analyst has been re-assigned from the responsibility to rate an obligor or the securities of an issuer, underwriter, or sponsor?
- Should the Commission require NRSROs to retain any communications containing a request from an obligor, issuer, underwriter, or sponsor that the NRSRO assign a specific analyst to a transaction in addition to the proposed requirement to retain complaints about analysts?

Clarifying Amendment to Rule 17g-2(b)(7)

Paragraph (b)(7) of Rule 17g-2 currently requires an NRSRO to retain all internal and external communications that relate to "initiating, determining, maintaining, changing, or withdrawing a credit rating." The Commission is proposing to add the word "monitoring" to this list. The intent is to clarify that NRSRO recordkeeping rules extend to all aspects of the credit rating surveillance process as well as the initial rating process. This was the intent when the Commission originally adopted the rule as indicated by the use of the term "maintaining." The Commission believes that adding the term "monitoring" – a term of art in the credit rating industry – would better clarify this requirement.

The Commission generally requests comment on all aspects of this proposed amendment. In addition, the Commission requests comment on the following question related to the proposal.

- Should the Commission delete the term "maintaining" from paragraph (b)(7) and proposed new paragraph (b)(8) of Rule 17g-2 as it has the same meaning as "monitoring?"

C. Amendments to the Instructions for Form NRSRO

Form NRSRO is the means by which credit rating agencies apply to be registered with the Commission and registered NRSROs update information they must publicly disclose. Much of the information elicited in Form NRSRO is required to be submitted to the

Commission pursuant to the statutory requirements of Section 15E(a)(1)(B) of the Exchange Act.[130] The Commission added certain additional information to be submitted in the Form.[131] As discussed below, the Commission, in part, under its authority pursuant to Section 15E(a)(1)(B)(x), is now proposing to amend Form NRSRO to further enhance the quality and usefulness of the information to be furnished and disclosed by registered NRSROs by requiring specified information in addition to that which is statutorily defined in the Section 15E of the Exchange Act.

1. Enhanced Ratings Performance Measurement Statistics on Form NRSRO

As discussed above, the Commission is proposing to require the disclosure of the historical rating actions relating to each current credit rating of an NRSRO through amendments to Rule 17g-2. The intent is to make available the raw data necessary for the marketplace to develop and apply credit ratings performance metrics. At the same time, the Commission is proposing to amend the instructions to Exhibit 1 to Form NRSRO to enhance the comparability of the performance measurement statistics the NRSROs are required to publicly disclose in the Form. Currently, the instructions require the disclosure of "performance measurement statistics of the credit ratings of the Applicant/NRSRO over short-term, mid-term, and long-term periods (as applicable) through the most recent calendar year-end." The Commission, in adopting this requirement, did not require disclosure of performance statistics in Form NRSRO beyond those specified in Section 1 5E(a)(1)(B)(i) of the Exchange Act.[132] In the Adopting Release, the Commission explained that it was not prepared to prescribe standard metrics at that time in light of the varying approaches suggested by some commenters and the opposition of other commenters to having the Commission impose any standards.[133] The Commission also stated that it would continue to consider the issue to determine the feasibility, as well as the potential benefits and limitations, of devising measurements that would allow reliable comparisons of the accuracy of the NRSROs' credit ratings.[134]

The Commission, with the benefit of further consideration of the issue, now preliminarily believes that the instructions to Exhibit 1 can prescribe greater specificity about how the performance statistics must be generated without intruding into the processes and methodologies by which NRSROs determine credit ratings. For example, through the examination process, the Commission has become more familiar with the procedures and methodologies used by the NRSROs to determine credit ratings. Through this experience, the Commission preliminarily believes it can prescribe generic requirements for the performance statistics that would accommodate the different procedures and methodologies used by the NRSROs.

The first proposed amendment would augment the instructions to Exhibit 1 by requiring the disclosure of separate sets of default and transition statistics for each asset class of credit rating for which an applicant is seeking registration as an NRSRO or an NRSRO is registered and any other broad class of credit ratings issued by the NRSRO. This would result in the generation of performance statistics that are specific to each class of credit ratings for which the NRSRO is registered (or an applicant is seeking registration). This proposal is designed to make it easier for users of credit ratings to compare the accuracy of NRSRO credit ratings on a class-by-class basis.

The proposed amendment also would require an NRSRO registered in the class of credit ratings described in Section 3(a)(62)(B)(iv) of the Rating Agency Act[135] (or an applicant seeking registration in that class) when generating the performance statistics for that class to include credit ratings of any security or money market instrument issued by an asset pool or as part of any asset-backed or mortgage-backed securities transaction. This is designed to ensure the inclusion of ratings actions for credit ratings of structured finance products that do not meet the narrower statutory definition of "issuers of asset- backed securities (as that term is defined is section 1101(c) of part 229 of title 17, Code of Federal Regulations)."[136]

The second proposed amendment would require that these class-by-class disclosures be broken out over 1, 3 and 10-year periods. Section 1 5E(a)(1)(B)(i) of the Exchange Act requires that the performance statistics be over short, mid, and long-term periods.[137] The proposed amendment would define those statutorily prescribed periods in specific years so that the performance statistics generated by the NRSROs cover comparable time periods. The Commission preliminarily believes that 1, 3, and 10 year periods are reasonable definitions of the terms "short-term, mid-term, and long-term periods" as used in Section 1 5E(a)(1)(B)(i) of the Exchange Act.[138] For example, the 1 year period would provide users with information about how the credit ratings are currently performing. In effect, it could serve as an early warning mechanism if a problem developed in an NRSRO's rating processes due to flaws or conflicts. Similarly, the 3 year period would provide information about the how the ratings were currently performing but, by including more historical data, smooth out spikes in the 1 year statistics to give a better sense of how the ratings perform over time. The 3 year statistics also would serve as a bridge to the longer term 10 year statistics. The 10 year statistics would show users how the ratings in a particular class of securities perform over the long range.

The third proposed amendment would modify what ratings actions are required to be included in these performance measurement statistics by replacing the term "downgrade and default rates" with "ratings transition and default rates." The proposed switch to "ratings transition" rates from "downgrade" rates is designed to clarify that upgrades (as well as downgrades) should be included in the statistics. The fact that an NRSRO upgrades a substantial amount of credit ratings may be just as indicative of a flaw in the initial rating as a large number of downgrades. For example, an NRSRO could try to manipulate its performance statistics by issuing overly conservative ratings.

The final proposed amendment would specify that the default statistics required under the exhibit must show defaults relative to the initial rating and incorporate defaults that occur after a credit rating is withdrawn. This amendment is designed to prevent an NRSRO from manipulating the performance statistics by not including defaults when generating statistics for a category of credit ratings (e.g., AA) because the defaults occur after the rating is downgraded to a lower category (e.g., CC) or withdrawn.

The Commission is proposing these amendments, in part, under authority to require such additional information in the application as it finds necessary or appropriate in the public interest or for the protection of investors.[139] The Commission preliminarily believes the proposed new disclosure requirements for Exhibit 1 are necessary and appropriate and in the public interest or for the protection of investors. Specifically, the information that would be required under the proposed amendments would aid investors by allowing them to evaluate how the credit ratings of an NRSRO perform (i.e., the percentage of credit ratings that migrate to another category of credit rating and the percentage of rated obligors and securities that default) on a class-by-class basis. This would provide better information on how an NRSRO's ratings have performed within the field of financial products relevant to any given user of credit ratings and investor. For example, an investor contemplating the purchase of a highly-rated subprime RMBS would be able to consider the performance of an NRSRO's ratings of structured finance products, which would be more useful than the NRSRO's general performance statistics across all classes of credit ratings. Specifically, an NRSRO may be much better at assessing the creditworthiness of corporate debt securities than of structured finance products. Consequently, performance statistics of such an NRSRO that incorporate all classes of credit ratings (e.g., corporate debt and structured finance products) would be less precise in terms of evaluating the performance of the NRSRO's credit ratings for structured finance products.

Furthermore, by defining "short-term, mid-term, and long-term" periods as 1, 3, and 10-year timeframes, the proposed amendment would provide a better basis for comparing the performance of different NRSROs as the statistics for each NRSRO would cover the same periods. Finally, the replacement of the "down-grade" requirement with a "ratings transition" requirement and the clarification of what default statistics would need to be incorporated into the ratings performance statistics would further enhance investor understanding of NRSRO performance by requiring that similar information be captured in the NRSROs' performance rating statistics and eliminating certain ways that could be used to "pad" statistics.

The Commission generally requests comment on all aspects of these proposed amendments. In addition, the Commission requests comment on the following questions related to the proposals.

- Should the Commission prescribe specific standards for the performance statistics, such as requiring an NRSRO to disclose how its credit ratings performed relative to metrics such as credit spreads? Commenters endorsing such an approach should provide specific details as to how it could be implemented; taking into consideration factors such as the issues related to the difficulty of obtaining timely and consistent pricing information for many debt instruments and the volatility of credit spreads.
- Should the Commission require performance statistics in a more granular form than by class of credit ratings? For example, should the Commission require for structured finance products statistics by more narrowly defined asset classes such as CDOs and RMBS or types of asset-backed securities such as those backed by home loans, credit cards, or commercial real estate? Commenters endorsing greater granularity should provide specific details, including definitions of the credit rating classes.
- Should the Commission prescribe different time periods for the short, medium, and long term statistics than 1, 3, and 10 years, respectively. For example, should the periods be 6 months, 2 years and 7 years or 2, 5, and 15 years or some other set of time periods?

2. Enhanced Disclosure of Ratings Methodologies

The Commission is proposing to amend the instructions for Exhibit 2 to Form NRSRO to require enhanced disclosures about the procedures and methodologies an NRSRO uses to determine credit ratings. Section 1 5E(a)(1)(B)(ii) of the Exchange Act requires that an application for registration as an NRSRO contain information regarding the procedures and methodologies used by the firm to determine credit ratings.[140] The Commission implemented this requirement by prescribing through the instructions to Form NRSRO that an applicant and NRSRO must provide general descriptions of their procedures and methodologies for determining credit ratings and that the descriptions must be sufficiently detailed to provide users of credit ratings with an understanding of the procedures and methodologies. The instructions also identified various areas that are required to be addressed in Exhibit 2, including, as applicable, descriptions of the NRSRO's policies for determining whether to initiate a credit rating; the public and nonpublic sources of information used in determining credit ratings, including information and analysis provided by third-party venders; and the quantitative and qualitative models and metrics used to determine credit ratings.

The Commission is proposing to add three additional areas that an applicant and a registered NRSRO would be required to address in the descriptions of its procedures and methodologies in Exhibit 2. The inclusion of these would serve to better disclose the actions an applicant and NRSRO is, or is not taking, in determining credit ratings. The additional areas required to be addressed in the exhibit would be:

- Whether and, if so, how information about verification performed on assets underlying or referenced by a security or money market instrument issued by an asset pool or as part of any asset-backed or mortgage-backed securities transaction is relied on in determining credit ratings;
- Whether and, if so, how assessments of the quality of originators of assets underlying or referenced by a security or money market instrument issued by an asset pool or as part of any asset-backed or mortgage-backed securities transaction play a part in the determination of credit ratings; and
- How frequently credit ratings are reviewed, whether different models or criteria are used for ratings surveillance than for determining initial ratings, whether changes made to models and criteria for determining initial ratings are applied retroactively to existing ratings, and whether changes made to models and criteria for performing ratings surveillance are incorporated into the models and criteria for determining initial ratings.

The Commission is proposing these amendments, in part, under authority to require such additional information in the application as it finds necessary or appropriate in the public interest or for the protection of investors.[141] The Commission preliminarily believes the proposed new disclosure requirements for Exhibit 2 are necessary and appropriate and in the public interest or for the protection of investors. Specifically, they are designed to provide greater clarity around three areas of the NRSROs' rating processes, particularly for structured finance products, where questions have been raised in the context of the credit market turmoil: namely, the verification performed on information provided in loan documents; the quality of loan originators; and the surveillance of existing ratings and how changes to models are applied to existing ratings. The amendments are designed to enhance the disclosures NRSROs make in these areas and, thereby, allow users of credit ratings to better evaluate the quality of their ratings processes.

The first proposed amendment would require an NRSRO to disclose whether it considers in its rating process for structured finance product steps taken to verify information about the assets in the pool backing the structured finance product. Underwriters and sponsors of structured finance products frequently take some steps to verify information provided by borrowers in loan documentation. Generally, they have been reluctant to provide this information to NRSROs for proprietary reasons. The proposed amendment would not require that the NRSROs incorporate verification (or the lack of verification) into their ratings processes. Rather, it would require an NRSRO to disclose whether and, if so, how information about verification performed on the assets is relied on in determining credit ratings for structured finance products. For example, an NRSRO would need to disclose, as applicable: if it does not consider steps taken to verify the information; if it requires some minimum level of verification to be performed before it will determine a credit rating for a structured finance product; and how it incorporates the level of verification performed into its procedures and methodologies for determining credit ratings (e.g., if it compensates for the lack of verification by requiring greater levels of credit enhancement for the tranche securities).

The Commission preliminarily believes this disclosure would benefit users of credit ratings by providing information about the potential accuracy of an NRSRO's credit ratings. As noted above, the NRSROs determine credit ratings for structured finance products based on assumptions in their models as to how the assets underlying the instruments will perform under varying levels of stress. These assumptions are based on the characteristics of the assets (e.g., value of the property, income of the borrower) as reported by the arranger of the structured finance product. If this information is inaccurate, the capacity of the model to predict the potential future performance of the assets may be significantly impaired. Consequently, information about whether an NRSRO requires that some level of verification be performed or takes other steps to account for the lack of verification or a low level of verification would be useful to users of credit ratings in assessing the potential for an NRSRO's credit ratings to be adversely impacted by bad information about the assets underlying a rated structured finance product.

The second proposed amendment would require an NRSRO to disclose whether it considers qualitative assessments of the originator of assets underlying a structured finance product in the rating process for such products. Certain qualities of an asset originator, such as its experience and underwriting standards, may impact the quality of the loans it originates and the accuracy of the associated loan documentation. This, in turn, could influence how the assets ultimately perform and the ability of the NRSRO's models to predict their performance. Consequently, the failure to perform any assessment of the loan originators could increase the risk that an NRSRO's credit ratings may not be accurate. Therefore, disclosures as to whether the NRSRO performs any qualitative assessments of the originators would be useful in comparing the efficacy of the NRSROs' procedures and methodologies.

The third proposed amendment would require an NRSRO to disclose the frequency of its surveillance efforts and how changes to its quantitative and qualitative ratings models are incorporated into the surveillance process. The Commission believes that users of credit ratings would find information about these matters useful in comparing the ratings methodologies of different NRSROs. For example, how often and with what models an NRSRO monitors its credit ratings would be relevant to assessing the accuracy of the ratings insomuch as ratings based on stale information and outdated models may not be as accurate as ratings of like products determined using newer data and models. Moreover, with respect to new types of rated obligors and debt securities, the NRSROs refine their models as more information about the performance of these obligors and debt securities is observed and incorporated into their assumptions. Consequently, as the models evolve based on more robust performance data, credit ratings of obligors or debt securities determined using older models may be at greater risk for being inaccurate than the newer ratings. Therefore, whether the NRSRO verifies the older ratings using the newer methodologies would be useful to users of credit ratings in assessing the accuracy of the credit ratings.

The Commission generally requests comment on all aspects of the proposed amendments. In addition, the Commission requests comment on the following question related to the proposals.

- Are there other areas of the ratings process where enhanced disclosure on Form NRSRO would benefit investors and other users of credit ratings? Commenters endorsing further disclosures should specifically identify them.

D. Amendment to Rule 17g-3 (Report of Credit Rating Actions)

The Commission adopted Rule 17g-3 pursuant to authority in Section 15E(k)[142] of the Exchange Act, which requires an NRSRO to furnish to the Commission, on a confidential basis[143] and at intervals determined by the Commission, such financial statements and information concerning its financial condition as the Commission, by rule, may prescribe as necessary or appropriate in the public interest or for the protection of investors. The statute also provides that the Commission may, by rule, require that the financial statements be certified by an independent public accountant.[144] In addition, Section 17(a)(1) of the Exchange Act[145] requires an NRSRO to make and keep such records, and make and disseminate such reports, as the Commission prescribes by rule as necessary or appropriate in the public interest, for the protection of investors, or otherwise in furtherance of the Exchange Act. [146]

Rule 17g-3 requires an NRSRO to furnish the Commission on an annual basis the following reports: audited financial statements; unaudited consolidated financial statements of the parent of the NRSRO, if applicable; an unaudited report concerning revenue categories of the NRSRO; an unaudited report concerning compensation of the NRSRO's credit analysts; and an unaudited report listing the largest customers of the NRSRO. The rule further requires an NRSRO to furnish the Commission these reports within 90 days of the end of its fiscal year.

The Commission is proposing to amend Rule 17g-3 to require an NRSRO to furnish the Commission with an additional annual report of the number of credit rating actions during the fiscal year in each class of security for which the NRSRO is registered. Specifically, the amendment would add a new paragraph (a)(6) to Rule 17g-3, which would require an NRSRO to provide the Commission with a report of the number of credit rating actions (upgrades, downgrades, and placements on watch for an upgrade or downgrade) during the fiscal year in each class of credit ratings for which the NRSRO is registered with the Commission. A note to paragraph (a)(6) would clarify that for the purposes of reporting credit rating actions in the asset-backed security class of credit ratings described in Section 3(a)(62)(B)(iv) of the Rating Agency Act[147] an NRSRO would need to include credit rating actions on any security or money market instrument issued by an asset pool or as part of any asset-backed or mortgage-backed securities transaction. This is designed to ensure the inclusion of information about ratings actions for credit ratings of structured finance products that do not meet the narrower statutory definition of "issuers of asset-backed securities (as that term is defined is section 1101(c) of part 229 of title 17, Code of Federal Regulations)."[148]

The Commission is proposing this amendment, in part, under authority to require an NRSRO to "make and disseminate such reports as the Commission, by rule, prescribes as necessary or appropriate in the public interest, for the protection of investors, or otherwise in furtherance of the purposes of [the Exchange Act]."[149] The Commission preliminarily believes this proposed amendment is necessary and appropriate in the public interest, for the protection of investors, or otherwise in furtherance of the purposes of the Exchange Act because it would assist the Commission in its examination function of NRSROs. Large spikes in ratings actions within a class of credit ratings could indicate the processes for determining the ratings may be compromised by inappropriate factors. For example, a substantial increase in the number of downgrades in a particular class of credit ratings may be indicative of the fact that the initial ratings were higher than the NRSRO's procedures and methodologies would have implied because the NRSRO sought to gain favor with issuers and underwriters by issuing higher ratings. A substantial increase in upgrades also could be the result of the NRSRO attempting to gain favor with issuers and underwriters.

The Commission recognizes that an increase in the number of ratings actions in a particular class of credit ratings may be the result of macroeconomic factors broadly impacting the rated obligors or securities. In this case, the ratings actions would be the result of appropriate credit analysis and not inappropriate extraneous factors. On the other hand, large numbers of actions could be a signal that the process for rating and monitoring ratings in the impacted class has been compromised by improper practices such as failing to adhere to disclosed and internally documented ratings procedures and methodologies, having prohibited conflicts, failing to establish reasonable procedures to manage conflicts, or engaging in unfair, coercive, or abusive conduct. Consequently, the report would be a valuable tool to improve the focus of examination resources.

The Commission generally requests comment on all aspects of this proposed amendment. In addition, the Commission requests comment on the following questions related to the proposal.

- Could the performance statistics currently required in Exhibit 1 to Form NRSRO, as well as the proposed enhancements to those statistics, be used to target potential problem areas in an NRSRO's credit rating processes in the same manner as this proposed report thereby making the report redundant?
- Should the Commission also require NRSROs to furnish an "early warning" report to the Commission when the number of downgrades in a class of credit ratings passes a certain percentage threshold (e.g., 5%, 10%, 15%, or 20%) within a number of calendar or business days (e.g., 2, 5, 10, or 15 days) after the threshold is passed, similar to the broker-dealer notification rule (See 17 CFR 240.17a-1 1)?

III. Proposed New Rule 17g-7 (Special Reporting or Use of Symbols to Differentiate Credit Ratings for Structured Finance Products)

The Commission is proposing a new rule, Rule 17g-7, to address concerns that certain investors assumed the risk characteristics for structured finance products, particularly highly rated instruments, were the same as for other types of similarly rated instruments. This proposal also is designed to address concerns that some investors may not have performed internal risk analysis on structured finance products before purchasing them, although at least one survey indicates that many institutional investors asserted that this was not a widespread problem.[150] Specifically, under proposed Rule 17g-7, each time an NRSRO published a credit rating for a structured finance product it also would be required to publish a report describing how the credit ratings procedures and methodologies and credit risk characteristics for structured finance products differ from those of other types of rated instruments such as corporate and municipal debt securities. The objective of this proposal is to alert investors that there are different rating methodologies and risk characteristics associated with structured finance products. As an alternative to publishing the report, an NRSRO would be allowed to use ratings symbols for structured finance products that differentiated them from the credit ratings for other types of debt securities.

More specifically, paragraph (a) of proposed Rule 17g-7 would require an NRSRO to publish a report accompanying every credit rating it publishes for a security or money market instrument issued by an asset pool or as part of any asset-backed or mortgage-backed securities transaction that describes the rating methodology used to determine the credit rating and how it differs from a rating for any other type of obligor or debt security and how the risks associated with a security or money market instrument issued by an asset pool or as part of any asset-backed or mortgage-backed securities transaction are different from other types of rated obligors and debt securities. A possible risk associated with this approach is that investors would come to view such reports as "boilerplate" and therefore would not review them.

However, the Commission preliminarily believes that requiring an NRSRO to publish such a report along with each publication of a credit rating for a structured finance product likely would provide certain investors with useful information about structured finance products. The goal of the proposal is to spur investors to perform more rigorous internal risk analysis on structure finance products so that they do not overly rely on NRSRO credit ratings in making investment decisions. A possible ancillary benefit of such reports is that they could cause certain investors to seek to better understand risks that are not necessarily addressed in credit ratings of structured products, such as market and liquidity risk.

Because the goal of the rule is to foster greater independent analysis by investors, the Commission preliminarily believes that permitting an NRSRO to comply with the rule by differentiating its structured finance product rating symbols would be an equally effective alternative. The differentiated symbol would alert investors that a structured product was being rated and, therefore, raise the question of how it differs from other types of debt instruments.

The Commission is not proposing to require that specific rating symbols be used to distinguish credit ratings for structured finance products. An NRSRO would be permitted to choose the appropriate symbol. The Commission preliminarily believes that methods for identifying credit ratings for structured finance products could include using a different rating symbol altogether, such as a numerical symbol, or appending identifying characters to existing ratings scales, e.g., "AAA.sf" or "AAASF."

The Commission is proposing these amendments under authority to require an NRSRO to "make and disseminate such reports as the Commission, by rule, prescribes as necessary or appropriate in the public interest, for the protection of investors, or otherwise in furtherance of the purposes of [the Exchange Act]."[151] The Commission preliminarily believes these proposed amendments are necessary and appropriate in the public interest, for the protection of investors, or otherwise in furtherance of the purposes of the Exchange Act because they are designed to encourage investors to perform greater levels of internal risk assessment of structured finance products by putting them on notice that these products have different characteristics than other types of rated debt instruments. The Commission does acknowledge the risks related to these proposals as outlined above.

The Commission generally requests comment on all aspects of this proposed rule. In addition, the Commission request comment on the following questions related to the proposal.

- Would the use of different rating symbols for structured products impact automated securities trading, routing, settlement, clearance, trade confirmation, reporting, processing, and risk management systems and any other systems that are programmed to use standard credit rating symbols across all product classes? Commenters should describe how these systems may be impacted and associated costs to address the impacts on the firm such as costs to change or update the systems. Commenters also should describe how the impacts to these systems could impact trading activity in the markets for structured finance products.
- Is the proposed rule sufficiently clear about the types of securities and money market instruments to which it applies? Are there securities to which the proposal applies that should not be subject to the requirement of a report or a differentiated symbol?
- Would the use of different rating symbols have consequences for investment guidelines and covenants in legal documents that use credit ratings to distinguish finance instruments? Commenters should describe the potential consequences and associated costs to market participants and to the finance markets more broadly.
- Would the use of different rating symbols or reports dissuade purchases of structured finance products?
- Would the reports or differentiated symbols achieve the Commission's stated goal of encouraging investors to perform more internal risk assessments of structured finance products? Could the reports cause investors to ignore other relevant disclosures or lead to confusion?
- Should the rule be expanded to require reports or different ratings symbols for each class of credit ratings identified in Section 3 (a)(62)(B) of the Exchange Act (15 U.S.C. 78c(a)(62)(B)); namely: (1) financial institutions, brokers, or dealers; (2) insurance companies; (3) corporate issuers; (4) issuers of asset-backed securities; and (5) issuers of government securities, municipal securities or securities issued

by a foreign government? Alternatively, should the rule be expanded to require reports or different ratings symbols for only certain of these classes or subclasses such as for municipal securities?

- Should the rule prohibit an NRSRO from using a common set of symbols (e.g., AAA, AA, A, BBB, BB, B, CCC, CC, C) to rate different types of obligors and debt securities (e.g., corporate debt and municipal debt) where the NRSRO uses different methodologies for determining such ratings? Would such a proposal raise any questions relating to the scope of the Commission's legal authority in this area?
- Should the rule allow the use of a common set of symbols only if the NRSRO determines additional types of ratings to distinguish the different risk characteristics of the different types of obligors and debt securities? For example, the rule could require the determination of ratings to distinguish the potential volatility of the credit ratings of different classes of obligors and debt securities or the differing levels of market and liquidity risk associated with different classes of debt securities. Would such disclosures raise any concerns regarding liability if they were found to be deficient?

IV. Paperwork Reduction Act

Certain provisions of the proposed rule amendments contain a "collection of information" within the meaning of the Paperwork Reduction Act of 1995 ("PRA").[152] The Commission is submitting these proposed amendments and proposed rule to the Office of Management and Budget ("OMB") for review in accordance with the PRA. An agency may not conduct or sponsor, and a person is not required to comply with, a collection of information unless it displays a currently valid control number. The titles for the collections of information are:

1 Rule 17g-1, Application for registration as a nationally recognized statistical rating agency; Form NRSRO and the Instructions for Form NRSRO (OMB Control Number 3235-0625);
2 Rule 17g-2, Records to be made and retained by national recognized statistical rating organizations (OMB Control Number 3235-0628) ;
3 Rule 17g-3, Annual reports to be furnished by nationally recognized statistical rating organizations (OMB Control Number 3235-0626);
4 Rule 1 7g-5, Conflicts of interest (a proposed new collection of information); and
5 Rule 17g-7, Credit rating reports to be furnished by national recognized statistical rating organizations (a proposed new collection of information).

A. Collections of Information under the Proposed Amendments

The Commission is proposing for comment rule amendments to prescribe additional requirements for NRSROs to address concerns that have arisen with respect to their role in the credit market turmoil. These proposed amendments would modify rules the Commission adopted in 2007 to implement registration, recordkeeping, financial reporting, and oversight rules under the Rating Agency Act. Additionally, the Commission is proposing a new rule under authority provided in the Rating Agency Act.[153] Certain of the proposed amendments and the proposed new rule would contain recordkeeping and disclosure requirements that would be subject to the PRA. The collection of information obligations imposed by the proposed amendments and proposed new rule would be mandatory. The proposed amendments and proposed new rule, however, would apply only to credit rating agencies that are registered with the Commission as NRSROs. Such registration is voluntary.[154]

In summary, the proposed rule amendments and proposed new rule would require: (1) an NRSRO to provide enhanced disclosure of performance measurements statistics and the procedures and methodologies used by the NRSRO in determining credit ratings for structured finance products and other debt securities on Form NRSRO; (2) an NRSRO to make, keep and preserve additional records under Rule 17g-2;[155] (3) an NRSRO to make its rating actions and the date of such actions from the initial credit rating to the current credit rating publicly available in an XBRL Interactive Data File no later than six months after the date of the rating action;[156] (4) an NRSRO to furnish the Commission with an additional annual report;[157] (5) disclosure of certain information about securities being rated beginning on the date the issuer or depositor sets the offering price of the securities being rated;[158] and (6) an NRSRO to attach a report to its credit ratings for structured finance products describing the rating methodology used and how it differs from the determination of ratings for other types of securities or use a symbol that identifies the rated security as a structured finance product.[159]

B. Proposed Use of Information

The proposed amendments and new rule would enhance the framework for Commission oversight of NRSROs in response to the recent credit market turmoil.[160] The collections of information in the proposed amendments and new rule are designed to assist the Commission in effectively monitoring, through its examination function, whether an NRSRO is conducting its activities in accordance with Section 15E of the Exchange Act[161] and the rules thereunder. In addition, these proposed amendments and the new rule are designed to assist users of credit ratings by proposing to require the disclosure of additional information with respect to an NRSRO that could be used to compare the credit ratings quality of different NRSROs, particularly with respect to structured finance products. The Commission believes that the information that NRSROs would have to make public as a result of the proposed amendments would advance one of the primary objectives of the Rating Agency Act, as noted in the accompanying Senate Report, to "facilitate informed decisions by giving investors the opportunity to compare ratings quality of different firms."[162]

C. Respondents

In adopting the final rules under the Rating Agency Act, the Commission estimated that approximately 30 credit rating agencies would be registered as NRSROs.[163] The

Commission believes that this estimate continues to be appropriate for identifying the number of respondents for purposes of the proposed amendments and for proposed new Rule 17g-7. Since the initial set of rules under the Rating Agency Act became effective in June 2007, nine credit rating agencies have registered with the Commission as NRSROs.[164] The registration program has been in effect for less than a year; consequently, the Commission expects additional entities will register. While 20 more entities may not ultimately register, the Commission believes the estimate is within reasonable bounds and appropriate given that it adds an element of conservatism as it increases paperwork burden estimates as well as cost estimates.

In addition, proposed Rule 17g-5(a)(3)[165] would require the disclosure of certain information provided to, and used by, an NRSRO in determining an initial rating for a security or money market instrument issued by an asset pool or as part of any asset- backed or mortgage-backed securities transaction and for monitoring those ratings. The rule would not specify which party would disclose such information: the NRSRO, sponsor, issuer, depositor, trustee or some other person. The Commission believes that the most likely persons to disclose this information would be structured finance product arrangers, managers, or trustees as they are the entities that generate the information and provide it to the NRSROs. For purposes of the PRA estimate for proposed Rule 17g- 5(a)(3), based on staff information gained from the NRSRO examination process, the Commission estimates that there would be approximately 200 respondents. As noted throughout the release, the number of arrangers bringing structured finance products to market is small relative to the number of deals.

The Commission generally requests comment on all aspects of these proposed estimates for the number of respondents. In addition, the Commission requests specific comment on the following items related to these estimates.

- Should the Commission use the number of credit rating agencies currently registered as NRSROs rather the estimated number of 30 ultimate registrants? Alternatively, is there a basis to estimate a different number of likely registrants?
- Is the Commission correct in believing that structured product arrangers, managers, and trustees would be the entities that disclose the information required under the proposed amendments to Rule 17g-5(a)?
- Are there sources that could provide credible information that could be used to determine the number of credit rating agencies and other NRSROs that would be subject to the proposed paperwork burdens? Commenters should identify any such sources and explain how a given source could be used to either support the Commission's estimate or arrive at a different estimate.

Commenters should provide specific data and analysis to support any comments they submit with respect to these burden estimates.

D. Total Annual Recordkeeping and Reporting Burden

As discussed in further detail below, the Commission estimates the total recordkeeping burden resulting from the proposed amendments and proposed new rule would be approximately 1,434,690 hours on an annual basis[166] and 64,500 hours on a one-time basis.[167]

The total annual and one-time hour burden estimates described below are averages across all types of NRSROs expected to be affected by the proposed amendment and new rule. The size and complexity of NRSROs range from small entities to entities that are part of complex global organizations employing thousands of credit analysts. Consequently, the burden hour estimates represent the average time across all NRSROs. The Commission further notes that, given the significant variance in size between the largest NRSROs and the smallest NRSROs, the burden estimates, as averages across all NRSROs, are skewed higher because the largest firms currently predominate in the industry.

1. Amendments to Form NRSRO

The proposed amendments to Form NRSRO would change the instructions for the Form to require that NRSROs provide more detailed credit ratings performance statistics in Exhibit 1 and disclose with greater specificity information about the procedures and methodologies used to determine structured finance and other credit ratings in Exhibit 2.[168] The Commission expects these proposed amendments would not have a material effect on the respondents' hour burden. The Commission believes that the total annual burden hours of 2,100 currently approved by OMB would not change for Rule 17g-1 and Form NRSRO materially because the additional disclosures would be included within the overall preparation of the initial Form NRSRO for new applicants. Additionally, the Commission believes that the nine currently registered NRSROs could be required to prepare and furnish an amended Form NRSRO to update their registration applications if the Commission were to adopt the proposed amendments (i.e., nine amended Form NRSROs). However, the Commission believes these potential nine furnishings of Form NRSRO are accounted for in the currently approved PRA collection for Rule 1 7g- 1, which includes an estimate that each NRSRO would file two amendments to Form NRSRO per year.[169]

The Commission generally requests comment on all aspects of these proposed burden estimates for Rule 17g-1 and Form NRSRO, proposed to be amended. In addition, the Commission requests specific comment on the following items related to these estimates:

- Would the proposed additional disclosure requirements increase the burden hours from the amount currently budgeted for Rule 17g-1 and Form NRSRO?

Commenters should provide specific data and analysis to support any comments they submit with respect to these burden estimates.

2. Amendments to Rule 17g-2

Rule 17g-2 requires an NRSRO to make and keep current certain records relating to its business and requires an NRSRO to preserve those and other records for certain prescribed time periods.[170] The Commission's current estimate for the average one-time burden of implementing a recordkeeping system to comply with Rule 17g-2 is 300 hours.[171] Additionally, the total annual burden currently approved by OMB for Rule 17g2 is 7,620 hours, which represents the average annual amount of time an NRSRO will spend to make and maintain these records (254 hours per year) multiplied by 30 respondents.[172]

The proposed amendments to Rule 17g-2 would require an NRSRO to make and retain two additional records and retain a third type of record. The records to be made and retained would be: (1) a record of the rationale for any material difference between the credit rating implied by the model and the final credit rating issued, if a quantitative model is a substantial component in the process of determining a credit rating;[173] and (2) a record showing the history and dates of all previous rating actions with respect to each current credit rating.[174] The proposed amendments to Rule 17g-2 would require an NRSRO to make the second set of records – rating actions related to current ratings – publicly available in an XBRL Interactive Data File.[175] In addition, the proposed amendments would require an NRSRO to retain communications that contain any complaints by an obligor, issuer, underwriter, or sponsor about the performance of a credit analyst.[176]

With respect to the proposed amendments to Rule 17g-2, the Commission estimates, based on staff information gained from the NRSRO examination process, that the total one-time and annual record recordkeeping burdens would increase approximately 10% and 5%, respectively.[177] Thus, the Commission estimates that the one-time burden that each NRSRO would spend implementing a recordkeeping system to comply with Rule 17g-2 as proposed to be amended would be approximately 330 hours,[178] for a total one-time burden of 9,900 hours for 30 NRSROs.[179] The Commission estimates that an NRSRO would spend an average of 267 hours per year[180] to make and retain records under Rule 17g-2 as proposed to be amended, for a total annual hour burden under Rule 17g-2 of 8,010 hours.[181] This estimate would result in an increase in the currently approved PRA burden under Rule 1 7g-2 of 390 annual burden hours.[182] As discussed above, the increase in annual burden hours would result from the increase in the number of records an NRSRO would be required to make and retain under the proposed amendments to Rule 17g-2.

In addition, the proposed amendments to Rule 17g-2 would require an NRSRO to make the records of its rating actions publicly available in an XBRL Interactive Data File.[183]

The Commission believes that an NRSRO would choose to make this information available through its Internet Web site and that each NRSRO already has, or would have, an Internet Web site. Therefore, based on staff information gained from the NRSRO examination process, the Commission estimates that, on average, an NRSRO would spend approximately 30 hours to publicly disclose the history of its rating actions for each credit rating in an XBRL Interactive Data File and, thereafter, 10 hours per year to update this information.[184] Accordingly, the total aggregate one-time burden to the industry to make the history of rating actions publicly available in an XBRL Interactive Data File would be 900 hours,[185] and the total aggregate annual burden hours would be 300 hours.[186]

Under the currently approved PRA collection for Rule 17g-2, the Commission estimated that an NRSRO may need to purchase recordkeeping system software to establish a recordkeeping system in conformance with Rule 17g-2[187] The Commission estimated that the cost of the software would vary based on the size and complexity of the NRSRO. Also, the Commission estimated that some NRSROs would not need such software because they already have adequate recordkeeping systems or, given their small size, such software would not be necessary. Based on these estimates, the Commission estimated that the average cost for recordkeeping software across all NRSROs would be approximately $1,000 per firm, with an aggregate one-time cost to the industry of $30,000. The Commission estimates that the proposed amendments to Rule 17g-2 would not alter this estimate or that any increases in the cost would be de minimis.

The Commission generally requests comment on all aspects of these proposed burden estimates for Rule 17g-2. In addition, the Commission requests specific comment on the following items related to these burden estimates:

- Are there publicly available reports or other data sources the Commission should consider in arriving at these burden estimates?
- Are the estimates that these amendments would result in an increase to the current total one-time and annual recordkeeping burdens of approximately 10% and 5% accurate? If not, should they be higher or lower?
- Are the estimates that the requirement to make records of rating actions publicly available in an XBRL Interactive Data File would result in an increased one-time burden for each NRSRO of approximately 30 hours to publicly disclose the history of its rating actions for each credit rating in an XBRL Interactive Data File and, thereafter, 10 hours per year to update this information accurate? If not, should they be higher or lower?
- Is the estimate that the NRSROs would incur no additional costs (or that any additional costs would be de minimis) to update recordkeeping systems to comply with the proposed new recordkeeping requirements accurate? If not, what would the additional costs be?

Commenters should provide specific data and analysis to support any comments they submit with respect to these burden estimates.

3. Proposed Amendment to Rule 17g-3

Rule 17g-3 requires an NRSRO to furnish certain financial reports to the Commission on an annual basis, including audited financial statements as well as other financial reports.[188] The Commission is proposing to amend Rule 17g-3 to require an NRSRO to furnish the Commission with an additional report: an unaudited report of the number of credit ratings that were changed during the fiscal year in each class of credit ratings for which the NRSRO is registered with the Commission.[189]

The total annual burden currently approved by OMB for Rule 17g-3 is 6,000 hours, based on the fact that it would take an NRSRO, on average, approximately 200 hours to prepare for and file the annual reports.[190] In addition, the total annual cost burden currently approved by OMB is $450,000 to engage the services of an independent public accountant to conduct the annual audit as part of the preparation of the first report required by Rule 17g-3.[191] This estimate is based on 30 NRSROs hiring an independent public accountant on an annual basis for an average of $15,000.[192]

The Commission believes that the proposed amendment to Rule 17g-3 that would require a report on an NRSRO's rating changes during a fiscal year would have a de minimis effect on the annual hour burden for the current PRA collection for Rule 1 7g-3. The Commission preliminarily believes that an NRSRO already would have this information with respect to each class of credit ratings for which it is registered. In addition, the proposed amendment does not prescribe a format for the report. Consequently, the Commission estimates that proposed Rule 17g-3(a)(6) would not have a significant effect on the total annual hour burden currently approved for the PRA for Rule 17g-3.

The Commission generally requests comment on all aspects of these proposed burden estimates for Rule 17g-3. In addition, the Commission requests specific comment on the following items related to these burden estimates:

- Are there publicly available reports or other data sources the Commission should consider in arriving at these burden estimates?

Commenters should provide specific data and analysis to support any comments they submit with respect to these burden estimates.

4. Amendments to Rule 17g-5

Rules 17g-5 requires an NRSRO to manage and disclose certain conflicts of interest.[193] The rule also prohibits specific types of conflicts of interest.[194] The proposed amendments to Rule 17g-5 would add an additional conflict to paragraph (b) of Rule 17g5. This proposed conflict of interest would be issuing or maintaining a credit rating for a security or money market instrument issued by an asset pool or as part of an asset-backed or mortgage-backed securities transaction that was paid for by the issuer, sponsor, or underwriter of the security or money market instrument.[195] Under the proposal, an NRSRO would be prohibited from issuing a credit rating for a structured finance product, unless certain information about the transaction and the assets underlying the structured finance product are disclosed.[196] Specifically, the following information would need to be made publicly available beginning on the date the underwriter, issuer or depositor set the offering price of the securities being rated: (1) all information provided to the NRSRO that is used in determining the initial credit rating, including information about the characteristics of the assets underlying or referenced by the security or money market instrument, and the legal structure; and (2) all information provided to the NRSRO by the issuer, underwriter, sponsor, depositor or trustee that is used by the NRSRO in undertaking credit rating surveillance on the security or money market instrument.[197] In a private offering, the above information would need to be made available on the date the underwriter and the issuer or depositor set the offering price of the securities being rated only to credit rating agencies and investors; it would need to be made publicly available, however, no later than one business day after the offering closes.

The proposed rule would not specify which party would disclose the information: the NRSRO, sponsor, issuer, depositor or trustee. The Commission preliminarily believes that in order to avoid conflicts with Securities Act prohibitions on general solicitations as well as to avoid making the NRSRO liable for the accuracy of information that would originally be supplied by the arrangers and trustees of structured products, this information would likely be disclosed by those arrangers and trustees. The Commission estimates that there would be approximately 200 such entities. For purposes of this PRA, the Commission estimates that it would take a respondent approximately 300 hours to develop a system, as well as policies and procedures, for the disclosures required by the proposed rule. This estimate is based on the Commission's experience with, and burden estimates for, the recordkeeping requirements for NRSROs.[198] Accordingly, the Commission believes, based on staff experience, that a respondent would take approximately 300 hours on a one-time basis to implement a disclosure system to comply with the proposal in that a respondent would need a set of policies and procedures for disclosing the information, as well as a system for making the information publicly available. This would result in a total one-time hour burden of 60,000 hours for 200 respondents.[199]

In addition to the one-time hour burden, disclosure would also be required under the proposed rule on a transaction by transaction basis when an initial rating is determined. Based on staff experience, the Commission estimates that each respondent would disclose information with respect to approximately 20 new transactions per year and that it would take approximately 1 hour per transaction to make the information publicly available. This estimate is based on the Commission's expectation that the respondent will have already implemented the system and policies and procedures for disclosure. The Commission estimates that a large NRSRO would have rated approximately 2,000 new RMBS and CDO transactions in a given year. The Commission is basing this estimate on the number of new RMBS and CDO deals rated in 2006 by two of the largest NRSROs which rated structured finance transactions. The Commission adjusted this number to approximately 4,000 transactions in order to include other types of structured finance products, including commercial MBS and other consumer assets. Therefore, the Commission estimates for purposes of the PRA that each respondent would arrange approximately 20 new transactions per year: 4,000 new transactions/200 arrangers = 20 new transactions. The Commission notes that the number of new transactions arranged per year would vary by the size of arranger and that this estimate would be an average across all respondents. Larger respondents may arrange in excess of 20 new deals per year, while a smaller entity may only arrange one or two new deals on an annual basis. Based on this analysis, the Commission estimates that it would take a respondent approximately 20 hours[200] to disclose this information under the proposed rule, on an annual basis, for a total aggregate annual hour burden of 4,000 hours.[201]

In addition, proposed Rule 17g-5(a)(ii) would require disclosure of information provided to an NRSRO that is used by an NRSRO in undertaking credit rating surveillance on a security or money market instrument. Because surveillance would cover more than just initial ratings, the Commission estimates based on staff information gained from the NRSRO examination process that monthly disclosure would be required with respect to approximately 125 transactions on an ongoing basis. Also based on staff information gained from the NRSRO examination process, the Commission estimates that it would take a respondent approximately 0.5 hours per transaction to disclose the information. Therefore, the Commission estimates that each respondent would spend approximately 750 hours[202] on an annual basis disclosing information under proposed Rule 17g-5, for a total aggregate annual burden hours of 150,000 hours.[203]

The Commission generally requests comment on all aspects of these proposed burden estimates for Rule 17g-5. In addition, the Commission requests specific comment on the following items related to these estimates:

- Are there publicly available reports or other data sources the Commission should consider in arriving at these burden estimates?
- Are the estimates of the one-time and recurring burdens of the proposed additional disclosures accurate? If not, should they be higher or lower?

Commenters should provide specific data and analysis to support any comments they submit with respect to these burden estimates.

5. Proposed Rule 17g-7

The Commission is proposing a new rule – Rule 17g-7 – which would address concerns that investors believe that the risk characteristics for a structured finance product are the same as for other types of obligors or debt securities. Proposed Rule 17g7 would require an NRSRO to attach a report each time it publishes a credit rating for a structured finance product describing how the ratings procedures and methodologies differ from those for other types of obligors or debt securities.[204] Proposed Rule 17g-7 would include an exemption to this requirement, however, if the NRSRO used credit rating symbols for structured finance products that identify the product as such as distinct from any other type of obligor or debt security. The Commission believes that proposed Rule 1 7g-7[205] would provide users of credit ratings with useful information either through the report or the differentiated symbol upon which to base their investment decisions.

The Commission expects that most NRSROs already have documented their methodologies and procedures in place to determine credit ratings for structured finance products and corporate debt securities, and have disclosed such policies and procedures if they have registered with the Commission as an NRSRO. The Commission expects, however, that an NRSRO would have to compile and/or modify these documents to comply with the specific reporting requirements that would be mandated by the proposed rule. Based on staff information gained from the NRSRO examination process, the Commission estimates that it would take an NRSRO approximately 50 hours[206] to draft the report required under the proposed rule for a total one-time hour burden of 1,500 hours.[207]

The Commission also estimates that it would take an NRSRO additional time to publish the report each time a credit rating for a structured finance product is published and to monitor the publications of structured finance credit ratings to ensure compliance with the proposed rule. Based on the average number of credit ratings of asset-backed securities outstanding as of the latest fiscal year of the three largest NRSROs, the Commission estimates that an NRSRO would publish approximately 128,000 asset- backed credit ratings per year.[208] The Commission notes that this number may not include all structured finance ratings, since some may not fit within the statutory definition of asset-backed security. However, the Commission also notes that the issuance of RMBS has dropped dramatically off recent highs. Accordingly, the Commission believes the number of asset-backed ratings reported in Form NRSRO is a reasonable proxy for the number of structured finance ratings. The Commission also notes that, as discussed below, the burden estimate identifies 30 respondents. However, most of the structured finance ratings are concentrated in the largest 3 or 4 NRSROs. Accordingly, the average number of structured finance ratings issued per NRSRO each year may be considerably lower than 128,000. For these reasons, the Commission believes the estimate is fairly conservative.

The Commission estimates that an NRSRO would publish a rating action with respect to a particular structured finance rating approximately 4 times per year for a total of 512,000 publications.[209] The Commission notes that this estimate would include publication of an initial rating, upgrades, downgrades and any affirmations published in a given year. Based on staff experience, the Commission estimates that an NRSRO would spend approximately 5 minutes ensuring that the required report was published along with the credit rating, for a total of 42,667 annual burden hours[210] per respondent, and a total of 1,280,000 hours[211] across 30 NRSROs. Finally, the Commission estimates, based on staff experience, that it would take an NRSRO approximately 10 hours per year to review and update the report to ensure that the disclosure was accurate and up-to-date for a total aggregate annual hour burden to the industry of 300 hours.[212] The Commission believes, therefore, that the aggregate one-time and annual burden hours under proposed Rule 17g-7(a) would be 1,280,000 and 1,800 hours,[213] respectively.

The Commission believes, however, that most, if not all, NRSROs would opt to differentiate their ratings under paragraph (b) of proposed Rule 17g-7,[214] rather than publish a report. The Commission believes that an NRSRO would likely choose to use a specific credit rating symbol to indicate that the particular credit rating relates to structured product as distinct from a credit rating for any other category of security or issuer. The Commission believes that an NRSRO would choose to employ this symbology approach because it would be more efficient and less burdensome than ensuring that the appropriate report was published along with the credit rating. The Commission believes that the implementation of a different rating symbol would entail a one-time burden of approximately 30 hours to develop the symbol for a total aggregate one-time burden to the industry of 900 hours.[215]

Because the Commission believes that NRSROs will choose to differentiate their ratings under paragraph (b) of proposed Rule 17g-7 rather than publish a report under paragraph (a) of the proposed new rule, the Commission believes that the appropriate estimate for the aggregate one-time burden to the industry under proposed Rule 17g-7 is 900 hours. The Commission generally requests comment on all aspects of these proposed burden estimates for Rule 17g-7. In addition, the Commission requests specific comment on the following items related to these burden estimates:

- Is the Commission incorrect in its belief that NRSROs would opt to use a different rating symbol rather than to publish a report with each structured product rating? If so, what percentage of NRSROs would be likely to opt to publish a report?

Commenters should provide specific data and analysis to support any comments they submit with respect to these burden estimates.

E. Collection of Information Is Mandatory

The recordkeeping and notice requirements for the proposed amendment and the proposed new rule would be mandatory.

F. Confidentiality

The disclosures proposed to be required under the amendments to Rule 17g-1 and Form NRSRO would be made publicly available on Form NRSRO. The books and records information proposed to be collected under the proposed amendments to Rule 1 7g-2 would be stored by the NRSRO and made available to the Commission and its representatives as required in connection with examinations, investigations, and enforcement proceedings. However, an NRSRO would be required to make the record of rating actions under proposed Rule 17g-2(a)(8) publicly available in an XBRL Interactive Data File no later than six months after the date of the rating action.[216] The information proposed to be collected under the proposed amendment to Rule 17g-3 would be generated from the internal records of the NRSRO and would be furnished to the Commission on a confidential basis, to the extent permitted by law.[217] The information under Rule 17g-5(a)(3) would be made publicly available or available to certain permitted persons. The information proposed to be required under proposed new Rule 17g-7 would be made publicly available.

G. Record Retention Period

The records required under the proposed amendments to Rule 17g-1 and Form NRSRO, Rule 17g-2, and 17g-3 would need to be retained by the NRSRO for at least three years.[218]

H. Request for Comment

The Commission requests comment on the proposed collections of information in order to: (1) evaluate whether the proposed collection of information is necessary for the proper performance of the functions of the Commission, including whether the information would have practical utility; (2) evaluate the accuracy of the Commission's estimates of the burden of the proposed collections of information; (3) determine whether there are ways to enhance the quality, utility, and clarity of the information to be collected; (4) evaluate whether there are ways to minimize the burden of the collection of information on those who respond, including through the use of automated collection techniques or other forms of information technology; and (5) evaluate whether the proposed rules would have any effects on any other collection of information not previously identified in this section.

Persons who desire to submit comments on the collection of information requirements should direct their comments to the OMB, Attention: Desk Officer for the Securities and Exchange Commission, Office of Information and Regulatory Affairs, Washington, DC 20503, and should also send a copy of their comments to Secretary, Securities and Exchange Commission, 100 F Street, NE, Washington, DC 20549-1090, and refer to File No. S7-13-08. OMB is required to make a decision concerning the collections of information between 30 and 60 days after publication of this document in the Federal Register; therefore, comments to OMB are best assured of having full effect if OMB receives them within 30 days of this publication. Requests for the materials submitted to OMB by the Commission with regard to these collections of information should be in writing, refer to File No. S7-13-08, and be submitted to the Securities and Exchange Commission, Records Management Office, 100 F Street, NE, Washington, DC 20549-1110.

V. Costs and Benefits of the Proposed Rules

The Commission is sensitive to the costs and benefits that result from its rules. The Commission has identified certain costs and benefits of the proposed amendments and the proposed new rule and requests comment on all aspects of this cost-benefit analysis, including identification and assessment of any costs and benefits not discussed in the analysis.[219] The Commission seeks comment and data on the value of the benefits identified. The Commission also welcomes comments on the accuracy of its cost estimates in each section of this cost-benefit analysis, and requests those commenters to provide data so the Commission can improve the cost estimates, including identification of statistics relied on by commenters to reach conclusions on cost estimates. Finally, the Commission seeks estimates and views regarding these costs and benefits for particular types of market participants, as well as any other costs or benefits that may result from the adoption of these proposed rule amendments.

A. Benefits

The purposes of the Rating Agency Act, as stated in the accompanying Senate Report, are to improve ratings quality for the protection of investors and in the public interest by fostering accountability, transparency, and competition in the credit rating industry.[220] As the Senate Report states, the Rating Agency Act establishes "fundamental reform and improvement of the designation process" to further the belief that "eliminating the artificial barrier to entry will enhance competition and provide investors with more choices, higher quality ratings, and lower costs."[221]

The proposed amendments and new rule would be issued pursuant to specific grants of rulemaking authority in the Rating Agency Act as well as the Commission's authority under the Exchange Act. The amendments are designed to further the goals of the Rating Agency Act and to enhance the Commission's oversight of NRSROs, in light of the recent credit market turmoil. Since the adoption of the final rules implementing the Rating Agency Act in 2007,[222] and in response to the recent concerns about the role of credit rating agencies in the credit market turmoil, the Commission has identified a number of areas where it would be appropriate to enhance the current regulatory program for NRSROs.

Consequently, the Commission is proposing amendments and a new rule that are designed to address concerns raised about the role NRSROs played in the credit turmoil by proposing to enhance the disclosure of credit ratings performance measurement statistics; increase the disclosure of information about the assets underlying structured finance products; require more information about the procedures and methodologies used to determine structured finance ratings; and address conflicts of interest arising from the structured finance rating process. As discussed below, the Commission believes that these proposed amendments and proposed new rule would further the purpose of the Rating Agency Act to improve the quality of credit ratings by fostering accountability, transparency, and competition in the credit rating industry, particularly with respect to credit ratings for structured finance products.[223]

Rule 1 7g- 1 prescribes a process for a credit rating agency to register with the Commission as an NRSRO using Form NRSRO, [224] and requires that a credit rating agency provide information required under Section 1 5E(a)(1)(B) of the Exchange Act and certain additional information.[225] Form NRSRO is also the means by which NRSROs update the information they must publicly disclose. The proposed amendments to the instructions to Exhibit 1 to Form NRSRO would require NRSROs to provide more detailed performance statistics and, thereby, make it easier for users of credit ratings to compare the ratings performance of the NRSROs.[226] In addition, these proposed amendments could make it easier for an NRSRO to demonstrate that it has a superior ratings methodology or competence and, thereby, attract clients.

The proposed amendments to the instructions to Exhibit 2 of Form NRSRO are designed to provide greater clarity around three areas of the NRSROs' rating processes for structured finance products that have raised concerns in the context of the recent credit market turmoil: the level of verification performed on information provided in loan documents; the quality of loan originators; and the on-going surveillance of existing ratings and how changes made to a model used for initial ratings are applied to existing ratings. The additional information provided by the proposed amendments would assist users of credit ratings in making more informed decisions about the quality of an NRSRO's ratings processes, particularly with regard to structured finance products.

The Commission preliminarily believes that these proposed enhanced disclosures in the Exhibits to Form NRSRO could make it easier for market participants to select the NRSROs that are performing best and have the highest quality processes for determining credit ratings. The potential result could be increased competition and the promotion of capital formation through a restoration of confidence in credit ratings.

The proposed amendments to Rule 17g-2 are designed to assist the Commission in its examination function and provide greater information to users of credit ratings about the performance of an NRSRO's credit ratings. The additional records would be: (1) a record of the rationale for any material difference between the credit rating implied by the model and the final credit rating issued, if a quantitative model is a substantial component in the process of determining a credit rating;[227] (2) a record showing the history and dates of all previous rating actions with respect to each current credit rating;[228] and (3) any complaints regarding the performance of a credit analyst in determining credit ratings.[229] These proposed records would assist the Commission in monitoring whether an NRSRO is complying with provisions of Section 1 5E of the Exchange Act and the rules thereunder. This would include monitoring whether an NRSRO is operating consistently with the methodologies and procedures it establishes (and discloses) to determine credit ratings and its policies and procedures designed to ensure the impartiality of its credit ratings, including its ratings of structured finance products.

In addition, the proposed amendments to Rule 17g-2, which would require an NRSRO to make its rating actions history publicly available in an XBRL Interactive Data File, would allow the marketplace to develop performance measurement statistics that would supplement those already required to be published by NRSROs in Exhibit 1 to Form NRSRO. This proposed amendment is designed to leverage the expertise of the marketplace and, thereby, provide users of credit ratings with innovative and potentially more useful metrics with which to compare NRSROs. This could make NRSROs more accountable for their ratings by enhancing the transparency of their ratings performance. By proposing to require an XBRL Interactive Data File the Commission also believes the proposed amendment would allow investors, analysts, and the Commission staff to capture and analyze the ratings action data more quickly and at less of a cost than is possible using another format.

The Commission preliminarily believes that the proposed amendments to Rule 17g-2 would enhance the Commission's oversight of NRSROs and, with respect to the public disclosure of ratings history, provide the marketplace with the raw materials to develop metrics for comparing the ratings performance of NRSROs. This could, in turn, help in restoring confidence in credit ratings and, thereby, promote capital formation. Increased disclosure of ratings history could make the ratings performance of the NRSROs more transparent to the marketplace and, thereby, highlight those firms that do a better job analyzing credit risk. This could benefit smaller NRSROs to the extent they have performed better than others by alerting the market to their superior competence.

The proposed amendment to Rule 17g-3 would require an NRSRO to furnish an additional annual report to the Commission: an unaudited report of the number of credit ratings that were changed during the fiscal year in each class of credit ratings for which the NRSRO is registered with the Commission.[230] The proposed new report is designed to enhance the Commission's oversight of NRSROs by providing the Commission with additional information to assist in the monitoring of NRSROs for compliance with their stated policies and procedures. For example, the proposed new report would allow examiners to target potential problem areas in an NRSRO's rating processes by highlighting spikes in rating actions within a particular class of credit rating.

The proposed amendments to Rule 17g-5 would prohibit an NRSRO from issuing a rating for a structured product unless information about the assets underlying the rated security is made available to certain persons.[231] These proposed rule amendments would prohibit an NRSRO from issuing or maintaining a credit rating where the NRSRO or an affiliate provided recommendations on the structure of the transaction being rated; a credit analyst or person involved in the ratings process participated in fee negotiations; or a credit analyst or a person responsible for approving a credit rating received gifts from the obligor being rated, or from the issuer, underwriter, or sponsor of the securities being rated, other than items provided in the context of normal business activities such as meetings that have an aggregate value of no more than $25.[232] The Commission believes that the proposed amendments to Rule 1 7g-5 would promote the disclosure and management of conflicts of interest and mitigate potential undue influences on an NRSRO's credit rating process, particularly with respect to credit ratings for structured finance products.[233] This would in turn increase confidence in the integrity of NRSRO ratings and, thereby, promote capital formation. In addition, the proposed disclosure of additional information regarding the assets underlying a structured finance transaction[234] would allow for unsolicited ratings that could help address ratings shopping by exposing an NRSRO whose ratings methodologies are less conservative in order to gain business. It also could mitigate the impact of rating shopping, since NRSROs not hired to rate a deal could nonetheless issue a credit rating. These potential impacts of the rule proposal could help to restore confidence in credit ratings and, thereby, promote capital formation. Also, by creating a mechanism for determining unsolicited ratings, they could increase competition by allowing smaller NRSROs to demonstrate proficiency in rating structured products.

Proposed Rule 17g-7 would address concerns that investors may believe that the risk characteristics for a structured finance product are the same as for other types of obligors or debt securities by requiring an NRSRO to attach a report each time it publishes a credit rating for a structured finance product describing how the ratings procedures and methodologies differ from those ratings for other types of obligors or debt securities.[235] Alternatively, an NRSRO would be permitted to use rating symbols for structured finance products that differentiate them from its other credit ratings. The Commission believes this proposed rule would address potential confusion by investors as to the different characteristics of structured finance products when compared to other types of obligors or debt securities and help them in assessing the risks involved with different types of securities and promote better informed investment decisions.

The Commission generally requests comment on all aspects of these proposed benefits. In addition, the Commission requests specific comment on the following items related to these benefits.

- Are there metrics available to quantify these benefits and any other benefits the commenter may identify, including the identification of sources of empirical data that could be used for such metrics.

Commenters should provide specific data and analysis to support any comments they submit with respect to these benefit estimates.

B. Costs

The cost of compliance with the proposed amendments and new rule to a given NRSRO would depend on its size and the complexity of its business activities. The size and complexity of NRSROs vary significantly. Therefore, the cost could vary significantly across NRSROs. Instead, the Commission is providing estimates of the average cost per NRSRO, as a result of the proposed amendments, taking into consideration the range in size and complexity of NRSROs and the fact that many already may have established policies, procedures and recordkeeping systems and processes that would comply substantially with the proposed amendments. Additionally, the Commission notes that nine credit rating agencies are currently registered with the Commission as NRSROs and subject to the Act and its implementing regulations. The cost of compliance would also vary depending on which classes of credit ratings an NRSRO issues. NRSROs which issue credit ratings for structured finance products would incur higher compliance costs than those NRSROs which do not issue such credit ratings or issue very few credit ratings in that class.

For these reasons, the cost estimates represent the average cost across all NRSROs and take into account that some firms would only need to augment existing policies, procedures and recordkeeping systems and processes to come into compliance with the proposed amendments.

1. Proposed Amendments to Form NRSRO

As discussed above, the Commission is proposing to amend the instructions to Exhibit 1 to Form NRSRO to provide more detailed performance statistics. Currently, the instructions require the disclosure of performance measurement statistics of the credit ratings of the "Applicant/NRSRO over the short-term, mid-term and long-term periods (as applicable) through the most recent calendar year end." The proposed amendments would augment these instructions to require the disclosure of separate sets of default and transition statistics for each class of credit ratings. In addition, the class-by-class disclosures would need to be broken out over 1, 3 and 10 year periods.[236]

The proposed amendments would also amend the instructions to Exhibit 2 to Form NRSRO to require enhanced disclosures about the procedures and methodologies an NRSRO uses to determine credit ratings, including whether and, if so, how information about verification performed on assets underlying a structured finance transaction is relied on in determining credit ratings; whether and, if so, how assessments of the quality of originators of assets underlying a structured finance transaction factor into the determination of credit ratings; and how frequently credit ratings are reviewed, whether different models are used for ratings surveillance than for determining credit ratings, and whether changes made to models and criteria for determining initial ratings are applied retroactively to existing ratings. As discussed above, the Commission estimates that for PRA purposes the total one-time and annual hour burdens and the cost would have a neutral effect, resulting in no overall change in hours or cost for the currently approved PRA collection.

The Commission preliminarily believes, however, NRSROs may incur a cost of compliance in updating their performance metric statistics to conform to the new requirements set forth in the proposed rule amendments. Under the current instructions to Exhibit 1 to Form NRSRO, an NRSRO must disclose its performance metrics over short, mid, and long-term periods. Thus, the current Form NRSRO instructions to Exhibit 1 allow an NRSRO to use its own definitions of "short, mid, and long-term periods" and to include all credit ratings, regardless of class of rating, in one set of metrics. Under the proposed amendments, an NRSRO would be required to break out on a class-by-class basis performance statistics over 1, 3 and 10-year periods. The Commission believes that existing NRSROs would incur costs to conform their current performance statistics with the requirements of this proposed amendment to Exhibit 1.

The Commission estimates that it would take each NRSRO currently registered with the Commission approximately 50 hours to review its performance measurement statistics and to develop and implement any changes necessary to comply with the proposed amendment. The Commission is basing this estimate on the amount of time the Commission estimated that it would take an NRSRO to establish procedures in conformance with Rule 17g-4 and on information gained from the NRSRO examination process.[237] For these reasons, the Commission estimates that the average one-time cost to an NRSRO would be $ 12,740[238] and the total aggregate cost to the currently registered NRSROs would be $1 14,660.[239]

The Commission generally requests comment on all aspects of these proposed cost estimates for the proposed amendments to Form NRSRO. In addition, the Commission requests specific comment on the following items related to these cost estimates:

- Would these proposals impose costs on other market participants, including persons who use credit ratings to make investment decisions or for regulatory purposes, and persons who purchase services and products from NRSROs?

Commenters should provide specific data and analysis to support any comments they submit with respect to these burden estimates.

2. Proposed Amendments to Rule 17g-2

Rule 1 7g-2 requires an NRSRO to make and preserve specified records related to its credit rating business.[240] As discussed above, the proposed amendments to Rule 17g-2 would require an NRSRO to make and retain two additional records and retain a third type of record. The records to be made and retained would be: (1) a record of the rationale for any material difference between the credit rating implied by the model and the final credit rating issued, if a quantitative model is a substantial component in the process of determining a credit rating;[241] and (2) a record showing the history and dates of all previous rating actions with respect to each current credit rating.[242] The proposed amendments to Rule 17g-2 would require an NRSRO to make the second record – rating actions related to current ratings – publicly available in an XBRL Interactive Data File.[243] In addition, the proposed amendments would require an NRSRO to retain communications that contain any complaints by an obligor, issuer, underwriter, or sponsor about the performance of a credit analyst.[244]

As discussed with respect to the PRA, the Commission estimates that, based on staff experience, that the total one-time and annual recordkeeping burdens would increase approximately 10% and 5%, respectively. Thus, the Commission estimates that the onetime hour burden that each NRSRO would spend implementing a recordkeeping system to comply with Rule 17g-2 would be approximately 330 hours (an increase of 30 hours)[245] for a total one-time burden of 9,900 hours (an increase of 900 hours).[246]

The Commission estimates that an NRSRO would spend an average of 267 hours per year (an increase of 13 hours[247] to make and maintain records under Rule 17g-2, for a total annual hour burden of 8,010 hours.[248] This estimate would increase the currently approved PRA burden under Rule 17g-2 by 390 hours.[249] For these reasons, the Commission estimates that an NRSRO would incur an average one-time cost of $7,350 and the average annual cost of $3,185, as a result of the proposed amendments.[250] Consequently, the total aggregate one-time cost attributable to the proposed amendments would be $220,500[251] and the total aggregate annual cost to the industry would be $95,550 .[252]

In addition, the proposed amendments to Rule 17g-2 would require an NRSRO to make the records of its rating actions publicly available in an XBRL Interactive Data File.[253] As discussed with respect to the PRA, the Commission estimates that, on average, an NRSRO would spend approximately 30 hours to publicly disclose this ratings history information in an XBRL Interactive Data File and, thereafter, 10 hours per year to update its rating action history.[254] Accordingly, the total aggregate one-time burden to the industry to make the history of its rating actions publicly available in an XBRL Interactive Data File would be 900 hours[255] and the total aggregate annual burden hours would be 300 hours.[256] Furthermore, as discussed in the PRA the Commission estimates there will be 30 NRSROs. For these reasons, the Commission estimates that an NRSRO would incur an average one-time cost of $8,670 and an average annual cost of $2,890, as a result of the proposed amendment.[257] Consequently, the total aggregate one-time cost to the industry would be $260,100[258] and the total aggregate annual cost to the industry would be $86,700.[259]

As discussed with respect to the PRA, the Commission estimated that an NRSRO may have to purchase recordkeeping software to establish a recordkeeping system in conformance with Rule 17g-2. The Commission estimated that the cost of the software will vary based on the size and complexity of the NRSRO. Also, the Commission estimated that some NRSROs would not need such software because they already have adequate recordkeeping systems or, given their small size, such software would not be necessary. Based on these estimates, the Commission estimated that the average cost for recordkeeping software across all NRSROs would be approximately $1,000 per firm. Therefore, the estimated one-time cost to the industry would be $30,000. The Commission estimates that the proposed amendments to Rule 17g-2 would not alter this estimate or that any increases in the cost would be de minimis.

Finally, proposed paragraph (a)(8) to Rule 17g-2 would require an NRSRO to create and maintain a record showing all rating actions and the date of such actions from the initial rating to the current rating identified by the name or rated security or obligor, and, if applicable, the CUSIP of the rated security or the Central Index Key (CIK) number of the rated obligor.[260] The Commission estimates that an NRSRO could be required to purchase a license from the CUSIP Service Bureau in order to access CUSIP numbers for the securities it rates. The CUSIP Service Bureau's operations are covered by fees paid by issuers and licensees of the CUSIP Service Bureau's data. Issuers pay a one-time fee for each new CUSIP assigned, and licensees pay a renewable subscription or a license fee for access and use of the CUSIP Service Bureau's various database services. The CUSIP Service Bureau's license fees vary based on usage, i.e., how many securities or by type of security or business line.[261] The Commission estimates that the license fees incurred by an NRSRO would vary depending on the size of the NRSRO and the number of credit ratings it issues. For purposes of this cost estimate, the Commission estimates that an NRSRO would incur a fee of $100,000 to obtain access to the CUSIP numbers for the securities it rates. Consequently, the estimated total one-time cost to the industry would be $3,000,000.[262]

The Commission generally requests comment on all aspects of these cost estimates for the proposed amendments to Rule 17g-2. In addition, the Commission requests specific comment on the following items related to these cost estimates:

- Would these proposals impose costs on other market participants, including persons who use credit ratings to make investment decisions or for regulatory purposes, and persons who purchase services and products from NRSROs?

Commenters should provide specific data and analysis to support any comments they submit with respect to these burden estimates.

3. Proposed Amendment to Rule 17g-3

Rule 17g-3 requires an NRSRO to furnish audited annual financial statements to the Commission, including certain specified schedules.[263] The proposed amendment to Rule 17g-3 would require an NRSRO to furnish the Commission with an additional annual report: an unaudited report of the number of credit ratings that were changed during the fiscal year in each class of credit ratings for which the NRSRO is registered with the Commission. The Commission believes that the annual costs to NRSROs to comply with the proposed amendment to Rule 17g-3 would be de minimis, as the Commission preliminarily believes that a credit rating agency already would have this information with respect to each class of credit ratings for which it is registered. In addition, the proposed amendment does not prescribe a format for the report. Consequently, the Commission estimates that proposed Rule 17g-3(a)(6) would not have a significant effect on the total average annual cost burden currently estimated for Rule 1 7g-3.

The Commission generally requests comment on all aspects of these cost estimates for the proposed amendment to Rule 17g-3. In addition, the Commission requests specific comment on the following items related to these cost estimates:

- Would this proposal impose costs on other market participants, including persons who use credit ratings to make investment decisions or for regulatory purposes, and persons who purchase services and products from NRSROs?

Commenters should provide specific data and analysis to support any comments they submit with respect to these burden estimates.

4. Proposed Amendments to Rule 17g-5

Rules 17g-5 requires an NRSRO to manage and disclose certain conflicts of interest.[264] The proposed amendments would add an additional conflict to paragraph (b) of Rule 17g-5. This proposed conflict of interest would be issuing or maintaining a credit rating for a security or money market instrument issued by an asset pool or as part of an asset-backed or mortgage-backed securities transaction that was paid for by the issuer, sponsor, or underwriter of the security or money market instrument.[265] Unlike the other conflicts of interest in paragraph (b) of Rule 17g-5, NRSROs would be prohibited from issuing a rating, unless certain information about the transaction and the assets underlying the structured product being rated were disclosed, pursuant to proposed Rule 1 7g5(a)(3)(i) and (ii).[266]

Specifically, proposed Rule 1 7g-5(a)(3)(i) and (ii) would require the disclosure of certain information about the assets underlying a structured product that is provided to an NRSRO and used in determining an initial rating and monitoring the rating. While the proposed rule would require disclosure of certain information, the rule would not specify which party would disclose the information. For purposes of this PRA, the Commission estimates that it would take a respondent approximately 300 hours to develop a system, as well as policies and procedures to disclose the information as required under the proposed rule. This would result in a total one-time hour burden of 60,000 hours for 200 respondents.[267] For these reasons, the Commission estimates that the average one-time cost to each respondent would be $65,850[268] and the total aggregate one-time cost to the industry would be $ 13,116,000.[269]

As discussed with respect to the PRA, in addition to the one-time hour burden, respondents also would be required to disclose the required information under proposed Rule 17g-5(a)(3)(i) on a transaction by transaction basis. Based on staff information gained from the NRSRO examination process, the Commission estimates that the proposed amendments would require each respondent to disclose information with respect to approximately 20 new transactions per year and that it would take approximately 1 hour per transaction to make the information publicly available.[270] Therefore, as discussed with respect to the PRA, the Commission estimates that it would take a respondent approximately 20 hours[271] to disclose this information under proposed Rule 17g-5(a)(i) and (ii), on an annual basis, for a total aggregate annual hour burden of 4,000.[272] For these reasons, the Commission estimates that the average annual cost to a respondent would be $4, 100[273] and the total annual cost to the industry would be $820,000.[274]

Proposed Rule 17g-5(a)(ii) would require respondents to disclose information provided to an NRSRO that is used by an NRSRO in undertaking credit rating surveillance on a structured product. Because surveillance would cover more than just initial ratings, the

Commission estimates that a respondent would be required to disclose information with respect to approximately 125 transactions on an ongoing basis and that the information would be provided to the NRSRO on a monthly basis. As discussed with respect to the PRA, the Commission estimates that each respondent would spend approximately 750 hours[275] on an annual basis disclosing the information for a total aggregate annual burden hours of 150,000 hours.[276] For these reasons, the Commission estimates that the average annual cost to a respondent would be $ 153,750[277] and the total annual cost to the industry would be $30,750,000.[278]

The Commission is also proposing to amend paragraph (c) to Rule 17g-5 to add three additional prohibited conflicts of interest.[279] The Commission estimates that the amendments to paragraph (c) to Rule 17g-5 generally would impose de minimis costs on an NRSRO. However, the Commission recognizes that an NRSRO may incur costs related to training employees about the requirements with respect to these proposed amendments. It also is possible that the proposed amendments could require some NRSROs to restructure their business models or activities, in particular with respect to their consulting services.

The Commission generally requests comment on all aspects of these cost estimates for the proposed amendments to Rule 17g-5. In addition, the Commission requests specific comment on the following items related to these cost estimates:

- Would the proposals for additional disclosure impose costs on issuers, underwriters, sponsors, depositors, or trustees?
- Would these proposals impose costs on other market participants, including persons who use credit ratings to make investment decisions or for regulatory purposes, and persons who purchase services and products from NRSROs?
- Would there be costs in addition to those identified above, such as costs arising from systems changes and restructuring business practices to account for the new reporting requirement?
- Would the proposed amendments to paragraph (c) of Rule 17g-5 impose training and restructuring costs?
- Would the proposed amendments to paragraph (c) of Rule 17g-5 impose personnel costs?
- Would the proposed amendments to paragraph (c) of Rule 17g-5 impose any additional costs on an NRSRO that is part of a large conglomerate related to monitoring the business activities of persons associated with the NRSRO, such as affiliates located in other countries, to comply with the proposed requirement? Commenters should provide specific data and analysis to support any comments they submit with respect to these burden estimates.

5. Proposed Rule 17g-7

The Commission is proposing a new rule – proposed Rule 17g-7 – which would require an NRSRO to attach a report each time it publishes a credit rating for a structured finance product describing how the ratings procedures and methodologies differ from those for corporate debt.[280] Alternatively, an NRSRO would be permitted to use rating symbols for structured finance products that differentiate them from its other credit ratings. The

Commission expects that most NRSROs already have methodologies in place to determine credit ratings for structured finance products and corporate debt securities, and disclosed such policies and procedures if they have registered as an NRSRO. The Commission expects, however, that an NRSRO would have to conform these disclosures into a report to comply with the specific requirements in the proposed rule. As discussed above with respect to PRA, the Commission estimates that it would take approximately 50 hours for an NRSRO to compile and write disclosures to comply with the proposed rule and that there would be 30 NRSROs. For these reasons, the Commission estimates that the average one-time cost to an NRSRO would be $ 12,250[281] and the total aggregate one-time cost to the industry would be $367,500.[282]

As discussed above with respect to the PRA, the Commission also estimates that it would take an NRSRO additional time to attach the report to each credit rating for a structured finance product and to monitor the report on an ongoing basis to ensure that the disclosure was accurate. Based on staff experience staff information gained from the NRSRO examination process, the Commission estimates that an NRSRO would spend approximately 5 minutes to attach each proposed report to the estimated 128,000 asset- backed credit ratings per NRSRO, four times per year, as discussed above, for a total of 42,667 annual burden hours[283] per respondent, and a total of 1,280,010 annual burden hours[284] for 30 NRSROs. For these reasons, the Commission estimates that the average annual cost to an NRSRO would be $4,373,265[285] and the total aggregate annual cost to the industry would be $131,197,950.[286]

Finally, as discussed with respect to the PRA, the Commission estimates, based on staff experience, that it would take an NRSRO approximately 10 hours per year to review and update the report to ensure the disclosure was accurate and up-to-date for a total aggregate annual hour burden to the industry of 300 hours.[287] For these reasons, the Commission estimates that the average annual cost to an NRSRO would be $2,700[288] and the total aggregate annual cost to the industry would be $8 1,000.[289]

The Commission generally requests comment on all aspects of these cost estimates for the proposed amendments to Rule 17g-7. In addition, the Commission requests specific comment on the following items related to these cost estimates:

- Would the use of different rating symbols for structured products impact automated securities trading, routing, settlement, clearance, trade confirmation, reporting, processing, and risk management systems and any other systems that are programmed to use standard credit rating symbols across all product classes?
- Would the use of different rating symbols have consequences for investment guidelines and covenants in legal documents that use credit ratings to distinguish finance instruments?
- Would these proposals impose costs on other market participants, including persons who use credit ratings to make investment decisions or for regulatory purposes, and persons who purchase services and products from NRSROs?
- Would there be costs in addition to those identified above, such as costs arising from systems changes and restructuring business practices to account for the new reporting requirement?

Commenters should provide specific data and analysis to support any comments they submit with respect to these burden estimates.

C. Total Estimated Costs and Benefits of this Rulemaking

As discussed above, the proposed amendments and new rules are expected to have both benefits and costs for investors and the credit rating industry as a whole. The Commission believes the benefits to investors and other users of credit ratings, especially with respect to investments in structured finance products would be quite substantial, but are difficult to quantify. Similarly difficult to quantify are the expected benefits to the Commission's oversight over NRSROs due to the enhanced recordkeeping, disclosure and reporting requirements. Moreover, not all the costs the Commission anticipates would result from this rulemaking are quantifiable. Based on the figures discussed above, however, the Commission estimates that the first year quantifiable costs related to this proposed rulemaking would be approximately $180, 175,81 0.[290]

VI. CONSIDERATION OF BURDEN ON COMPETITION AND PROMOTION OF EFFICIENCY, COMPETITION, AND CAPITAL FORMATION

Under Section 3(f) of the Exchange Act,[291] the Commission shall, when engaging in rulemaking that requires the Commission to consider or determine if an action is necessary or appropriate in the public interest, consider whether the action will promote efficiency, competition, and capital formation. Section 23(a)(2) of the Exchange Act[292] requires the Commission to consider the anticompetitive effects of any rules the Commission adopts under the Exchange Act. Section 23(a)(2) prohibits the Commission from adopting any rule that would impose a burden on competition not necessary or appropriate in furtherance of the purposes of the Exchange Act. As discussed below, the Commission's preliminary view is that the proposed amendments and new rules should promote efficiency, competition, and capital formation.

The proposed amendments to the Instructions to Exhibit 1 to Form NRSRO would require NRSROs to make more comparable disclosures about the performance of their credit ratings. These could make it easier for an NRSRO to demonstrate that it has a superior ratings methodology or competence and, thereby, attract clients. In addition, the proposed amendments to the instructions to Exhibit 2 are designed to enhance the disclosures NRSROs make with respect to their methodologies for determining credit ratings. The Commission believes these enhanced disclosures would make it easier for users of credit ratings to compare the quality of the NRSRO's procedures and methodologies for determining credit ratings. The greater transparency that would result from all these enhanced disclosures could make it easier for market participants to select the NRSROs that are performing best and have the highest quality processes for determining credit ratings. This could increase competition and promote capital formation by restoring confidence in the credit ratings, which are an integral part of the capital formation process.

The proposed amendments to Rule 17g-2 are designed to enhance the Commission's oversight of NRSROs and, with respect to the public disclosure of ratings history, provide the marketplace with the raw materials to develop metrics for comparing the ratings performance of NRSROs. Enhancing the Commission's oversight could help in restoring confidence in credit ratings and, thereby, promote capital formation. Increased disclosure of ratings history could make the ratings performance of the NRSROs more transparent to the marketplace and, thereby, highlight those firms that do a better job analyzing credit risk. This could benefit smaller NRSROs to the extent they have performed better than others by alerting the market to their superior competence.

The proposed amendment to Rule 17g-3 is designed to enhance the Commission's oversight of NRSROs. Enhancing the Commission's oversight could help in restoring confidence in credit ratings and, thereby, promote capital formation.

The proposed amendments to paragraphs (a) and (b) of Rule 17g-5 would enhance the disclosures made about assets underlying structured finance products. The goal of these proposals is to provide a mechanism for NRSROs to determine unsolicited credit ratings and other market participants and observers to independently assess the creditworthiness of structured finance products. This could expose NRSROs whose procedures and methodologies for determining credit ratings are less conservative in order to gain business. It also could mitigate the impact of rating shopping, since NRSROs not hired to rate a deal could nonetheless issue a credit rating. These potential impacts of the rule proposal could help to restore confidence in credit ratings and, thereby, promote capital formation. Also, by creating a mechanism for determining unsolicited ratings, they could increase competition by allowing smaller NRSROs to demonstrate proficiency in rating structured products.

The proposed amendments to paragraph (c) of Rule 17g-5 would prohibit NRSROs and their affiliates from providing consulting or advisory services, prohibit analysts from participating in fee negotiations, and prohibit credit analysts or persons responsible for approving a credit rating receiving gifts from the obligor being rated, or from the issuer, underwriter, or sponsor of the securities being rated, other than items provided in the context of normal business activities such as meetings that have an aggregate value of no more than $25. These proposals could increase confidence in the integrity of NRSROs and the credit ratings they issue. This could help to restore confidence in credit ratings and, thereby, promote capital formation.

Proposed new Rule 1 7g-7 would provide users of credit ratings with useful information about structured product ratings. This could help them in assessing the risk of securities and promote better informed investment decisions. This could increase the efficiency of the capital markets by making structured finance ratings more transparent.

The Commission generally requests comment on all aspects of this analysis of the burden on competition and promotion of efficiency, competition, and capital formation. In addition, the Commission requests specific comment on the following items related to this analysis:

- Would the proposed amendments have an adverse effect on efficiency, competition, and capital formation that is neither necessary nor appropriate in furtherance of the purposes of the Exchange Act?

Commenters should provide specific data and analysis to support any comments they submit with respect to these burden estimates.

VII. Consideration of Impact on the Economy

For purposes of the Small Business Regulatory Enforcement Fairness Act of 1996, or "SBREFA,"[293] the Commission must advise OMB whether a proposed regulation constitutes a major rule. Under SBREFA, a rule is "major" if it has resulted in, or is likely to result in:

- an annual effect on the economy of $100 million or more;
- a major increase in costs or prices for consumers or individual industries; or
- a significant adverse effect on competition, investment, or innovation.

If a rule is "major," its effectiveness will generally be delayed for 60 days pending Congressional review. The Commission requests comment on the potential impact of each of the proposed amendments on the economy on an annual basis. Commenters are requested to provide empirical data and other factual support for their view to the extent possible.

VIII. Initial Regulatory Flexibility Analysis

The Commission has prepared the following Initial Regulatory Flexibility Analysis ("IRFA"), in accordance with the provisions of the Regulatory Flexibility Act,[294] regarding proposed amendments to Form NRSRO, Rule 17g-2, Rule 17g-3, and Rule 17g-5 and regarding proposed Rule 17g-7 under the Exchange Act.

The Commission encourages comments with respect to any aspect of this IRFA, including comments with respect to the number of small entities that may be affected by the proposed amendments. Comments should specify the costs of compliance with the proposed amendments and suggest alternatives that would accomplish the goals of the amendments. Comments will be considered in determining whether a Final Regulatory Flexibility Analysis is required and will be placed in the same public file as comments on the proposed amendments. Comments should be submitted to the Commission at the addresses previously indicated.

A. Reasons for the Proposed Action

The proposed amendments would prescribe additional requirements for NRSROs to address concerns raised about the role of credit rating agencies in the recent credit market turmoil. The proposed amendments are designed to enhance and strengthen the rules the Commission adopted in 2007 to implement specific provisions of the Rating Agency Act.[295] The Rating Agency Act defines the term "nationally recognized statistical rating organization" as a credit rating agency registered with the Commission, provides authority for the Commission to implement registration, recordkeeping, financial reporting, and oversight rules with respect to registered NRSROs.

B. Objectives

The proposed amendments and new rules would enhance and strengthen the rules the Commission adopted in 2007 to implement specific provisions of the Rating Agency Act. The objectives of the Rating Agency Act are "to improve ratings quality for the protection of investors and in the public interest by fostering accountability, transparency, and competition in the credit rating industry."[296] The proposed amendments and new rules are designed to further enhance these objectives and assist the Commission in monitoring whether an NRSRO complies with the provisions of the Rating Agency Act and rules thereunder, consistent with the Commission's statutory mandate to adopt rules to implement the NRSRO regulatory program, and provide information regarding NRSROs to the public and to users of credit ratings. These proposed amendments would also prescribe additional requirements for NRSROs to address concerns raised about the role of credit rating agencies in the recent credit market turmoil, including concerns with respect to the determination of credit ratings for structured finance products.

C. Legal Basis

Pursuant to the Sections 3(b), 15E, 17(a), 23(a) and 36 of the Exchange Act.[297]

D. Small Entities Subject to the Rule

Paragraph (a) of Rule 0-10 provides that for purposes of the Regulatory Flexibility Act, a small entity "[w]hen used with reference to an 'issuer' or a 'person' other than an investment company" means "an 'issuer' or 'person' that, on the last day of its most recent fiscal year, had total assets of $5 million or less."[298] The Commission believes that an NRSRO with total assets of $5 million or less would qualify as a "small" entity for purposes of the Regulatory Flexibility Act.

As noted in the Adopting Release,[299] the Commission believes that approximately 30 credit rating agencies ultimately would be registered as an NRSRO. Of the approximately 30 credit rating agencies estimated to be registered with the Commission, the Commission estimates that approximately 20 may be "small" entities for purposes of the Regulatory Flexibility Act.[300]

E. Reporting, Recordkeeping, and Other Compliance Requirements

The proposals would amend Form NRSRO to elicit certain additional information regarding the performance data for the credit ratings and the methods used by a credit rating agency for issuing credit ratings.[301]

The proposals would amend Rule 17g-2 to establish additional recordkeeping requirements.[302] The proposed amendments would require an NRSRO to make and retain two additional records and retain a third type of record. The records would be: (1) a record of the rationale for any material difference between the credit rating implied by the model and the final credit rating issued, if a quantitative model is a substantial component in the process of determining a credit rating;[303] (2) a record showing the history and dates of all previous rating actions with respect to each current credit rating;[304] and (3) any complaints about the performance of a credit analyst.[305] These records would assist the Commission, through its examination process, in monitoring whether the NRSRO continues to maintain adequate financial and managerial resources to consistently produce credit ratings with integrity (as required under the Rating Agency Act) and whether the NRSRO was complying with the provisions of the Exchange Act including the provisions of the Rating Agency Act, the rules adopted thereunder, and the NRSRO's disclosed policies and procedures.

The proposals would amend Rule 17g-3 to require an NRSRO to furnish the Commission with an additional annual report: the number of downgrades in each class of credit ratings for which it is registered and the description of the findings from an independent review.[206] This requirement is designed to assist the Commission in its examination function and to require an NRSRO to assess the integrity of its rating process. It also is designed to assist the Commission in monitoring whether the NRSRO is complying with provisions of the Rating Agency Act and the rules adopted thereunder.

The proposals would amend paragraphs (a) and (b) of Rule 17g-5 to prohibit an NRSRO from issuing a credit rating for a structured product unless certain information about the assets underlying the product are disclosed. The proposals would amend paragraph (c) of Rule 17g-5 to prohibit NRSROs and their affiliates from providing consulting or advisory services, prohibit analysts from participating in fee negotiations, and prohibit credit analysts or persons responsible for approving a credit rating received gifts from the obligor being rated, or from the issuer, underwriter, or sponsor of the securities being rated, other than items provided in the context of normal business activities such as meetings that have an aggregate value of no more than $25.[307]

The proposals would amend Rule 17g-7 to require an NRSRO to attach a report each time it publishes a credit rating for a structured finance product describing how the ratings procedures and methodologies and credit risk characteristics for structured products differ from those for other types of obligors and debt securities. An NRSRO could avoid having to attach the report if it used ratings symbols for structured products that differentiate them from its other types of credit ratings.[308]

F. Duplicative, Overlapping, or Conflicting Federal Rules

The Commission believes that there are no federal rules that duplicate, overlap, or conflict with the proposed amendments or new rule.

G. Significant Alternatives

Pursuant to Section 3(a) of the RFA,[309] the Commission must consider certain types of alternatives, including: (1) the establishment of differing compliance or reporting requirements or timetables that take into account the resources available to small entities; (2) the clarification, consolidation, or simplification of compliance and reporting requirements under the rule for small entities; (3) the use of performance rather than design standards; and (4) an exemption from coverage of the rule, or any part of the rule, for small entities.

The Commission is considering whether it is necessary or appropriate to establish different compliance or reporting requirements or timetables; or clarify, consolidate, or simplify compliance and reporting requirements under the rule for small entities. Because the proposed amendments and proposed new rule are designed to improve the overall quality of ratings and enhance the Commission's oversight, the Commission is not proposing to exempt small entities from coverage of the rule, or any part of the rule. The proposed amendments and new rules allow NRSROs the flexibility to develop procedures tailored to their specific organizational structure and business models. The Commission also does not believe that it is necessary at this time to consider whether small entities should be permitted to use performance rather than design standards to comply with the proposed amendments as the amendments already propose performance standards and do not dictate for entities of any size any particular design standards that must be employed to achieve the Act's objectives.

H. Request for Comments

The Commission encourages the submission of comments to any aspect of this portion of the IRFA. Comments should specify costs of compliance with the proposed amendments and suggest alternatives that would accomplish the objective of the proposed amendments

IX. Statutory Authority

The Commission is proposing amendments to Form NRSRO and Rules 17g–2, 17g–3, and 17g–5 and is proposing new rule 17g–7 pursuant to the authority conferred by the Exchange Act, including Sections 3(b), 15E, 17, 23(a) and 36.[310]

Text of Proposed Rules

List of Subjects in 17 CFR Parts 240 and 249b

Brokers, Reporting and recordkeeping requirements, Securities.

In accordance with the foregoing, the Commission proposes to amend Title 17, Chapter II of the Code of Federal Regulations as follows.

Part 240—General Rules and Regulations, Securities Exchange Act of 1934

1. The authority citation for part 240 continues to read in part as follows: Authority: 15 U.S.C. 77c, 77d, 77g, 77j, 77s, 77z-2, 77z-3, 77eee, 77ggg, 77nnn, 77sss, 77ttt, 78c, 78d, 78e, 78f, 78g, 78i, 78j, 78j-1, 78k, 78k-1, 78l, 78m, 78n, 78o, 78p, 78q, 78s, 78u5, 78w, 78x, 78ll, 78mm, 80a-20, 80a-23, 80a-29, 80a-37, 80b-3, 80b-4, 80b-11, and 7201 et seq.; and 18 U.S.C. 1350, unless otherwise noted.

* * * * *

2. Section 240.17g–2 is amended by:

a Removing paragraph (a)(2)(iv);
b Redesignating paragraph (a)(2)(iii) as paragraph (a)(2)(iv);
c In newly redesignated paragraph (a)(2)(iv), removing "; and" and in its place adding a period;
d Adding new paragraph (a)(2)(iii);
e Adding paragraph (a)(8);
f In paragraph (b)(7), revising the phrase "maintaining, changing," to read "maintaining, monitoring, changing,";
g Redesignating paragraphs (b)(8), (b)(9), and (b)(10) as paragraphs (b)(9), (b)(10), and (b)(1 1), respectively;
h Adding new paragraph (b)(8); and
i In paragraph (d), adding a sentence to the end of the paragraph.

The additions read as follows:

§ 240.17g–2 Records to be made and retained by nationally recognized statistical rating organizations.

(a) * * * (2) * * * (iii) If a quantitative model was a substantial component in the process of determining the credit rating, a record of the rationale for any material difference between the credit rating implied by the model and the final credit rating issued; and

*****

(8) A record showing all rating actions and the date of such actions from the initial credit rating to the current credit rating identified by the name of the rated security or obligor and, if applicable, the CUSIP of the rated security or the Central Index Key (CIK) number of the rated obligor.

(b) * * *

(8) Any communications that contain complaints about the performance of a credit analyst in initiating, determining, maintaining, monitoring, changing, or withdrawing a credit rating.

*****

(d) * * * In addition, the records required to be retained pursuant to paragraph (a)(8) of this section must be made publicly available on the corporate Web site of the NRSRO in an XBRL Interactive Data File that uses a machine-readable computer code that presents information in eXtensible Business Reporting Language in electronic format no later than six months after the date of the rating action.

*****

3. Section 240.1 7g–3 is amended by:
Adding paragraph (a)(6); and
Revising paragraph (b).
The additions and revision read as follows:

§ 240.17g-3 Annual financial reports to be furnished by nationally recognized statistical rating organizations.

(a) * * *

(6) The number of credit ratings actions taken during the fiscal year in each class of credit ratings identified in section 3(a)(62)(B) of the Act (15 U.S.C. 78c(a)(62)(B)) for which the nationally recognized statistical rating organization is registered with the Commission.

Note to paragraph (a)(6): A nationally recognized statistical rating organization registered in the class of credit ratings described in section 3 (a)(62)(B)(iv) of the Act (15 U.S.C. 78c(a)(62)(B)(iv)) must include credit ratings actions taken on credit ratings of any security or money market instrument issued by an asset pool or as part of any asset-backed or mortgage-backed securities transaction for purposes of reporting the number of credit ratings actions in this class.

(b) The nationally recognized statistical rating organization must attach to the financial reports furnished pursuant to paragraphs (a)(1) through (a)(6) of this section a signed statement by a duly authorized person associated with the nationally recognized statistical rating organization stating that the person has responsibility for the financial reports and, to the best knowledge of the person, the financial reports fairly present, in all material respects, the financial condition, results of operations, cash flows, revenues, analyst compensation, and credit rating actions of the nationally recognized statistical rating organization for the period presented.

*****

4. Section 240.1 7g–5 is amended by:

a Removing the word “and” at the end of paragraph (a)(1);
b Removing the period at the end of paragraph (a)(2) and in its place adding “; and”;
c Adding paragraph (a)(3);
d Redesignating paragraph (b)(9) as paragraph (b)(10);
e Adding new paragraph (b)(9);
f Removing the word “or” at the end of paragraph (c)(3);
g Removing the period at the end of paragraph (c)(4) and in its place adding a semi-colon; and
h Adding paragraphs (c)(5), (c)(6), and (c)(7).

The additions read as follows:

§ 240.17g-5 Conflicts of interest.

(a) * * *

(3) In the case of the conflict of interest identified in paragraph (b)(9) of this section, the following information is disclosed through a means designed to provide reasonably broad dissemination:

(i) (A) All information provided to the nationally recognized statistical rating organization by the issuer, underwriter, sponsor, depositor, or trustee that is used in determining the initial credit rating for the security or money market instrument, including information about the characteristics of the assets underlying or referenced by the security or money market instrument, and the legal structure of the security or money market instrument, with such information to disclosed publicly in an offering registered under the Securities Act of 1933 (15 U.S.C. 77a et seq.) on the date the underwriter and the issuer or depositor set the offering price of the securities being rated;

(B) In offerings that are not registered under the Securities Act of 1933 (15 U.S.C. 77a et seq.), the information in paragraph (a)(3)(i)(A) of this section must be disclosed to investors and credit rating agencies on the date the underwriter and the issuer or depositor set the offering price of the securities being rated, and disclosed publicly on the first business day after the transaction closes; and

(ii) All information provided to the nationally recognized statistical rating organization by the issuer, underwriter, sponsor, depositor, or trustee that is used by the nationally recognized statistical rating organization in undertaking credit rating surveillance on the security or money market instrument, including information about the characteristics and performance of the assets underlying or referenced by the security or money market instrument, with such information to be disclosed publicly at the time such information is provided to the nationally recognized statistical rating organization.

* * *

(9) Issuing or maintaining a credit rating for a security or money market instrument issued by an asset pool or as part of any asset-backed or mortgage-backed securities transaction that was paid for by the issuer, sponsor, or underwriter of the security or money market instrument.

*****

(5) The nationally recognized statistical rating organization issues or maintains a credit rating with respect to an obligor or security where the nationally recognized statistical rating organization or a person associated with the nationally recognized statistical rating organization made recommendations to the obligor or the issuer, underwriter, or sponsor of the security about the corporate or legal structure, assets, liabilities, or activities of the obligor or issuer of the security;

(6) The nationally recognized statistical rating organization issues or maintains a credit rating where the fee paid for the rating was negotiated, discussed, or arranged by a person within the nationally recognized statistical rating organization who has responsibility for participating in determining credit ratings or for developing or approving procedures or methodologies used for determining credit ratings, including qualitative and quantitative models; or

(7) The nationally recognized statistical rating organization issues or maintains a credit rating where a credit analyst who participated in determining or monitoring the credit rating, or a person responsible for approving the credit rating received gifts, including entertainment, from the obligor being rated, or from the issuer, underwriter, or sponsor of the securities being rated, other than items provided in the context of normal business activities such as meetings that have an aggregate value of no more than $25.

*****

5. Section 240.17g–7 is added to read as follows:

§ 240.17g-7 Credit rating reports to be furnished by nationally recognized statistical rating organizations.

(a) A nationally recognized statistical rating organization must attach a report each time it publishes a credit rating for a security or money market instrument issued by an asset pool or as part of any asset-backed or mortgage-backed securities transaction that describes the rating methodology used to determine such credit rating and how it differs from the determination of ratings for any other type of obligor or debt security and how the credit risk characteristics associated with a security or money market instrument issued by an asset pool or as part of any asset-backed or mortgage-backed securities transaction differ from those of any other type of obligor or debt security.

(b) Exemption from attaching report. A nationally recognized statistical rating organization is not required to attach the report each time it publishes a credit rating as prescribed by paragraph (a) of this section if the credit rating symbol used by the nationally recognized statistical rating organization to indicate the credit rating identifies the credit rating as relating to a security or money market instrument issued by an asset pool or as part of any asset-backed or mortgage-backed securities transaction as distinct from a credit rating for any other type of obligor or debt security.

PART 249b—FURTHER FORMS, SECURITIES EXCHANGE ACT OF 1934

The authority citation for part 249b continues to read in part as follows: Authority: 15 U.S.C. 78a et seq., unless otherwise noted;

* * * * *

Form NRSRO (referenced in § 249b.300) is amended by revising Exhibits 1 and 2 in section H, Item 9 of the Form NRSRO Instructions to read as follows:

Note: The text of Form NRSRO and this amendment does not appear in the Code of Federal Regulations.

Form NRSRO

* * * * *

Form NRSRO Instructions

* * * * *

H. INSTRUCTIONS FOR SPECIFIC LINE ITEMS

* * * * *

Item 9. Exhibits. * * *

Exhibit 1

Provide in this Exhibit performance measurement statistics of the credit ratings of the Applicant/NRSRO, including performance measurement statistics of the credit ratings seperately for each class of credit rating for which the Applicant/NRSRO is seeking registration or is registered (as indicated in Item 6 and/or 7 of Form NRSRO) and any other broad class of credit rating issued by the Applicant/NRSRO. For the purposes of this Exhibit, an Applicant/NRSRO registered in the class of credit ratings described in Section 3(a)(62)(B)(iv) of the Act (15 U.S.C. 78c(a)(62)(B)(iv)) must include credit ratings of any security or money market instrument issued by an asset pool or as part of any asset-backed or mortgage-backed securities transaction for purposes of reporting the performance measurement statistics for this class. The performance measurement statistics must at a minimum show the performance of credit ratings in each class over 1 year, 3 year, and 10 year periods (as applicable) through the most recent calendar year-end, including, as applicable: historical ratings transition and default rates within each of the credit rating categories, notches, grades, or rankings used by the Applicant/NRSRO as an indicator of the assessment of the creditworthiness of an obligor, security, or money market instrument in each class of credit rating. The default statistics must include defaults relative to the initial rating and must incorporate defaults that occur after a credit rating is withdrawn. As part of this Exhibit, define the credit rating categories, notches, grades, and rankings used by the

Applicant/NRSRO and explain the performance measurement statistics, including the inputs, time horizons, and metrics used to determine the statistics. Also provide in this Exhibit the Web site address where the records of credit rating actions required under 17 CFR 240.1 7g-2(a)(8) are, or will be, made publicly available in an XBRL Interactive Data File pursuant to the requirements of 17 CFR 240.17g-2(d).

Exhibit 2

Provide in this Exhibit a general description of the procedures and methodologies used by the Applicant/NRSRO to determine credit ratings, including unsolicited credit ratings within the classes of credit ratings for which the Applicant/NRSRO is seeking registration or is registered. The description must be sufficiently detailed to provide users of credit ratings with an understanding of the processes employed by the Applicant/NRSRO in determining credit ratings, including, as applicable, descriptions of: policies for determining whether to initiate a credit rating; a description of the public and non-public sources of information used in determining credit ratings, including information and analysis provided by third-party vendors; whether and, if so, how information about verification performed on assets underlying or referenced by a security or money market instrument issued by an asset pool or as part of any asset-backed or mortgage-backed securities transaction is relied on in determining credit ratings; the quantitative and qualitative models and metrics used to determine credit ratings, including whether and, if so, how assessments of the quality of originators of assets underlying or referenced by a security or money market instrument issued by an asset pool or as part of any asset-backed or mortgage-backed securities transaction factor into the determination of credit ratings; the methodologies by which credit ratings of other credit rating agencies are treated to determine credit ratings for securities or money market instruments issued by an asset pool or as part of any asset-backed or mortgaged- backed securities transaction; the procedures for interacting with the management of a rated obligor or issuer of rated securities or money market instruments; the structure and voting process of committees that review or approve credit ratings; procedures for informing rated obligors or issuers of rated securities or money market instruments about credit rating decisions and for appeals of final or pending credit rating decisions; procedures for monitoring, reviewing, and updating credit ratings, including how frequently credit ratings are reviewed, whether different models or criteria are used for ratings surveillance than for determining initial ratings, whether changes made to models and criteria for determining initial ratings are applied retroactively to existing ratings, and whether changes made to models and criteria for performing ratings surveillance are incorporated into the models and criteria for determining initial ratings; and procedures to withdraw, or suspend the maintenance of, a credit rating. An Applicant/NRSRO may provide in Exhibit 2 the location on its Web site where additional information about the procedures and methodologies is located.

*****

By the Commission.
Florence E. Harmon Acting Secretary
Dated: June 16, 2008

REFERENCES

[1] There is no standard definition of a subprime loan. However, such a loan can broadly be described as a mortgage loan that does not conform to the underwriting standards required for sale to the government sponsored enterprises (non-conforming loans) and are made to borrowers who: (1) have weakened credit histories such as payment delinquencies, charge-offs, judgments, and bankruptcies; (2) have reduced repayment capacity as measured by credit scores (e.g., FICO), debt-to-income ratios, loan-to-value rations, or other criteria; (3) have not provided documentation to verify all or some of the information, particularly financial information, in their loan applications; or (4) have any combination of these factors. Non-conforming loans made to less risky borrowers fall into two other classifications: jumbo and Alt-A.

[2] See e.g., Testimony of John C. Dugan, Comptroller of the Currency, before the U.S. Senate Committee on Banking, Housing, and Urban Affairs (March 4, 2008) ("Dugan March 4, 2008 Senate Testimony"), pp. 8-12; Statement of Sheila C. Bair, Chairman, Federal Deposit Insurance Corporation, before U.S. Senate Committee on Banking, Housing, and Urban Affairs (March 4, 2008) ("Bair March 4, 2008 Senate Statement"), pp. 5-6.

[3] See e.g., Dugan March 4, 2008 Senate Testimony, pp. 12-14; Bair March 4, 2008 Senate Statement, pp. 6-7.

[4] See e.g., Statement of Ben S. Bernanke, Chairman, Board of Governors of the Federal Reserve System, before the U.S. Senate Committee on Banking, Housing, and Urban Affairs (February 28, 2008) ("Bernanke February 28, 2008 Senate Statement"), pp. 1-3; Dugan March 4, 2008 Senate Testimony, pp. 12-15.

[5] Report of the Senate Committee on Banking, Housing, and Urban Affairs to Accompany S. 3850, Credit Rating Agency Reform Act of 2006, S. Report No. 109-326, 109th Cong., 2d Sess. (Sept. 6, 2006) ("Senate Report"), p. 1.

[6] See Oversight of Credit Rating Agencies Registered as Nationally Recognized Statistical Rating Organizations, Securities Exchange Act of 1934 ("Exchange Act") Release No. 55857 (June 5, 2007), 72 FR 33564 (June 18, 2007) ("Adopting Release"). The rules adopted by the Commission prescribe: how a credit rating agency must apply to the Commission for registration as an NRSRO (Rule 1 7g-1 (17 CFR 240.1 7g-1)); the form of the application and the information that must be provided in the application (Form NRSRO and the Instructions to Form NRSRO (17 CFR 240.249b.300)); the records an NRSRO must make and maintain (Rule 17g-2 (17 CFR 240.17g-2)); the reports an NRSRO must furnish to the Commission annually (Rule 17g-3 (17 CFR 240.17g-3)); the areas that must be addressed in an NRSRO's procedures to prevent the misuse of material nonpublic information (Rule 1 7g-4 (17 CFR 240.1 7g-4)); the types of conflicts of interest an NRSRO must disclose and manage or is prohibited from having (Rule 17g-5 (17 CFR 240.17g5)); and certain unfair, coercive, or abusive practices an NRSRO is prohibited from engaging in (Rule 1 7g-6 (17 CFR 240.1 7g-6)).

[7] See Commission Orders granting registration of A.M. Best Company, Inc. (34-56507, September 24, 2007), DBRS Ltd. (34-56508, September 24, 2007), Fitch,

Inc. (34-56509, September 24, 2007), Japan Credit Rating Agency, Ltd, (34-56510, September 24, 2007), Moody's Investor Services, Inc. (34-56511, September 24, 2007), Rating and Investment Information, Inc. (34- 56512, September 24, 2007), Standard & Poor's Rating Services (34-56513, September 24, 2007), Egan-Jones Rating Company (34-57031, December 21, 2007) and LACE Financial Corp. (34- 57300, February 11, 2008).

[8] According to their most recent Annual Certifications on Form NRSRO, S&P rates 197,700 issuers of asset-backed securities, the category that includes RMBS, Moody's rates 110,000 such issuers, and Fitch rates 75,278 such issuers. No other registered NRSRO reports rating more than 1,000 issuers of asset-backed securities. See Standard & Poor's 2007 Annual Certification on Form NRSRO, available at www.standardandpoors.com; Moody's Investor Services 2007 Annual Certification on Form NRSRO, available at www.moodys.com; Fitch, Inc. 2007 Annual Certification on Form NRSRO, available at www.fitchratings.com.

[9] See Testimony of Christopher Cox, Chairman, Commission, before the U.S. Senate Committee on Banking, Housing, and Urban Affairs (April 22, 2008) ("Cox April 22, 2008 Senate Testimony"), pp. 2-3.

[10] See Id, p. 4.

[11] A copy of the policy statement is available at: www.ustreas.gov.

[12] A copy of the report is available at: www.iosco.org.

[13] A copy of the report is available at: www.fsforum.org.

[14] See Cox April 22, 2008 Senate Testimony, pp. 6-8.

[15] The term "structured finance product" as used throughout this release refers broadly to any security or money market instrument issued by an asset pool or as part of any asset-backed or mortgage-backed securities transaction. This broad category of financial instrument includes, but is not limited to, asset-backed securities ("ABS") such as RMBS and to other types of structured debt instruments such as CDOs, including synthetic and hybrid CDOs.

[16] See Senate Report, p. 2.

[17] See e.g., Statement of Sheila C. Bair, Chairman, Federal Deposit Insurance Corporation, before U.S. Senate Committee on Banking, Housing, and Urban Affairs (January 31, 2008) ("Bair January 31, 2008 Senate Statement"), p. 4.

[18] According to Moody's, subprime mortgage loans represented $421 billion of $3.03 8 trillion total mortgage origination in 2002 and $640 billion of $2.8 86 trillion total mortgage origination in 2006. See A Short Guide to Subprime, Moody's, March 25, 2008, p. 1.

[19] See e.g., Dugan March 4, 2008 Senate Testimony, pp. 8-11.

[20] Id.

[21] Subprime Residential Mortgage Securitizations: Frequently Asked Questions, Moody's, April 19, 2007, p. 1.

[22] See e.g., Bernanke February 28, 2008 Senate Testimony, p. 1; Dugan March 4, 2008 Senate Testimony, pp. 8-10.

[23] Rating Stability of Fitch-Rated Global Cash Mezzanine Structured Finance CDOs with Exposure to U.S. Subprime RMBS, Fitch, April 2, 2007, p. 1.

[24] See, e.g., Inside the Ratings: What Credit Ratings Mean, Fitch, August 2007 ("Inside the Ratings"), p. 2; Testimony of Michael Kanef, Group Managing

Director, Moody's Investors Service, Before the United States Senate Committee on Banking, Housing, and Urban Affairs (September 26, 2007) ("Kanef September 26, 2007 Senate Testimony"), p. 2; Principles-Based Rating Methodology For Global Structured Finance Securities, S&P, May 29, 2007, p. 3. Since credit ratings are issued for tranches of RMBS and CDOs individually, rather than for the issuers of those tranches, the NRSRO credit ratings are estimates of the probability of default of each RMBS or CDO tranche as an independent instrument.

[25] As bankruptcy remote stand-alone legal entities, RMBS and CDO trusts had no employees. Consequently, they relied on third-parties to create and manage them. The term "arranger" is used herein to refer to the party that oversees the creation of the RMBS and CDO, which would include the process of obtaining credit ratings for the various tranches. Frequently, the arranger also served as the underwriter of the securities.

[26] See, e.g., Kanef September 26, 2007 Senate Testimony, p. 7.

[27] To the extent that the RMBS included other forms of credit enhancement besides the subordination and over-collateralization provided in this example, e.g., excess spread, this 20 percent subordination figure would be reduced accordingly.

[28] Principal parties are not rated de novo in each RMBS transaction; rather, each NRSRO has its own procedures and schedules for reviewing those parties on a periodic basis in order to incorporate its assessment of those entities into the rating process.

[29] See e.g., Dugan March 4, 2008 Senate Testimony, p. 10; Bernanke February 28, 2008 Senate Testimony, p. 1.

[30] See e.g., Id; Bair March 4, 2008 Senate Statement, pp. 5-8; Bair January 31, 2008 Senate Statement, p.3.

[31] See e.g., Bair January 31, 2008 Senate Statement, p. 3.

[32] Id.

[33] See e.g., Bair March 24, 2008 Senate Statement, p. 6 ("Serious delinquency rates on subprime mortgages securitized in 2006 are significantly higher than those for any of the previous three years.").

[34] Early Defaults Rise In Mortgage Securitizations: Updated Data Show Continued Deterioration, Moody's, September 19, 2007, pp. 3-4.

[35] U.S. Subprime RMBS Performance Update: January 2008 Distribution Date, S&P, February 25, 2008, p. 1.

[36] Defined as 90-plus day delinquencies, foreclosures, and real estate owned. Id.

[37] Id.

[38] Id.

[39] U.S. Subprime RMBS 2005-2007 Vintage Rating Actions Update: January 2008, Moody's, February 1, 2008, pp. 2-4.

[40] Transition Study: Structured Finance Rating Transition And Default Update As Of March 21, 2008, S&P, March 28, 2008, pp. 2-3.

[41] U.S. RMBS Update, Fitch, February 20, 2008 p. 5.

[42] Update On U.S. Subprime And Alt-A: Performance And Rating Reviews, Fitch, March 20, 2008, p. 13.

[43] For example, in November 2007, Fitch announced that in rating CDOs with asset pools which included subprime RMBS, it would adjust all subprime RMBS

securities on Rating Watch Negative downwards by three categories – or notches – (six in the case of 2007 subprime RMBS rated BBB+ or lower) before factoring them into a re-assessment of the CDO's rating. See Global Criteria For The Review Of Structured Finance CDOs With Exposure To US Subprime RMBS, Fitch, November 15, 2007, p. 4.

[44] 2008 U.S. CDO Outlook And 2007 Review, Moody's, March 3, 2008, p. 6.

[45] 86 Ratings Lowered On 20 U.S. CDOs Of ABS Deals; $9.107 Billion In Issuance Affected, S&P, April 1, 2008, p. 1.

[46] Summary of Global Structured Finance CDO Rating Actions, Fitch, December 14, 2007, p. 1.

[47] Id, p. 6.

[48] See e.g., Dugan March 4, 2008 Senate Testimony, p. 13.

[49] Id; Bair March 4, 2008 Senate Statement, p. 7.

[50] Id; Bernanke February 28, 2008 Senate Testimony, p. 3.

[51] See e.g., Dugan March 4, 2008 Senate Testimony, p. 13; Bair January 31, 2008 Senate Testimony, pp. 3-4.

[52] See, e.g., Opening Statement of Senator Richard C. Shelby for the Hearing of the U.S. SenateCommittee on Banking, Housing, and Urban Affairs (September 26, 2007), p. 1-2.

[53] See, e.g., Testimony of Professor John C. Coffee, Jr., Adolf A. Berle Professor of Law, Columbia University Law School, before the U.S. Senate Committee on Banking, Housing, and Urban Affairs (September 26, 2007), pp. 4-5.

[54] See, e.g., Opening Statement of Senator Jack Reed for the Hearing of the U.S. Senate Committee on Banking, Housing, and Urban Affairs (September 26, 2007), pp. 1-2.

[55] See Section 1 5E(h)(2) of the Exchange Act (15 U.S.C. 78o-7(h)(2)).

[56] 17 CFR 240.17g-5(a).

[57] 17 CFR 240.17g-5(b)(1).

[58] 17 CFR 240.17g-5(b)(5).

[59] Adopting Release, 72 FR at 33598.

[60] 17 CFR 240.17g-5.

[61] 17 CFR 240.17g-5(b)(1). As the Commission noted when adopting Rule 17g-5, the concern with conflict identified in paragraph (b)(1) "is that an NRSRO may be influenced to issue a more favorable credit rating than warranted in order to obtain or retain the business of the issuer or underwriter." Adopting Release, 72 FR at 33595.

[62] See e.g., Testimony of Professor John C. Coffee, Jr., Adolf A. Berle Professor of Law, Columbia University Law School, before the U.S. Senate Committee on Banking, Housing, and Urban Affairs (April 22, 2008) ("Coffee April 22, 2008 Senate Testimony"), pp. 4-6.

[63] Id.

[64] This proposed requirement would be in addition to the current requirements of paragraph (a) that an NRSRO disclose the type of conflict of interest in Exhibit 6 to Form NRSRO; and establish, maintain and enforce written policies and procedures to address and manage the conflict of interest. 17 CFR 240 17g-5(a)(1) and (2).

[65] As used herein, an "unsolicited rating" is one that is determined without the consent and/or payment of the obligor being rated or issuer, underwriter, or arranger of the securities being rated.

[66] The Commission notes that "unsolicited" ratings could be used to obtain business with arrangers by creating a track record of favorable ratings. The Commission believes the potential to expose such conduct would be equal to that of exposing an NRSRO influenced by the "arranger-pay" conflict insomuch as the paid for ratings (usually at least two) would be consistently lower than the "unsolicited" ratings.

[67] See proposed paragraph (a)(3)(i)(A) and (B) of Rule 17g-5.

[68] See proposed paragraph (a)(3)(ii) of Rule 17g-5.

[69] See Sections II.A. 1 .b.i – iii below for a broader discussion of the scope of the disclosures that would be required under the proposed amendments.

[70] See proposed paragraph (a)(3)(i)(A) of Rule 17g-5.

[71] 15 U.S.C. 78c(a)(61).

[72] Proposed paragraph (a)(3)(ii) of Rule 17g-5.

[73] 15 U.S.C. 78o-7(h)(2).

[74] Id.

[75] As discussed below, for private offerings and offshore offerings, this information would not be disclosed publicly before the offering closes but instead would be provided via a password- protected Internet Web site to credit rating agencies and accredited investors. After the offering closes, the information would be required to be disclosed publicly and, therefore, made available to market observers such as academics.

[76] 15 U.S.C. 77a et seq.

[77] Securities Act Section 2(a)(3) (15 U.S.C. 77b(a)(3)) defines an "offer" as any attempt to offer to dispose of, or solicitation of any offer to buy, a security or interest in a security for value. The term "offer" has been interpreted broadly and goes beyond the common law concept of an offer. See Diskin v. Lomasney & Co., 452 F. 2d 871 (2d Cir. 1971); SEC v. Cavanaugh, 1 F. Supp. 2d 337 (S.D.N.Y. 1998). The Commission has explained that "the publication of information and publicity efforts, made in advance of a proposed financing which have the effect of conditioning the public mind or arousing public interest in the issuer in its securities constitutes an offer * * *." Guidelines for the Release of Information by Issuers Whose Securities are in Registration, Securities Act Release No. 5180 (August 16, 1971), 36 FR 16506.

[78] Before the registration statement is filed, all offers, in whatever form, are prohibited. See Securities Act Section 5(c) (15 U.S.C. 77e(c)). Between the filing of the registration statement and its effectiveness, offers made in writing (including by e-mail or Internet), by radio, or by television are limited to a "statutory prospectus" that conforms to the information requirements of Securities Act Section 10. See Securities Act Section 5(b)(1) (15 U.S.C. 77e(b)(1)) and Securities Act Section 10 (15 U.S.C. 77j). After the registration statement is declared effective, offering participants may make written offers only through a statutory prospectus, except that they may use additional offering materials if a final prospectus that meets the requirements of Securities Act Section 10(a) is sent or given prior to or with those materials. See Securities Act Section 2(a)(10) (15 U.S.C. 77b(a)(10)) and Section 5(b)(1).

[79] This may be the case even if the information relates to pools backing prior issuances. In an offering of securities backed by the same class of assets, the information provided for surveillance and required to be disclosed pursuant to proposed Rule 1 7g-5(a)(3)(iii) may be static pool data as described in Item 1105 of Regulation AB (17 CFR 229.1105).

[80] See Securities Offering Reform, Securities Act Release 33-8591 (July 19, 2005), 70 FR 44722 (August 3, 2005) (the "Securities Offering Reform Release") for a discussion of the definition of written communications and rules relating to permitted communications in registered offerings. See also Asset-Backed Securities, Securities Act Release No. 8518 (December 22, 2004) 70 FR 1506 (January 7, 2005) (the "Asset-Backed Securities Release") for rules applicable to offerings of asset-backed securities.

[81] Under the Securities Act, purchasers of an issuer's securities in a registered offering have private rights of action for materially deficient disclosure in registration statements under Section 11 and in prospectuses and oral communications under Section 12(a)(2). Under Securities Act Section 12(a)(2) and Securities Act Rule 159, the liability determination as to an oral communication, prospectus, or statement, as the case may be, does not take into account information conveyed to a purchaser only after the time of sale (including the contract of sale), including information contained in a final prospectus, prospectus supplement, or Exchange Act filing that is filed or delivered subsequent to the time of sale (including the contract of sale) where the information is not otherwise conveyed at or prior to that time. The time of sale under the Securities Act includes the time of the contract of sale – the time at which an investor has taken the action the investor must take to become committed to purchase the securities and therefore entered into a contract of sale.

[82] See Section III.D.3.b.iii(C)(3)(a)(iii) of the Securities Offering Reform Release, 70 FR at 44722, 44751.

[83] 17 CFR 239.13. An ABS issuer is eligible to use Form S-3 if the conditions of General Instruction V are met.

[84] 17 CFR 229.1101. Item 1101 of Regulation AB provides the following definition: (a) ABS informational and computational material means a written communication consisting solely of one or some combination of the following: Factual information regarding the asset-backed securities being offered and the structure and basic parameters of the securities, such as the number of classes, seniority, payment priorities, terms of payment, the tax, Employment Retirement Income Security Act of 1974, as amended, (29 U.S.C. 1001 et seq.) ("ERISA") or other legal conclusions of counsel, and descriptive information relating to each class (*e.g.*, principal amount, coupon, minimum denomination, anticipated price, yield, weighted average life, credit enhancements, anticipated ratings, and other similar information relating to the proposed structure of the offering); Factual information regarding the pool assets underlying the asset-backed securities, including origination, acquisition and pool selection criteria, information regarding any prefunding or revolving period applicable to the offering, information regarding significant obligors, data regarding the contractual and related characteristics of the underlying pool assets (*e.g.*, weighted average coupon, weighted average maturity, delinquency and loss

information and geographic distribution) and other factual information concerning the parameters of the asset pool appropriate to the nature of the underlying assets, such as the type of assets comprising the pool and the programs under which the loans were originated; Identification of key parties to the transaction, such as servicers, trustees, depositors, sponsors, originators and providers of credit enhancement or other support, including a brief description of each such party's roles, responsibilities, background and experience; Static pool data, as referenced in Item 1105 of this Regulation AB, such as for the sponsor's and/or servicer's portfolio, prior transactions or the asset pool itself; Statistical information displaying for a particular class of asset-backed securities the yield, average life, expected maturity, interest rate sensitivity, cash flow characteristics, total rate of return, option adjusted spread or other financial or statistical information relating to the class or classes under specified prepayment, interest rate, loss or other hypothetical scenarios. Examples of such information under the definition include: Statistical results of interest rate sensitivity analyses regarding the impact on yield or other financial characteristics of a class of securities from changes in interest rates at one or more assumed prepayment speeds; Statistical information showing the cash flows that would be associated with a particular class of asset-backed securities at a specified prepayment speed; and Statistical information reflecting the financial impact of losses based on a variety of loss or default experience, prepayment, interest rate and related assumptions. The names of underwriters participating in the offering of the securities, and their additional roles, if any, within the underwriting syndicate; The anticipated schedule for the offering (including the approximate date upon which the proposed sale to the public will begin) and a description of marketing events (including the dates, times, locations, and procedures for attending or otherwise accessing them); and A description of the procedures by which the underwriters will conduct the offering and the procedures for transactions in connection with the offering with an underwriter or participating dealer (including procedures regarding account-opening and submitting indications of interest and conditional offers to buy). The Commission confirmed in the Asset-Backed Securities Release that loan level information could be included in ABS information and computational materials.

[85] 17 CFR 249.308.

[86] 17 CFR 230.167 and 17 CFR 230.426.

[87] 17 CFR 23 0.405. The contents of free writing prospectuses are not limited to ABS informational and computational materials.

[88] 17 CFR 230.164 and 17 CFR 230.433. Rule 433 also provides that a free writing prospectus or portion thereof required to be filed under Rule 433 containing only ABS informational and computational materials may be filed under Rule 433 but within the time frame required for satisfaction of the conditions of Rule 426, and that such filing will satisfy the conditions of Rule 433.

[89] Depending on whether the materials constitute a free writing prospectus or ABS informational and computational materials, the liability provisions governing the disclosure may differ. Free writing prospectuses are subject to liability under Section 12(a)(2) and Section 17(a) of the Securities Act. 15 U.S.C. 77l(a)(2) and 15 U.S.C. 77q(a). A free writing prospectus will not be part of a registration statement subject to liability under Securities Act Section 11 unless the issuer elects to file

it as part of the registration statement. See also Asset-Backed Securities Release at footnote 335. On the other hand, ABS informational and computational materials also are subject to Section 12(a)(2) and Section 17(a) liability, but they must be filed on Form 8-K and therefore, by virtue of incorporation by reference into a registration statement, are subject to Section 11 liability.

[90] 17 CFR 230.433 and 17 CFR 230.426.

[91] An "ineligible issuer," as the term is defined in Rule 405 of the Securities Act, includes, in the case of asset-backed issuers, the depositor or any issuing entities previously established, directly or indirectly by the depositor, who are not current in their Exchange Act reports and other materials required to be filed during the prior 12 months (or such shorter period that the issuer was required to file such reports and materials), other than reports on Form 8-K required solely pursuant to an item specified in General Instruction I.A.4 of Form S-3.

[92] In asset-backed offerings by ineligible issuers, free writing prospectuses used by ineligible issuers are limited to the following information: factual information regarding the asset-backed securities being offered and the structure and basic parameters of the securities, such as the number of classes, seniority, payment priorities, terms of payment, the tax, ERISA or other legal conclusions of counsel, and descriptive information relating to each class (e.g., principal amount, coupon, minimum denomination, anticipated price, yield, weighted average life, credit enhancements, anticipated ratings, and other similar information relating to the proposed structure of the offering); factual information regarding the pool assets underlying the asset-backed securities, including origination, acquisition and pool selection criteria, information regarding any prefunding or revolving period applicable to the offering, information regarding significant obligors, data regarding the contractual and related characteristics of the underlying pool assets (e.g., weighted average coupon, weighted average maturity, delinquency and loss information and geographic distribution) and other factual information concerning the parameters of the asset pool appropriate to the nature of the underlying assets, such as the type of assets comprising the pool and the programs under which the loans were originated; identification of key parties to the transaction, such as servicers, trustees, depositors, sponsors, originators and providers of credit enhancement or other support, including a brief description of each such party's roles, responsibilities, background and experience; static pool data; the names of underwriters participating in the offering of the securities, and their additional roles, if any, within the underwriting syndicate; the anticipated schedule for the offering (including the approximate date upon which the proposed sale to the public will begin) and a description of marketing events (including the dates, times, locations, and procedures for attending or otherwise accessing them); and a description of the procedures by which the underwriters will conduct the offering and the procedures for transactions in connection with the offering with an underwriter or participating dealer (including procedures regarding account opening and submitting indications of interest and conditional offers to buy).

[93] See Form S-3 (17 CFR 239.13), Form 8-K (17 CFR 249.308) and Item 601(b)(4) of Regulation S-K (17 CFR 229.601).

[94] 17 CFR 243.100 to 103.

[95] See Asset-Backed Securities Release.

[96] 15 U.S.C. 77d(2).

[97] 17 CFR 230.501 through 230.508.

[98] See Securities Act Section 4(2) (15 U.S.C. 77d(2)) and Securities Act Rules 504, 505 and 506 of Regulation D (17 CFR 230.504, 230.505 and 230.506). An exception to the prohibition against general solicitation applies to some limited offerings under Rule 504(b)(1) (17 CFR 230.504(b)(1)) when an issuer has satisfied state securities laws of specified types. See Revision of Rule 504 of Regulation D, the "Seed Capital" Exemption, Securities Act Release No. 7644 (February 25, 1999), 64 FR 11090. The restriction on general solicitation or advertising applies to all methods by which the communication can be made, including electronic, paper, mail, radio, television, or in newspapers or magazines.

[99] See Use of Electronic Media, Securities Act Release No. 7856 (April 28, 2000), 65 FR 25843 (the "Electronic Media Release"). The Commission noted in the Electronic Media Release that the federal securities laws apply equally to information contained on an issuer's Web site as they do to other communications made by or attributed to the issuer.

[100] 15 U.S.C. 78c(a)(61).

[101] A password-protected Web site would meet the requirements of an amended Rule 17g-5 in the context of private offerings.

[102] The Commission noted in Interpretative Release on Regulation D, Securities Act Release No. 6455 (March 3, 1983), 17 CFR 231, that Rule 502(c) relates to the nature of the offering, not the nature of the offerees.

[103] Rule 901 of Regulation S, 17 CFR 230.901.

[104] Rule 903(a)(1).

[105] Rule 903(a)(2).

[106] See Statement of the Commission Regarding Use of Internet Web Sites to Offer Securities, Solicit Securities Transactions or Advertise Investment Services Offshore, Securities Act Release No. 7516 (March 23, 1998).

[107] Id.

[108] 15 U.S.C. 78c(a)(63).

[109] 15 U.S.C. 78o-7(h)(2).

[110] Id.

[111] See e.g., Coffee April 22, 2008 Senate Testimony, pp. 2-3.

[112] 17 CFR 240.17g-5.

[113] 15 U.S.C. 78o-7(h)(2).

[114] Id.

[115] See Adopting Release, 72 FR at 33618.

[116] 17 CFR 240.17g-5.

[117] 15 U.S.C. 78o-7(h)(2).

[118] Id.

[119] See Section 5 of the Rating Agency Act and 15 U.S.C 78q(a)(1).

[120] 17 CFR 240.17g-2.

[121] See Extension of Interactive Data Voluntarily Reporting Program in the EDGAR System to Include Mutual Fund Risk/Return Summary Information, Securities Act Release No. 8823 (August 20, 2007).

[122] The accommodation of subscriber-pay models acknowledges the Rating Agency Act's intent to encourage the subscriber-pays model (see Senate Report, p. 7) while simultaneously ensuring equal treatment for NRSROs operating under an issuer-pays model.
[123] See Section 17(a)(1) of the Exchange Act (15 U.S.C. 78q(a)(1)).
[124] The Commission notes that it would consider the RMBS and CDO rating process described above in Section I.C.2 as using a quantitative model as a substantial component in the ratings process.
[125] See Section 17(a)(1) of the Exchange Act (15 U.S.C. 78q(a)(1)).
[126] 17 CFR 240.17g-6. Rule 17g-6 prohibits an NRSRO from engaging in certain unfair, abusive or coercive practices such as issuing a credit rating that is not determined in accordance with the NRSRO's established procedures and methodologies for determining credit ratings based on whether the rated person will purchase the credit rating. See 17 CRF 240.1 7g-6(a)(2).
[127] 17 CFR 240.17g-2.
[128] See Section 17(a)(1) of the Exchange Act (15 U.S.C. 78q(a)(1)).
[129] See e.g., Coffee April 22, 2008 Senate Testimony, pp. 4-6.
[130] 15 U.S.C. 78o-7(a)(1)(B).
[131] 15 U.S.C. 78o-7(a)(1)(B)(x).
[132] See 15 U.S.C. 78o-7(a)(1)(B)(i).
[133] See Adopting Release, 72 FR at 33574.
[134] Id.
[135] 15 U.S.C. 78c(a)(62)(B)(iv).
[136] See Id.
[137] 15 U.S.C. 78o-7(a)(1)(B)(i).
[138] 15 U.S.C. 78o-7(a)(1)(B)(i).
[139] See Section 1 5E(a)(1)(B)(x) of the Exchange Act (15 U.S.C. 78o–7(a)(1)(B)(x)).
[140] 15 U.S.C. 78o-7(a)(1)(B)(ii).
[141] See Section 1 5E(a)(1)(B)(x) of the Exchange Act (15 U.S.C. 78o–7(a)(1)(B)(x)).
[142] 15 U.S.C. 78o-7(k).
[143] An applicant can request that the Commission keep this information confidential. See Section 24 of the Exchange Act (15 U.S.C. 78x), 17 CFR 240.24b-2, 17 CFR 200.80 and 17 CFR 200.83.
[144] Id.
[145] 15 U.S.C. 78q(a)(1).
[146] See Section 5 of the Rating Agency Act and 15 U.S.C. 78q(a)(1).
[147] 15 U.S.C. 78c(a)(62)(B)(iv).
[148] See Id.
[149] See Section 17(a)(1) of the Exchange Act (15 U.S.C. 78q(a)(1)).
[150] See Introducing Assumption Volatility Scores and Loss Sensitivities for Structured Finance Securities, Moody's, May 14, 2007, p. 3.
[151] See Section 17(a)(1) of the Exchange Act (15 U.S.C. 78q(a)(1)).
[152] 44 U.S.C. 3501 et seq.; 5 CFR 1320.11.
[153] Proposed Rule 1 7g-7.
[154] See Section 15E of the Exchange Act (15 U.S.C. 78o-7).
[155] 17 CFR 240.17g-2.

[156] See proposed Rule 1 7g-2(a)(2)(iv) and (d).
[157] See proposed Rule 17g-3(a)(6).
[158] See proposed Rule 1 7g-5(a)(3) and (b)(9).
[159] See proposed Rule 17g-7.
[160] See 17 CFR 17g-1 through 17g-6, and Form NRSRO.
[161] 15 U.S.C. 78o-7.
[162] See Senate Report, p. 8.
[163] See Adopting Release, 72 FR at 33606-33607.
[164] A.M. Best Company, Inc.; DBRS Ltd.; Fitch.; Japan Credit Rating Agency, Ltd.; Moody's; Rating and Investment Information, Inc.; S&P; LACE Financial Corp.; and Egan-Jones Rating Company.
[165] See proposed Rule 1 7g-5(a)(3)(i) and (iii).
[166] This total is derived from the total annual hours set forth in the order that the totals appear in the text: 390 + 300 + 4,000 + 150,000 + 1,280,000 = 1,434,690.
[167] This total is derived from the total one-time hours set forth in the order that the totals appear in the text: 900 + 900 + 60,000 + 1,500 + 300 + 900 = 64,500.
[168] 17 CFR 240.17g-1 and Form NRSRO.
[169] See Adopting Release, 72 FR at 33609. To date, only one of the seven NRSROs that have been registered with the Commission since September 2007 has furnished the Commission with an amended Form NRSRO since registering with the Commission.
[170] 17 CFR 240.17g-2.
[171] See Adopting Release, 72 FR at 33608.
[172] See Adopting Release, 72 FR at 33610.
[173] Proposed paragraph (a)(2)(iii) of Rule 1 7g-2.
[174] Proposed paragraph (a)(8) of Rule 17g-2.
[175] Proposed amendment to Rule 1 7g-2(d).
[176] Proposed paragraph (b)(8) of Rule 17g-2.
[177] The Commission believes that the one-time burden to set up and/or modify a recordkeeping system to comply with the proposed amendments would be greater than the ongoing annual burden. Once an NRSRO has set up or modified its recordkeeping system to comply with the proposed amendments, its annual hour burden would be increased only to the extent it would be required to make and retain additional records.
[178] 300 hours x 1.10 = 330 hours. This would result in an increase of approximately 30 hours per NRSRO for the one-time hour burden.
[179] 330 hours x 30 respondents = 9,900 hours. The proposed amendments would result in an increase of 900 total one-time burden hours.
[180] 254 hours x 1.05 = 267 hours. The proposed amendments would result in an increase of approximately 13 annual burden hours per NRSRO for Rule 1 7g-2.
[181] 267 hours x 30 respondents = 8,010 hours.
[182] 8,010 hours – 7,620 hours = 390 hours.
[183] See proposed amendment to Rule 17g-2(d).
[184] The Commission also bases this estimate on the current one-time and annual burden hours for an NRSRO to publicly disclose its Form NRSRO. No alternatives

to these estimates as proposed were suggested by commenters. See Adopting Release, 72 FR at 33609.

[185] 30 hours x 30 NRSROs = 900 hours.

[186] 10 hours x 30 NRSROs = 300 hours.

[187] See Adopting Release, 72 FR at 33609, 33610.

[188] 17 CFR 240.17g-3.

[189] See proposed Rule 17g-3(a)(6).

[190] 200 hours x 30 NRSROs = 6,000 hours. See Adopting Release, 72 FR at 33610.

[191] Rule 17g-3 currently requires five reports. Only the first report – financial statements – need be audited. The two new reports proposed to be required by the amendments would not need to be audited.

[192] $15,000 x 30 NRSROs = $450,000. See Adopting Release, 72 FR at 33610.

[193] 17 CFR 240.17g-5.

[194] 17 CFR 240.17g-5(c).

[195] See proposed Rule 17g-5(b)(9). The current paragraph (b)(9) would be renumbered as (b)(10).

[196] See proposed Rule 1 7g-5(a)(3).

[197] See proposed Rule 1 7g-5(a)(3)(i)-(iii).

[198] See Adopting Release, 72 FR at 33609.

[199] 300 hours x 200 respondents = 60,000 hours.

[200] 20 transactions x 1 hour = 20 hours.

[201] 20 hours x 200 respondents = 4,000 hours.

[202] 125 transactions x 30 minutes x 12 months = 45,000 minutes/60 minutes = 750 hours.

[203] 750 hours x 200 respondents = 150,000 hours.

[204] See proposed Rule 1 7g-7.

[205] See proposed Rule 1 7g-7.

[206] The Commission based this estimate on the estimated number of hours it would take an NRSRO to comply with Rule 17g-4 to develop policies and procedures to prevent the misuse of material nonpublic information. See Adopting Release, 72 FR at 33611.

[207] 50 hours x 30 NRSROs = 1,500 hours.

[208] This estimate uses the average of the approximate number of credit ratings for asset-based securities as defined in 17 CFR 229.1101(c) that S&P, Moody's and Fitch had outstanding as of the most recent calendar year end as reported in their annual certifications. (S&P: 197,700; Moody's: 110,000; and Fitch: 75,278).

[209] 128,000 x 4 = 512,000 ratings publications.

[210] 512,000 x 5 minutes per report = 2,560,000 minutes/60 minutes per hour = 42,667 hours.

[211] 42,667 hours x 30 NRSROs = 1,280,000 hours.

[212] This estimate is based on the number of hours it would take an NRSRO to complete an annual certification on Form NRSRO. See Adopting Release, 72 FR at 33609. 10 hours x 30 NRSROs = 300 hours.

[213] 1,500 + 300 hours.

[214] See proposed Rule 1 7g-7(b).

[215] 30 hours x 30 NRSROs.

[216] See proposed Rule 17g-2(a)(8) and (d).
[217] 15 U.S.C. 78o-7(k).
[218] 17 CFR 240.17g-2(c).
[219] For the purposes of this cost/benefit analysis, the Commission is using salary data from the Securities Industry and Financial Markets Association ("SIFMA") Report on Management and Professional Earnings in the Securities Industry 2007, which provides base salary and bonus information for middle-management and professional positions within the securities industry. The Commission believes that the salaries for these securities industry positions would be comparable to the salaries of similar positions in the credit rating industry. Finally, the salary costs derived from the report and referenced in this cost benefit section, are modified to account for an 1800-hour work year and multiplied by 5.35 to account for bonuses, firm size, employee benefits and overhead. The Commission used comparable assumptions in adopting the final rules implementing the Rating Agency Act in 2007, requested comments on such assumptions, and received no comments in response to its request. See Adopting Release, 72 FR at 33611, note 576. Hereinafter, references to data derived from the report as modified in the manner described above will be cited as "SIFMA 2007 Report as Modified."
[220] Senate Report, p. 2.
[221] Id, p. 7.
[222] See Adopting Release.
[223] See Senate Report, p. 2.
[224] See Rule 17g-1.
[225] See Section 1 5E(a)(1)(B) of the Exchange Act. 15 U.S.C. 78o-7(a)(1)(B).
[226] 17 CFR 240.17g-1 and Form NRSRO.
[227] Proposed paragraph (a)(2)(iii) of Rule 1 7g-2.
[228] Proposed paragraph (a)(8) of Rule 17g-2.
[229] Proposed paragraph (b)(8) of Rule 17g-2.
[230] See proposed Rule 17g-3(a)(6).
[231] See proposed Rule 17g-5(a)(3) and (b)(9).
[232] See proposed Rule 17 CFR 240.1 7g-5(c)(5)-(7).
[233] See 15 U.S.C. 78o-7(a)(1)(B)(vi) and (h).
[234] See proposed Rule 17 CFR 240.1 7g-5(a)(3).
[235] See proposed Rule 1 7g-7.
[236] See proposed instructions to Exhibit 1, Form NRSRO.
[237] See 17 CFR 240.17g-4; Adopting Release, 72 FR at 33616.
[238] The Commission estimates that a Compliance Attorney (40 hours) and a Programmer Analyst (10 hours) would perform these responsibilities. The SIFMA 2007 Report as Modified indicates that the average hourly rates for a Compliance Attorney and a Programmer Analyst are $270 and $194 per hour, respectively. Therefore, the average one-time cost to an NRSRO would be $12,740 [(40 hours x $270) + (10 hours x $194)].
[239] $12,740 x 9 NRSROs = $114,660.
[240] 17 CFR 240.17g-2.
[241] Proposed paragraph (a)(2)(iii) of Rule 17g-2.
[242] Proposed paragraph (a)(8) of Rule 17g-2.

[243] Proposed amendment to Rule 1 7g-2(d).
[244] Proposed paragraph (b)(8) of Rule 17g-2.
[245] 300 hours x 1.10 = 330 hours.
[246] 330 hours x 30 respondents = 9,900 hours.
[247] 254 hours x 1.05 = 267 hours.
[248] 267 hours x 30 respondents = 8,010 hours.
[249] 8,010 hours – 7,620 hours = 390 hours.
[250] The Commission estimates that an NRSRO will have a Compliance Manager perform these responsibilities. Based on the average hourly rate for a Compliance Manager of $245, the average one time cost will be $7,350 (30 hours x $245 per hour) and the average annual cost will be $3,185 (13 hours x $245 per hour).
[251] $7,350 x 30 NRSROs = $220,500.
[252] $3,185 x 30 NRSROs = $95,550.
[253] See proposed amendment to Rule 17g-2(d).
[254] The Commission also bases this estimate on the estimated one time and annual burden hours it would take an NRSRO to publicly disclose its Form NRSRO on its Web site. No comments were received on these estimates in the final rule release. See Adopting Release, 72 FR at 33609.
[255] 30 hours x 30 NRSROs = 900 hours.
[256] 10 hours x 30 NRSROs = 300 hours.
[257] The Commission estimates that an NRSRO would have a Senior Programmer perform these responsibilities. The SIFMA 2007 Report as Modified indicates that the average hourly cost for a Senior Programmer is $289. Therefore, the average one-time cost would be $8,670 [(30 hours) x ($289 per hour)] and the average annual cost would be $2,890 [(10 hours per year) x ($289 per hour)].
[258] 900 hours x $289 per hour.
[259] 300 hours x $289 per hour.
[260] See proposed Rule 17g-2(a)(8). The Central Index Key (CIK) is used on the Commission's computer systems to identify corporations and individual people who have filed disclosure with the Commission. Anyone may search www.edgarcompany.sec.gov for a company, fund, or individual CIK. There is no fee for this service. CUSIP stands for Committee on Uniform Securities Identification Procedures. A CUSIP number identifies most securities, including: stocks of all registered U.S. and Canadian companies, U.S. government and municipal bonds, as well as structured finance issuances. The CUSIP system—owned by the American Bankers Association and operated by Standard & Poor's—facilitates the clearing and settlement process of securities. The CUSIP number consists of nine characters (including letters and numbers) that uniquely identify a company or issuer and the type of security.
[261] See https://www.cusip.com/static/html/webpage/service_fees.html#lic_fees.
[262] $100,000 x 30 NRSROs = $3,000,000.
[263] 17 CFR 240.17g-3.
[264] 17 CFR 240. 17g-5.
[265] See proposed Rule 17g-5(b)(9). The current paragraph (b)(9) would be renumbered as (b)(10).
[266] See proposed Rule 1 7g-5(a)(3).

[267] 300 hours x 200 respondents = 60,000 hours.

[268] The Commission estimates an NRSRO would have a Compliance Manager and a Programmer Analyst perform these responsibilities, and that each would spend 50% of the estimated hours performing these responsibilities. The SIFMA 2007 Report as Modified indicates that the average hourly cost for a Compliance Manager is $245 and the average hourly cost for a Programmer Analyst is 194. Therefore, the average one-time cost to an NRSRO would be $[1 50 hours x $245) + (150 hours x $194)] = $65,850.

[269] $65,580 x 200 respondents = $13,116,000.

[270] This estimate assumes the respondent has already implemented the system and policies and procedures for disclosure. The Commission cannot estimate the number of initial transactions per year with certainty. The Commission believes that the number of deals that each respondent will disclose information on will vary widely based on the size of the entity. In addition, the Commission preliminarily believes that the number of asset-backed or mortgaged-backed issuances being rated by NRSROs in the next few years would be difficult to predict given the recent credit market turmoil.

[271] 20 transactions x 1 hour = 20 hours.

[272] 20 hours x 200 respondents = 4,000 hours.

[273] The Commission estimates an NRSRO would have a Webmaster perform these responsibilities. The SIFMA 2007 Report as Modified indicates that the average hourly cost for a Webmaster is $205. Therefore, the average one-time cost to a respondent would be 20 hours x $205 = $4,100.

[274] $4,100 x 200 respondents = $820,000.

[275] 125 transactions x 30 minutes x 12 months = 45,000 minutes/60 minutes = 750 hours.

[276] 750 hours x 200 respondents = 150,000 hours.

[277] The Commission estimates an NRSRO would have a Webmaster perform these responsibilities. The SIFMA 2007 Report as Modified indicates that the average hourly cost for a Webmaster is $205. Therefore, the average one-time cost to a respondent would be 750 hours x 205 = $153,750.

[278] $153,750 x 200 respondents = $30,750,000.

[279] See proposed Rule 1 7g-5(c)(5)-(7).

[280] See proposed Rule 1 7g-3A.

[281] The Commission estimates an NRSRO would have a Compliance Manager perform these responsibilities. The SIFMA 2007 Report as Modified indicates that the average hourly cost for a Compliance Manager is $245. Therefore, the average one-time cost to an NRSRO would be $12,250 (50 hours x $245).

[282] 30 NRSROs x $12,250 = $367,500.

[283] 128,000 x 4 = 512,000 reports x 5 minutes per report = 2,560,000 minutes/60 minutes per hour =42,667 hours.

[284] 42,667 hours x 30 NRSROs = 1,280,010 hours.

[285] The Commission estimates an NRSRO would have a Webmaster perform these responsibilities. The SIFMA 2007 Report as Modified indicates that the average hourly cost for a Webmaster is $205. Therefore, the average one-time cost to an NRSRO would be $4,373,265 (21,333 hours x $205).

[286] $4,373,265 x 30 NRSROs = $131,197,950.

[287] This estimate is based on the number of hours it would take an NRSRO to complete an annual certification on Form NRSRO. See Exchange Act Release No. 55857 (June 5, 2007), 72 FR 33564, 33609 (June 18, 2007). 10 hours x 30 NRSROs = 300 hours.

[288] The Commission estimates an NRSRO would have a Compliance Attorney perform these responsibilities. The SIFMA 2007 Report as Modified indicates that the average hourly cost for a Compliance Attorney is $270. Therefore, the average one-time cost to an NRSRO would be $2,700 (10 hours x $270).

[289] $2,700 x 30 NRSROs = $81,000.

[290] $17,078,760 (total one-time costs) + $163,097,810 (total annual costs) = $180,175,810.

[291] 15 U.S.C. 78c(f).

[292] 15 U.S.C. 78w(a)(2).

[293] Pub. L. No. 104-121, Title II, 110 Stat. 857 (1996) (codified in various sections of 5 U.S.C., 15 U.S.C. and as a note to 5 U.S.C. 601).

[294] 5 U.S.C. 603.

[295] Pub. L. No. 109-291 (2006); see also Exchange Act Release No. 55857 (June 5, 2007), 72 FR 33564, 33609 (June 18, 2007).

[296] See Senate Report.

[297] 15 U.S.C. 78c(b), 78o-7, 78q(a), and 78w.

[298] 17 CFR 240.0-10(a).

[299] Adopting Release, 72 FR at 33618.

[300] See 17 CFR 240.0-10(a).

[301] See proposed amendments to Form NRSRO.

[302] See proposed amendments to Rule 1 7g-2.

[303] Proposed paragraph (a)(2)(iii) of Rule 1 7g-2.

[304] Proposed paragraph (a)(8) of Rule 17g-2.

[305] Proposed paragraph (b)(8) of Rule 17g-2.

[306] See proposed amendment to Rule 17g-3.

[307] See proposed amendment to Rule 17g-5.

[308] See proposed Rule 1 7g-7.

[309] 5 U.S.C. 603(c).

[310] 15 U.S.C. 78c(b), 78o–7, 78q, 78w, and 78mm.

In: Credit Rating Agency Reform
Editors: John De Luca and Paul Russo, pp. 95-128
ISBN: 978-1-60692-192-0

Chapter 2

SUMMARY REPORT OF ISSUES IDENTIFIED IN THE COMMISSION STAFF'S EXAMINATIONS OF SELECT CREDIT RATING AGENCIES

Staff of the Securities and Exchange Commission
July 8, 2008

I. SUMMARY

In August 2007, the Securities and Exchange Commission's Staff initiated examinations of three credit rating agencies -- Fitch Ratings, Ltd. ("Fitch"), Moody's Investor Services, Inc. ("Moody's") and Standard & Poor's Ratings Services ("S&P") -- to review their role in the recent turmoil in the subprime mortgage-related securities markets. These firms registered with the Commission as nationally recognized statistical rating organizations in September 2007 (collectively, the examined firms are referred to in this report as the "rating agencies" or "NRSROs"). These firms were not subject to the Credit Rating Agency Reform Act of 2006 or Commission regulations for credit rating agencies until September 2007. The focus of the examinations was the rating agencies' activities in rating subprime residential mortgage-backed securities ("RMBS") and collateralized debt obligations ("CDOs") linked to subprime residential mortgage-backed securities. The purpose of the examinations was to develop an understanding of the practices of the rating agencies surrounding the rating of RMBS and CDOs. This is a summary report by the Commission's Staff of the issues identified in those examinations.[1]

In sum, as described in Section IV of this report, while the rating agencies had different policies, procedures and practices and different issues were identified among the firms examined, the Staff's examinations revealed that:

- there was a substantial increase in the number and in the complexity of RMBS and CDO deals since 2002, and some of the rating agencies appear to have struggled with the growth;
- significant aspects of the ratings process were not always disclosed;

- policies and procedures for rating RMBS and CDOs can be better documented;
- the rating agencies are implementing new practices with respect to the information provided to them;
- the rating agencies did not always document significant steps in the ratings process -- including the rationale for deviations from their models and for rating committee actions and decisions -- and they did not always document significant participants in the ratings process;
- the surveillance processes used by the rating agencies appear to have been less robust than the processes used for initial ratings;
- issues were identified in the management of conflicts of interest and improvements can be made; and
- the rating agencies' internal audit processes varied significantly.

This report also summarizes generally the remedial actions that the examined NRSROs have said they will take as a result of these examinations. In addition, this report also describes the Commission's proposed rules, which, if adopted, would require that the NRSROs take further actions.[2]

In conjunction with the Staff's examinations of the three rating agencies, the Staff of the Office of Economic Analysis ("OEA Staff") reviewed the processes used by these firms with respect to rating RMBS and CDOs that held subprime RMBS securities. The purpose of the OEA Staff's review was to gain insight into the conflicts of interest in the ratings process for RMBS and CDOs, and to gain an understanding of the ratings methodologies employed by the rating agencies so that the Staff could better evaluate the extent to which conflicts of interest may have entered into and affected the ratings process. Section V of this report summarizes conflicts of interest that are unique to these products and provides a factual summary of the models and methodologies used by the rating agencies. This information is provided in this report solely to provide transparency to the ratings process and the activities of the rating agencies in connection with the recent subprime mortgage turmoil. The Staff does not make recommendations or seek to regulate the substance of the methodologies used.[3]

II. Background

A. The Examinations

Beginning in 2007, delinquency and foreclosure rates for subprime mortgage loans in the United States dramatically increased, creating turmoil in the markets for residential mortgage-backed securities backed by such loans and collateralized debt obligations linked to such securities. As the performance of these securities continued to deteriorate, the three rating agencies most active in rating these instruments downgraded a significant number of their ratings. The rating agencies performance in rating these structured finance products raised questions about the accuracy of their credit ratings generally as well as the integrity of the ratings process as a whole.

On August 31, 2007, the Staff in the Commission's Office of Compliance Inspections and Examinations ("OCIE"), Division of Trading and Markets ("Trading & Markets") and Office of Economic Analysis ("OEA Staff") (collectively "the Staff") initiated examinations of Fitch, Moody's and S&P with respect to their activities in rating subprime RMBS and CDOs.[4] Specifically, key areas of review included:

- the NRSROs' ratings policies, procedures and practices, including gaining an understanding of ratings models, methodologies, assumptions, criteria and protocols;
- the adequacy of the disclosure of the ratings process and methodologies used by the NRSROs;
- whether the NRSROs complied with their ratings policies and procedures for initial ratings and ongoing surveillance;
- the efficacy of the NRSROs' conflict of interest procedures; and
- whether ratings were unduly influenced by conflicts of interest related to the NRSROs' role in bringing issues to market and the compensation they receive from issuers and underwriters.

The examinations also included a review of whether the examined rating agencies had policies and procedures to detect and address ratings determined to be inaccurate as a result of errors in ratings models used. Initial observations as a result of this aspect of the examinations are also included in this report.

The examination review period generally covered January 2004 through the present. The firms under examination became subject to regulation as NRSROs when they registered with the Commission as NRSROs in September 2007. Although these rating agencies were not subject to legal obligations applicable to NRSROs during most of the review period, the Staff nonetheless sought to make relevant factual findings and observations with respect to the activities of these firms in rating subprime RMBS and CDOs during the period, as well as to identify possible areas for improvement in their practices going forward.

The examinations included extensive on-site interviews with the rating agencies' staff, including senior and mid-level managers, initial ratings analysts and surveillance analysts, internal compliance personnel and auditors, personnel responsible for building, maintaining and upgrading the ratings models and methodologies used in the ratings process and other relevant rating agency staff.

In addition, the Staff reviewed a large quantity of the rating agencies' internal records, including written policies, procedures and other such documents related to initial ratings, the ongoing surveillance of ratings, the management of conflicts of interest and the public disclosures of the procedures and methodologies for determining credit ratings. The Staff also reviewed deal files for subprime RMBS and CDO ratings, internal audit reports and records and other internal records, including a large quantity of email communications (the rating agencies produced over two million emails and instant messages that were sorted, analyzed and reviewed using software filtering tools). Finally, the Staff reviewed the rating agencies' public disclosures, filings with the Commission and other public documents.

B. Current Regulatory Requirements and Proposed New Rules and Rule Amendments with Respect to Credit Rating Agencies

The Rating Agency Reform Act was enacted on September 29, 2006. The Act created a new Section 15E of the Securities Exchange Act of 1934 ("Exchange Act"), providing for Commission registration of NRSROs if specific requirements are met. Section 15E also provides authority for the Commission to implement financial reporting and oversight rules with respect to registered NRSROs. The Rating Agency Reform Act amended Section 17(a) of the Exchange Act to provide for Commission authority to require reporting and recordkeeping requirements for registered NRSROs, as well as examination authority with respect to ratings activity conducted by the NRSROs. The Rating Agency Reform Act expressly prohibits the Commission from regulating "the substance of the credit ratings or the procedures and methodologies" by which any NRSRO determines credit ratings. The Commission voted to adopt rules related to NRSROs on June 18, 2007, which became effective on June 26, 2007.

Under the new law and rules, NRSROs are required to make certain public disclosures, make and retain certain records, furnish certain financial reports to the Commission, establish procedures to manage the handling of material non-public information and disclose and manage conflicts of interest. The Commission's rules additionally prohibit an NRSRO from having certain conflicts of interest and engaging in certain unfair, abusive, or coercive practices.

In order to increase transparency in the ratings process and to curb practices that contributed to recent turmoil in the credit market, on June 11, 2008 the Commission proposed additional rules with respect to NRSROs.[5] The Commission was informed by, among other things, the information from these then-ongoing Staff examinations. In sum, the Commission proposed to:

- Prohibit an NRSRO from issuing a rating on a structured product unless information on the characteristics of assets underlying the product is available, in order to allow other credit rating agencies to use the information to rate the product and, potentially, expose a rating agency whose ratings were unduly influenced by the product's sponsors.
- Prohibit an NRSRO from issuing a rating where the NRSRO or a person associated with the NRSRO has made recommendations as to structuring the same products that it rates.
- Require NRSROs to make all of their ratings and subsequent rating actions publicly available, to facilitate comparisons of NRSROs by making it easier to analyze the performance of the credit ratings the NRSROs issue in terms of assessing creditworthiness.
- Prohibit anyone who participates in determining a credit rating from negotiating the fee that the issuer pays for it, to prevent business considerations from undermining the NRSRO's objectivity.

- Prohibit gifts from those who receive ratings to those who rate them, in any amount over $25.
- Require NRSROs to publish performance statistics for one, three and ten years within each rating category, in a way that facilitates comparison with their competitors in the industry.
- Require disclosure by the NRSROs of whether and how information about verification performed on the assets underlying a structured product is relied on in determining credit ratings.
- Require disclosure of how frequently credit ratings are reviewed; whether different models are used for ratings surveillance than for initial ratings; and whether changes made to models are applied retroactively to existing ratings.
- Require NRSROs to make an annual report of the number of ratings actions they took in each ratings class.
- Require documentation of the rationale for any material difference between the rating implied by a qualitative model that is a "substantial component" in the process of determining a credit rating and the final rating issued.
- Require NRSROs to differentiate the ratings they issue on structured products from other securities, either through issuing a report disclosing how procedures and methodologies and credit risk characteristics for structured finance products differ from other securities, or using different symbols, such as attaching an identifier to the rating.

III. The Ratings Process

The general processes used to create and rate RMBS and CDOs are described below.

A. The Creation of RMBS and CDOs

The process for creating a RMBS begins when an arranger, generally an investment bank, packages mortgage loans -- generally thousands of separate loans -- into a pool, and transfers them to a trust that will issue securities collateralized by the pool. The trust purchases the loan pool and becomes entitled to the interest and principal payments made by the borrowers. The trust finances the purchase of the loan pool through the issuance of RMBS to investors. The monthly interest and principal payments from the loan pool are used to make monthly interest and principal payments to the investors in the RMBS.

The trust typically issues different classes of RMBS (known as "tranches"), which offer a sliding scale of coupon rates based on the level of credit protection afforded to the security. Credit protection is designed to shield the tranche securities from the loss of interest and principal due to defaults of the loans in the pool. The degree of credit protection afforded a tranche security is known as its "credit enhancement" and is provided through several means, each of which is described below.

The primary source of credit enhancement is subordination, which creates a hierarchy of loss absorption among the tranche securities. For example, if a trust issued securities in 10 different tranches, the first (or senior) tranche would have nine subordinate tranches, the next highest tranche would have eight subordinate tranches and so on down the capital structure. Any loss of interest and principal experienced by the trust from delinquencies and defaults in loans in the pool are allocated first to the lowest tranche until it loses all of its principal amount and then to the next lowest tranche and so on up the capital structure. Consequently, the senior tranche would not incur any loss until all the lower tranches have absorbed losses from the underlying loans.

A second form of credit enhancement is over-collateralization, which is the amount that the principal balance of the mortgage pool exceeds the principal balance of the tranche securities issued by the trust. This excess principal creates an additional "equity" tranche below the lowest tranche security to absorb losses. In the example above, the equity tranche would sit below the tenth tranche security and protect it from the first losses experienced as a result of defaulting loans.

A third form of credit enhancement is excess spread, which is the amount that the trust's monthly interest income exceeds its monthly liabilities. Excess spread is comprised of the amount by which the total interest received on the underlying loans exceeds the total interest payments due to investors in the tranche securities (less administrative expenses of the trust, such as loan servicing fees, premiums due on derivatives contracts, and bond insurance). This excess spread can be used to build up loss reserves or pay off delinquent interest payments due to a tranche security.

The process for creating a typical CDO is similar to that of an RMBS. A sponsor creates a trust to hold the CDO's assets and issue its securities. Generally, a CDO is comprised of 200 or so debt securities (rather than mortgage loans that are held in RMBS pools). The CDO trust uses the interest and principal payments from the underlying debt securities to make interest and principal payments to investors in the securities issued by the trust. Similar to RMBS, the trust is structured to provide differing levels of credit enhancement to the securities it issues through subordination, over-collateralization, excess spread and bond insurance. In addition to the underlying assets, one significant difference between a CDO and an RMBS is that the CDO may be actively managed such that its underlying assets change over time, whereas the mortgage loan pool underlying an RMBS generally remains static.

In recent years, CDOs have been some of the largest purchasers of subprime RMBS and the drivers of demand for those securities. According to one NRSRO, the average percentage of subprime RMBS in the collateral pools of CDOs it rated grew from 43.3% in 2003 to 71.3% in 2006. As the market for mortgage-related CDOs grew, CDO issuers began to use credit default swaps to replicate the performance of subprime RMBS and CDOs. In this case, rather than purchasing subprime RMBS or CDOs, the CDO entered into credit default swaps referencing subprime RMBS or CDOs, or indexes on RMBS. These CDOs, in some cases, are composed entirely of credit default swaps ("synthetic CDOs") or a combination of credit default swaps and cash RMBS ("hybrid CDOs").

B. Determining Credit Ratings for RMBS and CDOs

A key step in the process of creating and ultimately selling a subprime RMBS and CDO is the issuance of a credit rating for each of the tranches issued by the trust (with the exception of the most junior "equity" tranche). The credit rating for each rated tranche indicates the credit rating agency's view as to the creditworthiness of the debt instrument in terms of the likelihood that the issuer would default on its obligations to make interest and principal payments on the debt instrument.

The three examined rating agencies generally followed similar procedures to develop ratings for subprime RMBS and CDOs. The arranger of the RMBS initiates the ratings process by sending the credit rating agency a range of data on each of the subprime loans to be held by the trust (e.g., principal amount, geographic location of the property, credit history and FICO score of the borrower, ratio of the loan amount to the value of the property and type of loan: first lien, second lien, primary residence, secondary residence), the proposed capital structure of the trust and the proposed levels of credit enhancement to be provided to each RMBS tranche issued by the trust. Upon receipt of the information, the rating agency assigns a lead analyst who is responsible for analyzing the loan pool, proposed capital structure and proposed credit enhancement levels and, ultimately, for formulating a ratings recommendation for a rating committee composed of analysts and/or senior-level analytic personnel.

The next step in the ratings process is for the analyst to develop predictions, based on a quantitative expected loss model and other qualitative factors, as to how many of the loans in the collateral pool would default under stresses of varying severity. This analysis also includes assumptions as to how much principal would be recovered after a defaulted loan is foreclosed. To assess the potential future performance of the loan under various possible scenarios, each rating agency generally uses specific credit characteristics to analyze each loan in the collateral pool. These characteristics include the loan information described above as well as the amount of equity that the borrowers have in their homes, the amount of documentation provided by borrowers to verify their assets and/or income levels and whether the borrowers intend to rent or occupy their homes.

The purpose of this loss analysis is to determine how much credit enhancement a given tranche security would need for a particular category of credit rating. The severest stress test (i.e., the one that would result in the greatest number of defaults among the underlying loans) is run to determine the amount of credit enhancement required for an RMBS tranche issued by the trust to receive the highest rating. The next severest stress test is run to determine the amount of credit enhancement required of the next highest tranche and so on down the capital structure. The lowest rated tranche is analyzed under a more benign market scenario. Consequently, its required level of credit enhancement -- typically provided primarily or exclusively by a subordinate equity tranche -- is based on the number of loans expected to default in the normal course given the lowest possible level of macroeconomic stress.

The next step in the ratings process is for the analyst to check the proposed capital structure of the RMBS against requirements for a particular rating. Typically, if the analyst concludes that the capital structure of the RMBS does not support the desired ratings, this preliminary conclusion would be conveyed to the arranger. The arranger could accept that determination and have the trust issue the securities with the proposed capital structure and the lower rating or adjust the structure to provide the requisite credit enhancement for the senior tranche to get the desired highest rating. Generally, arrangers aim for the largest possible senior tranche, i.e., to provide the least amount of credit enhancement possible, since the senior tranche -- as the highest rated tranche -- pays the lowest coupon rate of the RMBS' tranches and, therefore, costs the arranger the least to fund.

The next step in the process is for the analyst to conduct a cash flow analysis on the interest and principal expected to be received by the trust from the pool of subprime loans to determine whether it will be sufficient to pay the interest and principal due on each RMBS tranche issued by the trust. The rating agency uses quantitative cash flow models that analyze the amount of principal and interest payments expected to be generated from the loan pool each month over the terms of the RMBS tranche securities under various stress scenarios. The outputs of this model are compared against the priority of payments (the "waterfall") to the RMBS tranches specified in the trust legal documents. The waterfall documentation could specify over-collateralization and excess spread triggers that, if breached, reallocated principal and interest payments from lower tranches to higher tranches until the minimum levels of over-collateralization and excess spread were reestablished. Ultimately, the monthly principal and interest payments derived from the loan pool need to be enough to satisfy the monthly payments of principal and interest due by the trust to the investors in the RMBS tranches as well as to cover the administrative expenses of the trust. The analyst also reviews the legal documentation of the trust to evaluate whether it is bankruptcy remote, i.e., isolated from the effects of any potential bankruptcy or insolvency of the arranger.

Following these steps, the analyst develops a rating recommendation for each RMBS tranche and then presents it to a rating committee composed of analysts and/or senior- level analytic personnel. The rating committee votes on the ratings for each tranche and usually communicates its decision to the arranger. In most cases, an arranger can appeal a rating decision, although the appeal is not always granted (and, if granted, may not necessarily result in any change in the rating decision). Final ratings decisions are published and subsequently monitored through surveillance processes. Typically, the rating agency is paid only if the credit rating is issued, though sometimes it receives a breakup fee for the analytic work undertaken even if the credit rating is not issued.

The rating agencies' process for assigning ratings to subprime CDOs is similar and also involves a review of the creditworthiness of each tranche of the CDO. As with RMBS, the process centers on an examination of the pool of assets held by the trust and an analysis of how they would perform individually and in correlation during various stress scenarios. However, this analysis is based primarily on the credit rating of each RMBS or CDO in the underlying pool (or referenced through a credit default swap entered into by the CDO) and does not include an analysis of the underlying asset pools in the RMBS.

CDOs collateralized by RMBS or by other CDOs often are actively managed. Consequently, there can be frequent changes to the composition of the cash assets (RMBS or CDOs), synthetic assets (credit default swaps), or combinations of cash and synthetic assets in the underlying pool. As a result, ratings for managed CDOs are based not on the composition of the pool but instead on covenanted limits for each potential type of asset that could be put in the pool. Typically, following a post-closing period in which no adjustments can be made to the collateral pool, the CDO's manager has a predetermined period of several years in which to adjust that asset pool through various sales and purchases pursuant to covenants set forth in the CDO's indenture. These covenants set limitations and requirements for the collateral pools of CDOs, often by establishing minimum and maximum concentrations for certain types of securities or certain ratings.

In developing a rating for a CDO, the analyst uses the CDO's indenture guidelines to run "worst-case" scenarios based on the collateral that is permitted under the indenture. In preparing a rating for that CDO, an analyst will run the rating agency's models based on all possible collateral pools permissible under the indenture guidelines, placing the most weight on the results from the weakest potential pools (i.e., the minimum permissible amount, 10%, of the highest-rated securities and the lowest-rated investment grade securities for the remaining 90%). As with RMBS ratings, the analyst then compares the model results against the capital structure of the proposed CDO to confirm that the level of subordination, over-collateralization and excess spread available to each tranche

provides the necessary amount of credit enhancement to sustain a particular rating. The process is the same as for an RMBS rating, the analyst makes a recommendation for a rating to a ratings committee, which votes on the rating for each tranche and usually communicates its decision to the arranger.

IV. The Staff's Examinations: Summary of Factual Findings, Observations and Recommendations

The Staff's general factual findings, observations and recommendations from the examinations are summarized below. This is a general summary of the issues identified, and the practices, policies and procedures varied among the firms examined.[6] Not all of the issues described below were found at each rating agency. The Staff notes that the rating agencies cooperated with the Staff's examinations. Each of the rating agencies examined has agreed to implement the Staff's recommendations, though individual firms may not have agreed with the Staff's factual findings giving rise to the recommendation.

A. There was a Substantial Increase in the Number and in the Complexity of RMBS and CDO Deals Since 2002, and Some Rating Agencies Appeared to Struggle with the Growth

From 2002 to 2006, the volume of RMBS and CDO deals rated by the rating agencies examined substantially increased, as did the revenues the firms derived from rating these products. As the number of RMBS and CDOs rated by these agencies increased, each rating agency also increased, to varying degrees, the number of staff assigned to rate these securities. With respect to RMBS, each rating agency's staffing increase approximately matched the percentage increase in deal volume. With respect to CDOs, however, two rating agencies' staffing increases did not appear to match their percentage increases in deal volume.

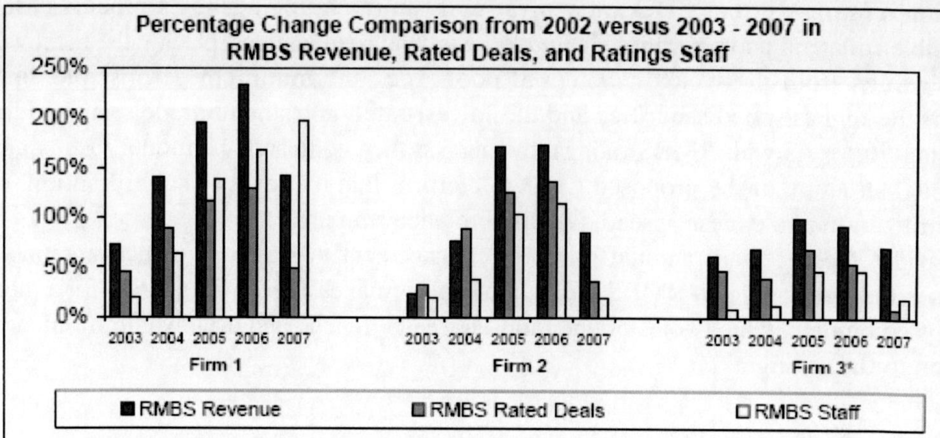

* Firm 3 provided 9 months of RMBS revenue for 2006. Therefore, 12 months of estimated 2006 revenue was extrapolated for RMBS by multiplying 9 months of revenue by 1.3.

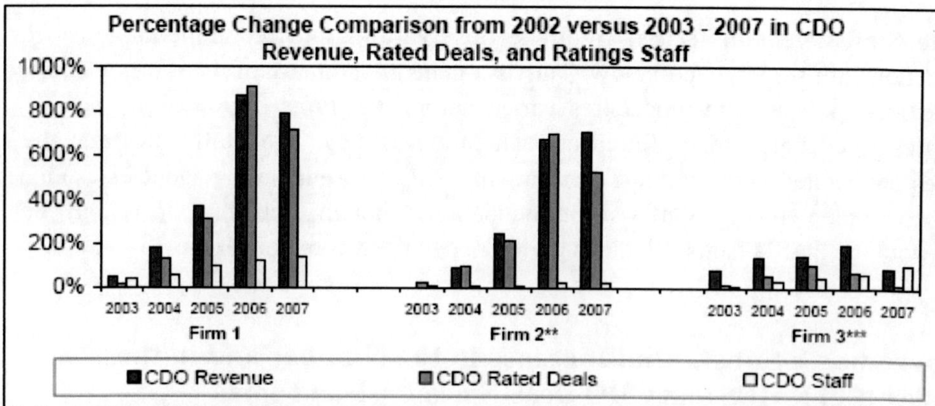

** Firm 2 did not provide 2002 CDO revenue data. Therefore, the CDO revenue percentage change is based upon the 2003 balance as opposed to 2002.

*** Firm 3 provided 9 months of CDO revenue for 2006. Therefore, 12 months of estimated 2006 revenue was extrapolated for CDO by multiplying 9 months of revenue by 1.3.

The structured finance products that the rating agencies were asked to evaluate also became increasingly complex, including the expanded use of credit default swaps to replicate the performance of mortgage-backed securities. Further, the loans to retail borrowers being securitized into RMBS, particularly subprime RMBS, became more complex and less conservative.

- Internal documents at two of the rating agencies appear to reflect struggles to adapt to the increase in the volume and complexity of the deals.

  - There are indications that ratings were issued notwithstanding that one or more issues raised during the analysis of the deal remained unresolved.[7]

- For example, in one exchange of internal communications between two analysts at one rating agency, the analysts were concerned about whether they should be rating a particular deal. One analyst expressed concern that her firm's model did not capture "half" of the deal's risk, but that "it could be structured by cows and we would rate it."[8]
- Resource issues appear to have existed in other structured finance groups outside of the RMBS and CDO areas. For instance, at one rating agency, an analytical manager in the firm's real estate group stated in one email that "[o]ur staffing issues, of course, make it difficult to deliver the value that justifies our fees"[9] and in another email that "[t]ensions are high. Just too much work, not enough people, pressure from company, quite a bit of turnover and no coordination of the non-deal 'stuff' they want us and our staff to do."[10] Similarly, an email from an employee in the same firm's asset backed securities group stated that "[w]e ran our staffing model assuming the analysts are working 60 hours a week and we are short on resources. . . . The analysts on average are working longer than this and we are burning them out. We have had a couple of resignations and expect more."[11]

Remedial Action

The Staff has recommended that each examined NRSRO evaluate, both at this time and on a periodic basis, whether it has sufficient staff and resources to manage its volume of business and meet its obligations under the Section 15E of the Exchange Act and the rules applicable to NRSROs. Each examined NRSRO stated that it will implement the Staff's recommendation.

B. Significant Aspects of the Ratings Process Were Not Always Disclosed

The rating agencies stated to the Staff that, prior to being registered as NRSROs, they disclosed their ratings process.[12] It appears, however, that certain significant aspects of the ratings process and the methodologies used to rate RMBS and CDOs were not always disclosed, or were not fully disclosed, as described below.

- *Relevant ratings criteria were not disclosed.* Documents reviewed by the Staff indicate the use of unpublished ratings criteria.

  - At one firm, communications by the firm's analytical staff indicate that they were aware of the use of unpublished criteria. For example:
  - "[N]ot all our criteria is published. [F]or example, we have no published criteria on hybrid deals, which doesn't mean that we have no criteria."[13]
  - A criteria officer in the Structured Finance Surveillance group noted "our published criteria as it currently stands is a bit too unwieldy and all over the map in terms of being current or comprehensive. It might be too much of a stretch to say that we're complying with it because our SF [structured finance] rating approach is inherently flexible and subjective, while much of our written criteria is detailed and prescriptive. Doing a complete inventory of our criteria and documenting all of the

areas where it is out of date or inaccurate would appear to be a huge job - that would require far more man-hours than writing the principles- based articles."[14]

- Another rating agency, from 2004 to 2006, reduced its model's raw loss numbers for second lien loans based upon internal matrices. The raw loss outputs from the model were adjusted to set numbers from the matrices depending on the issuer and the raw loss numbers. The rating agency did not publicly disclose its use of matrices to adjust model outputs for second lien loans.
- This rating agency also maintained a published "criteria report" that was no longer being used in its ratings process. The criteria report stated the rating agency conducted an extensive review of origination and servicing operations and practices, despite the fact that the RMBS group no longer conducted a formal review of origination operations and practices. This rating agency identified this discrepancy in its internal audit process and corrected it.
- At a third rating agency in certain instances there was a time lag from the date at which the firm implemented changes to its criteria and the date at which it published notice of these changes to the market.[15] Additionally, the Staff discovered emails indicating that the firm's analysts utilized an unpublished model to assess data.[16]

- *Rating agencies made "out of model adjustments" and did not document the rationale for the adjustment*. In certain instances, the loss level that was returned by application of the rating agency's quantitative model was not used, and another loss level was used instead. These decisions to deviate from the model were approved by ratings committees but in many cases the rating agency did not have documentation explaining the rationale for the adjustments, making it difficult or impossible to identify the factors that led to the decision to deviate from the model. Two rating agencies frequently used "out of model" adjustments in issuing ratings.

  - One rating agency regularly reduced loss expectations on subprime second lien mortgages from the loss expectations output by its RMBS model, in some cases reducing the expected loss. While the rating agency's analysts might have discussed the adjustment with issuers in the course of rating a deal, it appears that the firm did not publicly disclose the practice of overriding model outputs regarding loss expectations on subprime second liens.
  - Another rating agency indicated to the Staff that its ratings staff, as a general practice, did not adjust its collateral or cash flow analysis based upon factors that were not incorporated into the firm's models. However, the Staff observed instances in the firm's deal files that demonstrated adjustments from the cash flow models as well as instances where the firm implemented changes to its ratings criteria which were utilized prior to disclosure or used before being incorporated into its models.

Current Regulatory Requirements

The Exchange Act and rules applicable to NRSROs specifically address the importance of disclosure (the firms examined became subject to these rules in September 2007). An NRSRO is required to disclose in its application for registration the procedures and methodologies that the applicant uses in determining ratings.[17] An NRSRO is required to include a description of the procedures and methodologies it uses (but is not required to include each such written procedure or methodology) on its registration form (Form NRSRO). The instructions to the form require that the description must be sufficiently detailed to provide users of credit ratings with an understanding of the processes the applicant or NRSRO employs to determine credit ratings. The instructions also identify a number of areas that must be addressed in the description, to the extent they are applicable.[18]

Remedial Action

The Staff has recommended that each NRSRO examined conduct a review of its current disclosures relating to processes and methodologies for rating RMBS and CDOs to assess whether it is fully disclosing its ratings methodologies in compliance with Section 15E of the Exchange Act and the rules applicable to NRSROs. Further, the Staff has recommended that each NRSRO examined review whether its policies governing the timing of disclosure of a significant change to a process or methodology are reasonably designed to comply with these requirements. Each examined NRSRO stated that it will implement the Staff's recommendations.

Proposed Rules and Rule Amendments that Would Address These Issues

The Commission has proposed to require enhanced disclosures about the procedures and methodologies that an NRSRO uses to determine credit ratings.[19] The Commission also proposed to add additional areas that an applicant and a registered NRSRO would be required to address in its description of its procedures and methodologies in its Form NRSRO. Disclosure would be enhanced regarding the actions that an NRSRO is, or is not taking, in determining credit ratings. The additional areas proposed to be required to be addressed in its Form NRSRO would be:

- How frequently credit ratings are reviewed, whether different models or criteria are used for ratings surveillance than for determining initial ratings, whether changes made to models and criteria for determining initial ratings are applied retroactively to existing ratings and whether changes made to models and criteria for performing ratings surveillance are incorporated into the models and criteria for determining initial ratings;
- Whether and, if so, how information about verification performed on assets underlying or referenced by a security or money market instrument issued by an asset pool or as part of any asset-backed or mortgage-backed securities transaction is relied on in determining credit ratings; and
- Whether and, if so, how assessments of the quality of originators of assets underlying or referenced by a security or money market instrument issued by an asset pool or as part of any asset-backed or mortgage-backed securities transaction play a part in the determination of credit ratings.

C. Policies and Procedures for Rating RMBS and CDOs Can be Better Documented

Each of the rating agencies has policies that emphasize the importance of providing accurate ratings with integrity. Upon their registration as NRSROs in September 2007, each of the rating agencies examined became subject to a requirement to make and retain certain internal documents relating to their business, including the procedures and methodologies they use to determine credit ratings.[20] The Staff noted that the rating agencies improved their policies and procedures during the examination period, particularly in connection with their registration as NRSROs.

- *None of the rating agencies examined had specific written procedures for ating RMBS and CDOs*. One rating agency maintained comprehensive written procedures for rating structured finance securities, but these procedures were not specifically tailored to rating RMBS and CDOs. The written procedures for the two other rating agencies were not comprehensive and did not address all significant aspects of the RMBS and/or CDO ratings process. For example, written materials set forth guidelines for the structured finance ratings committee process (including its composition, the roles of the lead analyst and chair, the contents of the committee memo and the voting process) but did not describe the ratings process and the analyst's responsibilities prior to the time a proposed rating is presented to a ratings committee.

The lack of full documentation of policies and procedures made it difficult for the Staff to confirm that the actual practice undertaken in individual ratings was consistent with the firm's policies and procedures. This lack of full documentation could also impede the effectiveness of internal and external auditors conducting reviews of rating agency activities.

In addition, the Staff is examining whether there were any errors in ratings issued as a result of flaws in ratings models used. While this aspect of the examinations is ongoing, as a result of the examinations to date, the Staff notes that:

- Rating agencies do not appear to have specific policies and procedures to identify or address errors in their models or methodologies. For example, policies and procedures would address audits and other measures to identify possible errors, and what should be done if errors or deficiencies are discovered in models, methodologies, or other aspects of the ratings process (e.g., the parameters of an investigation, the individuals that would conduct the investigation, the disclosures that should be made to the public about errors and guidelines for rectifying errors).

Current Regulatory Requirements

An NRSRO is required to make and retain certain records relating to its business and to retain certain other business records made in the normal course of business operations.[21] Among the records required to be kept is a record documenting the established procedures and methodologies used by the NRSRO to determine credit ratings.[22] These rules applied to these rating agencies in September 2007.

Remedial Action

The Staff has recommended that each NRSRO examined conduct a review to determine whether its written policies and procedures used to determine credit ratings for RMBS and CDOs are fully documented in accordance with the requirements of Rule 17g-2. Each examined NRSRO stated that it will implement the Staff's recommendation.

D. Rating Agencies are Implementing New Practices with Respect to the Information Provided to Them

There is no requirement that a rating agency verify the information contained in RMBS loan portfolios presented to it for rating. Additionally, rating agencies are not required to insist that issuers perform due diligence, and they are not required to obtain reports concerning the level of due diligence performed by issuers. The observations in this section are included in the report to describe how the rating agencies approached due diligence during the review period, and how they have stated that they intend to approach it in the future.

The Staff notes that each rating agency publicly disclosed that it did not engage in any due diligence or otherwise seek to verify the accuracy or quality of the loan data underlying the RMBS pools they rated during the review period. Each rating agency's "Code of Conduct" (available on each rating agency's website) clearly stated that it was under no obligation to perform, and did not perform, due diligence. Each also noted that the assignment of a rating is not a guarantee of the accuracy, completeness, or timeliness of the information relied on in connection with the rating. The rating agencies each relied on the information provided to them by the sponsor of the RMBS. They did not verify the integrity and accuracy of such information as, in their view, due diligence duties belonged to the other parties in the process. They also did not seek representations from sponsors that due diligence was performed.

- All of the rating agencies examined have implemented, or announced that they will implement, measures that are designed to improve the integrity and accuracy of the loan data they receive on underlying RMBS pools.
  - One rating agency began conducting "Enhanced Originator/Issuer Reviews" for all subprime transactions in January 2008. These reviews involve a more extensive review of mortgage originations and their practices, including a review of originator/conduit/issuer due diligence reports and a sample of mortgage origination files.[23]
  - Another rating agency recently announced that for transactions closing after May 1, 2008, it is requesting updated loan level performance data from issuers on a monthly basis. In addition, it intends to incorporate the quality of an originator's fraud tools and detection policies into its ratings criteria by mid-year 2008.
  - In addition, as reported in press accounts of a May 2008 agreement with the New York State Attorney General, the rating agencies examined each agreed to develop and publicly disclose due diligence criteria to be performed by underwriters on all mortgages comprising RMBS, and to review those results prior to issuing ratings.[24]

Proposed Rules and Rule Amendments that Would Address Verification

The Commission proposed to add two additional areas that an NRSRO (or an applicant to become an NRSRO) would be required to address in its descriptions of its procedures and methodologies in Form NRSRO.[25] These disclosures would provide information about how the NRSROs treat due diligence in the NRSROs' ratings process. The additional proposed disclosures would include:

- Whether and, if so, how information about verification performed on assets underlying or referenced by a security or money market instrument issued by an asset pool or as part of any asset-backed or mortgage-backed securities transaction is relied on in determining credit ratings; and
- Whether and, if so, how assessments of the quality of originators of assets underlying or referenced by a security or money market instrument issued by an asset pool or as part of any asset-backed or mortgage-backed securities transaction play a part in the determination of credit ratings.

E. Rating Agencies Did Not Always Document Significant Steps in the Ratings Process -- Including the Rationale for Deviations from Their Models and for Rating Committee Actions and Decisions -- and They Did Not Always Document Significant Participants in the Ratings Process

Following their registration as NRSROs in September 2007, the rating agencies became subject to a requirement to retain their internal records, including non-public information and workpapers, which were used to form the basis of a credit rating they issued. Prior to being registered as NRSROs, all of the rating agencies examined had established policies and procedures generally requiring documentation of the ratings committee process and its key deliberations.

The Staff notes, however, that the rating agencies examined did not always fully document certain significant steps in their subprime RMBS and CDO ratings process. This made it difficult or impossible for Commission examiners to assess compliance with their established policies and procedures, and to identify the factors that were considered in developing a particular rating. This lack of documentation would similarly make it difficult for the rating agencies' internal compliance staff or internal audit staff to assess compliance with the firms' policies and procedures when conducting reviews of rating agency activities. Examples include:

- *The rationale for deviations from the model or out of model adjustments was not always documented in deal records.* As a result, in its review of rating files, the Staff could not always reconstruct the process used to arrive at the rating and identify the factors that led to the ultimate rating.
- *There was also a lack of documentation of committee actions and decisions.* At one rating agency, the vote tallies of rating committee votes were rarely documented despite being a required item in the rating committee memorandum or

addendum; in addition, numerous deal files failed to include the required addenda and/or included no documentation of the ratings surveillance process. At two of the rating agencies, there were failures to make or retain committee memos and/or minutes as well as failures to include certain relevant information in committee reports.

The Staff noted instances where the rating agencies failed to follow their internal procedures and document the ratings analyst and/or ratings committee participants who approved credit ratings. For example:

- *There was sometimes no documentation of committee attendees.* At one rating agency, approximately a quarter of the RMBS deals reviewed lacked an indication of the chairperson's identity, and a number lacked at least one signature of a committee member, although internal procedures called for this documentation. At another rating agency, an internal audit indicated that certain relevant information, including committee attendees and quorum confirmation, were sometimes missing from committee memos, though the Staff noted improvements in this area during the review period.

Current Regulatory Requirements

An NRSRO is required to make and retain certain records relating to its business and to retain certain other business records made in the normal course of business operations.[26] An NRSRO is specifically required to make and retain certain records, including records with respect to each current credit rating that indicate: (1) the identity of any credit analyst(s) that participated in determining the credit rating; (2) the identity of the person(s) that approved the credit rating before it was issued; (3) whether the credit rating was solicited or unsolicited; and (4) the date the credit rating action was taken.[27] These rules applied to these rating agencies in September 2007.

Remedial Action

The Staff has recommended that each NRSRO examined conduct a review of its current policies and practices for documenting the credit ratings process and the identities of RMBS and CDO ratings analysts and committee members to review whether they are reasonably designed to ensure compliance with Rule 17g-2 and to address weaknesses in the policies or in adherence to existing policies that result in gaps in documentation of significant steps and participants in the credit ratings process. Each examined NRSRO stated that it will implement the Staff's recommendations.

Proposed Rules and Rule Amendments that Would Address These Issues

The Commission proposed an amendment to its rules that, if adopted, would require that if a quantitative model is a substantial component of the credit ratings process, an NRSRO would be required to keep a record of the rationale for any material difference between the credit rating implied by the model and the final credit rating is sued.[28]

F. The Surveillance Processes Used by the Rating Agencies Appear to Have Been Less Robust than Their Initial Ratings Processes

While NRSROs are not required under the law to perform surveillance, a rating agency will generally monitor the accuracy of its ratings on an ongoing basis in order to change the ratings when circumstances indicate that a change is required. This process is generally called "monitoring" or "surveillance," and each rating agency charges issuers, upfront or annually, ratings surveillance fees. Performing adequate and timely surveillance is important, particularly when issuers of structured products do not make publicly available their due diligence information and underlying loan performance information, which would enable independent analysis by investors and third parties.

Each of the rating agencies examined conducts some type of surveillance of its ratings. The Staff notes that weaknesses existed in the rating agencies' surveillance efforts, as described below:

- Resources appear to have impacted the timeliness of surveillance efforts. For example:
  - In an internal email at one firm, an analytical manager in the structured finance surveillance group noted: "I think the history has been to only re- review a deal under new assumptions/criteria when the deal is flagged for some performance reason. I do not know of a situation where there were wholesale changes to existing ratings when the primary group changed assumptions or even instituted new criteria. The two major reasons why we have taken the approach is (i) lack of sufficient personnel resources and (ii) not having the same models/information available for surveillance to relook [sic] at an existing deal with the new assumptions (i.e., no cash flow models for a number of assets)."[29]
  - At the same firm, internal email communications appear to reflect a concern that surveillance criteria used during part of review period were inadequate.[30]

- *There was poor documentation of the surveillance conducted.* One rating agency could not provide documentation of the surveillance performed (copies of monthly periodic reports, exception reports and exception parameters), though it asserted that such surveillance was conducted. Internal communications by the surveillance staff indicate awareness of this issue.[31] At this firm, the Staff was unable to assess the information generated by the surveillance group during the review period. Another rating agency did not run monthly "screener reports" required by its own procedures for three months during the review period. It stated that the entire vintage of high risk subprime RMBS and CDOs were under a targeted review for two of the months. As a result, the Staff could not assess the information generated by the rating agency's surveillance staff for those months.
- *Lack of Surveillance Procedures.* Two rating agencies do not have internal written procedures documenting the steps that their surveillance staff should undertake to monitor RMBS and CDOs.

Current Regulatory Requirements

Under the Exchange Act and the rules applicable to NRSROs, an NRSRO is required to disclose publicly the procedures and methodologies it uses in determining credit ratings. Further, the Commission may censure, limit the activities, functions, or operations of, suspend, or revoke the registration of an NRSRO that fails to maintain adequate financial and managerial resources to produce credit ratings with integrity (the provisions of the Act applied to the rating agencies examined upon their registration in September 2007).[32]

Remedial Action

The Staff has recommended that each NRSRO examined conduct a review to determine if adequate resources are devoted to surveillance of outstanding RMBS and CDO ratings. This review should include, for example, whether the rating agency maintains adequate staffing and has adequate expertise dedicated to performing ongoing surveillance. The Staff has also recommended that the NRSROs ensure that they have comprehensive written surveillance procedures. Finally, the Staff has recommended that all appropriate surveillance records be maintained. Each examined NRSRO stated that it will implement the Staff's recommendations.

Proposed Rules and Rule Amendments that Would Address These Issues

The Commission has proposed to enhance disclosures about the procedures and methodologies that an NRSRO uses to determine credit ratings.[33] Among other things, the Commission proposed to require an NRSRO to disclose how frequently credit ratings are reviewed, whether different models or criteria are used for ratings surveillance than for determining initial ratings, whether changes made to models and criteria for determining initial ratings are applied retroactively to existing ratings and whether changes made to models and criteria for performing ratings surveillance are incorporated into the models and criteria for determining initial ratings.

G. Issues Were Identified in the Management of Conflicts of Interest and Improvements Can be Made

Each of the rating agencies examined has established its own policies and procedures to address and mitigate conflicts of interest. Generally, the Staff notes that the rating agencies enhanced their procedures at the time they sought registration as NRSROs. The Staff reviewed these policies and procedures in the following areas: procedures to address the "issuer pays" conflict of interest and procedures to address conflicts of interest due to personal financial interests by analysts and other firm employees. Each area is summarized below.

1. The "Issuer Pays" Conflict

Each of the NRSROs examined uses the "issuer pays" model, in which the arranger or other entity that issues the security is also seeking the rating, and pays the rating agency for the rating. The conflict of interest inherent in this model is that rating agencies have an interest in generating business from the firms that seek the rating, which could conflict with providing ratings of integrity. The Commission's rules specify that it is a conflict of interest for an NRSRO being paid by issuers or underwriters to determine credit ratings with respect to securities they issue or underwrite.[34] They are required to establish, maintain and enforce policies and procedures reasonably designed to address and manage conflicts of interest.[35] Such policies and procedures are intended to maintain the integrity of the NRSRO's judgment, and to prevent an NRSRO from being influenced to issue or maintain a more favorable credit rating in order to obtain or retain business of the issuer or underwriter.[36]

Each of the NRSROs has policies that emphasize the importance of providing accurate ratings with integrity. To further manage the conflicts of interest arising from the "issuer pays" model, each of the examined NRSROs established policies to restrict analysts from participating in fee discussions with issuers. These policies are designed to separate those individuals who set and negotiate fees from those employees who rate the issue, in order to mitigate the possibility or perception that a rating agency would link its ratings with its fees (e.g., that an analyst could explicitly or implicitly link the fee for a rating to a particular rating).

- While each rating agency has policies and procedures restricting analysts from participating in fee discussions with issuers, these policies still allowed key participants in the ratings process to participate in fee discussions.

  - One rating agency allowed senior analytical managers to participate directly in fee discussions with issuers until early 2007 when it changed its policy.
  - At another rating agency an analyst's immediate supervisor could engage in fee negotiations directly with issuers. The firm changed its procedure in October 2007 so that analytical staff (including management) may no longer engage in fee discussions with issuers; only business development personnel may do so.
  - One rating agency permits an analytical manager to participate in internal discussions regarding which considerations are appropriate for determining a fee for a particular rated entity.
  - Only one rating agency actively monitors for compliance with its policy against analysts participating in fee discussions with issuers, and, as a result was able to detect and correct certain shortcomings in its process.

Proposed Rules and Rule Amendments that Would Address These Issues

The Commission has proposed amendments to its rules that would address the conflict created by NRSRO employees being involved in both fee discussions and ratings decisions by prohibiting an NRSRO from having the conflict that arises when a person within an NRSRO who has responsibility for participating in determining credit ratings, or for developing or approving procedures or methodologies used for determining credit ratings, participate in any fee discussions or arrangements.[37]

- Analysts appeared to be aware, when rating an issuer, of the rating agency's business interest in securing the rating of the deal. The Staff notes multiple communications that indicated that some analysts were aware of the firm's fee schedules, and actual (negotiated) fees.[38] There does not appear to be any internal effort to shield analysts from emails and other communications that discuss fees and revenue from individual issuers.[39] In some instances, analysts discussed fees for a rating. Examples are set forth below:

- At one firm, an analyst wrote to his manager asking about whether the firm would be charging a fee for a particular service and what the fee schedule will be.[40]
- At another firm, a business manager in the RMBS group wrote to several analysts: ". . . if you have not done so please send me any updates to fees on your transactions for this month. It is your responsibility to look at the deal list and see what your deals are currently listed at."[41]
- At two rating agencies, there were indications that analysts were involved in fee discussions with employees of the rating agency's billing department.[42]

- Rating agencies do not appear to take steps to prevent considerations of market share and other business interests from the possibility that they could influence ratings or ratings criteria. At one firm, internal communications appear to expose analytical staff to this conflict of interest by indicating concern or interest in market share when firm employees were discussing whether to make certain changes in ratings methodology. In particular, employees discussed concerns about the firm's market share relative to other rating agencies, or losing deals to other rating agencies. While there is no evidence that decisions about rating methodology or models were made based on attracting or losing market share, in most of these instances, it appears that rating agency employees who were responsible for obtaining ratings business (i.e., marketing personnel) would notify other employees, including those responsible for criteria development, about business concerns they had related to the criteria.

- For instance, a senior analytical manager in the Structured Finance group wrote "I am trying to ascertain whether we can determine at this point if we will suffer any loss of business because of our decision [on assigning separate ratings to principal and interest] and if so, how much?" "Essentially, [names of staff] ended up agreeing with your recommendations but the CDO team didn't agree with you because they believed it would negatively impact business."[43]
- In another example, after noting a change in a competitor's ratings methodology, an employee stated: "[w]e are meeting with your group this week to discuss adjusting criteria for rating CDOs of real estate assets this week because of the ongoing threat of losing deals."[44] In another email, following a discussion of a competitor's market share, an employee of the same firm states that aspects of the firm's ratings methodology would have to be revisited to recapture market share from the competing rating agency.[45] An additional email by an employee stated, following a discussion of losing a rating to a competitor, "I had a discussion with the team leaders here and we think that the only way to compete is to have a paradigm shift in thinking, especially with the interest rate risk."[46]
- Another rating agency reported to the Staff that one of its foreign ratings surveillance committees had knowledge that the rating agency had issued ratings on almost a dozen securities using a model that contained an error.[47] The rating agency reported to the Staff that, as a result, the committee was aware that the

ratings were higher than they should have been. Nonetheless, the committee agreed to continue to maintain the ratings for several months, until the securities were downgraded for other reasons. Members of the committee, all analysts or analytical managers, considered the rating agency's reputational interest in not making its error public, according to the rating agency.

Current Regulatory Requirements

An NRSRO is required to establish, maintain and enforce policies and procedures reasonably designed, taking into consideration the nature of its business, to address and manage conflicts of interest.[48] An NRSRO is further prohibited from having certain conflicts unless it has disclosed the type of conflict of interest, and has implemented policies and procedures to address and manage it.[49] Included among these conflicts is being paid by issuers or underwriters to determine credit ratings with respect to securities or money market instruments they issue or underwrite.[50] These requirements applied to these firms in September 2007.

Remedial Action

The Staff recommended that each NRSRO examined review its practices, policies and procedures for mitigating and managing the "issuer pays" conflict of interest. In particular, the Staff recommended that each NRSRO examined consider and implement steps that would insulate or prevent the possibility that considerations of market share and other business interests could influence ratings or ratings criteria. Each examined NRSRO stated that it would implement the Staff's recommendations.

Proposed Rules and Rule Amendments that Would Address These Issues

The Commission proposed rules that would prohibit a credit rating agency from issuing or maintaining a rating on a structured product unless information on assets underlying the product was disclosed.[51] The intent of the disclosure is to create the opportunity for other credit rating agencies, including those not registered with the Commission as NRSROs, to use the information to rate and monitor the rating of the instrument as well. Any resulting "unsolicited ratings" could be used by market participants to evaluate the ratings issued by the rating agency hired to rate the product and, in turn, potentially expose a rating agency whose ratings were influenced by the desire to gain favor with the product sponsor in order to obtain more business. The proposal is also designed to make it more difficult for product sponsors to exert influence on the rating agencies. Specifically, by opening up the ratings process to greater scrutiny, the proposal is designed to make it easier for the hired rating agency to resist pressure from the product sponsors by increasing the likelihood that any steps taken to inappropriately favor the product sponsor could be exposed to the market.

2. Analysts' Compensation

Each of the rating agencies examined has a similar policy with respect to compensating their analysts. These policies generally provide that an analyst may not be compensated or evaluated based upon the amount of revenue that the rating agency derives from issuers or issues that the analyst rates, or with whom the analyst regularly interacts. The internal compensation guidelines reviewed by the Staff indicated that analysts' salaries generally were based on seniority and experience, and bonuses were determined both by individual performance and the overall success of the firm. The Staff's review did not find indications that rating agencies compensated analysts in a manner contrary to their stated policies.

3. Securities Transactions by Employees of Credit Rating Agencies

To minimize the possibility that an analyst's objectivity could be compromised by the analyst's individual financial interests, each of the rating agencies examined prohibits persons with significant business or any economic ties (including stock ownership) to a rated entity from participating in the ratings process for that issuer. Each rating agency also monitors and restricts the securities trading activity of employees (particularly with respect to rated issuers).

Each rating agency examined has adopted policies prohibiting employees (and their immediate family members) from owning any security that is subject to a credit rating by a team on which the employee is a member.

- While each rating agency has policies and procedures with respect to employees' personal securities holdings, the rating agencies vary in how rigorously they monitor or prevent prohibited transactions, including personal trading, by their employees from occurring.

  - Two of the rating agencies require employees to have duplicate copies of brokerage statements sent to the rating agency, and the third requires its ratings staff to either have an account with a brokerage firm that has agreed to provide the firm with reports of the employee's transactions or to manually report transactions to the firm within ten days of execution.
  - One rating agency reviews requested transactions by employees against a list of prohibited securities before clearing the proposed transactions for execution; the other rating agencies employ exception reports to identify restricted transactions after execution.
  - Only one rating agency employs a third-party service to identify undisclosed brokerage accounts, thus monitoring whether employees are submitting complete information about their brokerage accounts.
  - Two rating agencies do not appear to prohibit structured finance analysts from owning shares of investment banks that may participate in RMBS and CDO transactions.[52]
  - The Staff discovered indications that an employee of one rating agency appears to have engaged in personal trading practices inconsistent with the firm's policies.

Current Regulatory Requirements

An NRSRO is required to establish, maintain and enforce policies and procedures reasonably designed to address and manage conflicts of interest.[53] An NRSRO is prohibited from having certain conflicts relating to the issuance of a credit rating unless it has disclosed the type of conflict of interest, and has implemented policies and procedures to address and manage it.[54] A conflict is created when persons within the rating agency directly own securities or have other direct ownership interests in issuers or obligors subject to a credit rating issued by the rating agency.[55] In addition, an NRSRO is prohibited from having certain conflicts -- regardless of whether it discloses them or establishes procedures to manage them. Among these absolute prohibitions is issuing or maintaining a credit rating, when the rating agency, a credit analyst that participated in determining the credit rating, or a person responsible for approving the credit rating, directly owns securities of, or has any other direct ownership interest in, the person that is subject to the credit rating.[56]

Remedial Action

The Staff has recommended that each NRSRO examined conduct a review of its policies and procedures for managing the securities ownership conflict of interest to determine whether these policies are reasonably designed to ensure that their employees' personal trading is appropriate and comply with the requirements of Rule 17g-5. Each examined NRSRO stated that it will implement the Staff's recommendation.

H. Internal Audit Processes

The examined rating agencies each maintained internal audit programs that were designed to provide verification that the firm and its employees were complying with the firms' internal policies and procedures. Internal audit programs are an important internal control used by many organizations. In general, internal auditors conduct routine and special reviews of different aspects of an organization's operations, and report results and recommendations to management. A firm's internal audit staff generally operates in an organizational unit that is independent of the firm's business operations.

The Staff reviewed each rating agency's internal audit programs and activities related to its RMBS and CDO groups for the time period January 2003 to November 2007. The Staff concluded that the rating agencies' internal audit programs varied in terms of scope and depth of the reviews performed.

- The internal audit program of one rating agency appeared adequate in terms of assessing compliance with internal control procedures.

  - One rating agency maintained an internal audit program that appeared to be adequate during the entire examination period. It regularly conducted both substantive audits of ratings business units (e.g., RMBS or CDOs) as well as functional reviews across units for particular concerns (e.g., email, employee securities trading and issuer requested review of rating). In addition, these internal audits produced substantial recommendations that were responded to in an adequate manner by management.

- The internal audit or management response processes at two examined rating agencies appeared inadequate.

  - At one rating agency, its internal audits of its RMBS and CDO groups appeared to be cursory. The reviews essentially constituted a one-page checklist limited in scope to evaluate the completeness of deal files. The rating agency provided only four examples where the reviewer forwarded findings to management and no examples of management's response thereto.

- Another rating agency's internal audits of its RMBS and CDO groups uncovered numerous shortcomings, including non-compliance with document retention policies, lack of adherence to rating committee guidelines and most significantly, the failure of management to formally review/validate derivatives models prior to posting for general use. The rating agency did not provide documentation demonstrating management follow-up.

Current Regulatory Requirements

NRSROs are required to maintain internal audit plans, reports and related follow-up documents, including internal audit plans and reports, documents relating to audit follow-up measures and documents identified by auditors as necessary to audit an activity relating to the NRSRO's business as a rating agency.[57] Retention of these records will identify the rating agency's activities that its internal auditors had determined, raised, or did not raise, and compliance or control issues. In addition, this requirement is also meant to assist the Commission in determining whether the rating agency is complying with its methods, procedures and policies.

Remedial Action

The Staff has recommended that two of the NRSROs examined review whether their internal audit functions, particularly in the RMBS and CDO ratings areas, are adequate and whether they provide for proper management follow-up. Both of these NRSROs stated that it will implement the Staff's recommendation.

With respect to the NRSRO that maintained an adequate internal audit program, Staff recommended that it continue to conduct appropriate audits and periodically review whether improvements are warranted. That NRSRO committed to do so.

V. Observations by the Office of Economic Analysis

In conjunction with the Staff's examinations of the three rating agencies, the Staff of the Office of Economic Analysis ("OEA Staff") reviewed the processes used by these firms with respect to rating RMBS and CDOs that held subprime RMBS securities.

The purpose of the OEA Staff's review was to gain an understanding of the ratings methodologies employed by the rating agencies. The review assisted the Staff to better evaluate the extent to which conflicts of interest may have entered into and affected the ratings process. Review of the models helped provide a base-line for understanding the processes used by the NRSROs. This type of review can also assist the Staff in its assessment of whether the processes used in developing the models, their application, any adjustments made and their upkeep may have been potentially subject to conflicts of interest.

In conducting this review, the Staff, including OEA Staff, was mindful that the Commission is expressly prohibited from regulating "the substance of the credit ratings or the procedures and methodologies" by which any NRSRO determines credit ratings.[58] The

Staff does not make recommendations or seek to regulate the substance of the methodologies used.

Described below are conflicts of interest that are inherent, and in some cases unique, to these products and a factual summary of the models and methodologies used by the rating agencies. This information is provided in this public report solely to provide transparency to the ratings process and the activities of the rating agencies in connection with the recent subprime mortgage turmoil. The following description does not draw any conclusion as to whether conflicts of interest affected the ratings methodology or surrounding processes.

A. Conflicts of Interest

As the Commission noted in its recent release, some observers have indicated that while conflicts of interest due to the "issuer pays" model exist with respect to all asset classes that receive ratings, the conflicts created from the "issuer pays" model in rating structured finance products, particularly RMBS and related-CDOs, may be exacerbated for a number of reasons. First, the arranger is often the primary designer of the deal and as such, has more flexibility to adjust the deal structure to obtain a desired credit rating as compared to arrangers of non-structured asset classes. As well, arrangers that underwrite RMBS and CDO offerings have substantial influence over the choice of rating agencies hired to rate the deals.

Second, there is a high concentration in the firms conducting the underwriting function. Based on data provided by the three rating agencies examined, the Staff reviewed a sample of 642 deals. While 22 different arrangers underwrote subprime RMBS deals, 12 arrangers accounted for 80% of the deals, in both number and dollar volume. Similarly, for 368 CDOs of RMBS deals, although 26 different arrangers underwrote the CDOs, 11 arrangers accounted for 92% of the deals and 80% of the dollar volume.[59] In addition, 12 of the largest 13 RMB S underwriters were also the 12 largest CDO underwriters, further concentrating the underwriting function, as well as the sources of the rating agencies' revenue stream.

Achieving accuracy in ratings in a fast-changing market for a relatively new security may require frequent updating of the models used to produce the ratings, leading to quickly-changing ratings processes. The combination of the arrangers' influence in determining the choice of rating agencies and the high concentration of arrangers with this influence appear to have heightened the inherent conflicts of interest that exist in the "issuer pays" compensation model. One area where arrangers could have benefited in this context is in the ratings process itself. In discussions with OEA Staff, the ratings agencies indicated that arrangers preferred that the ratings process be fast and predictable. For instance, arrangers and their employees are generally compensated, at least in part, by the volume of deals completed and the total dollar volume of those deals. The Staff understands that at least one rating agency allowed deals that were already in the ratings process to continue to use older criteria, even when new criteria had been introduced.

Pressure from arrangers could also come in the form of requiring more favorable ratings or reduced credit enhancement levels. Such outcomes would reduce the cost of the debt for a given level of cash inflows from the asset pool. This benefit is particularly valuable to an arranger when it also serves as the sponsor of the RMBS or CDO trust. Such pressure could influence the rating agencies' decisions on whether to update a model when such an update would lead to a less favorable outcome.

High profit margins from rating RMBS and CDOs may have provided an incentive for a rating agency to encourage the arrangers to route future business its way.[60] Unsolicited ratings were not available to provide an independent check on the rating agencies' ratings, and the structures of these securities were complex, and information regarding the composition of the portfolio of assets, especially prior to issuance, was difficult to obtain for parties unrelated to the transaction.

B. Factual Summary of the Ratings Process for RMBS

Subprime mortgage origination has grown substantially over the last 12 years both in terms of absolute dollar volume and as a percentage of all mortgage origination. In its recent release, the Commission noted that one rating agency reported that subprime mortgages had increased (in dollars) from $421 billion to $640 billion between 2002 and 2006. As a percentage of all mortgages originated, subprime mortgages grew to represent from 14% to 22% of the pool over the same period. The dollar value of originations of subprime mortgages rose from $96.8 billion in 1996[61] to approximately $600 billion in 2006.[62]

In addition to the recent growth in subprime origination, there has also been a growth in the risk factors associated with subprime mortgages. Studies indicate that the percentage of subprime loans with less-than-full documentation, high combined loan to total value (CLTVs), and second liens grew substantially between 1999 and 2006.[63] Notably, while 2/28 adjustable rate mortgages comprised just 31% of subprime mortgages in 1999, they comprised almost 69% of subprime loans in 2006.[64] Further, 40-year mortgages were virtually non-existent prior to 2005, but they made up almost 27% of the subprime loans in 2006. These data provide evidence that the majority of subprime origination occurred within the last five years, and the loans containing very high risk combinations are even more recent.

Based on publications by the ratings agencies describing their methods, as well as other studies, the OEA Staff observed that all three of the examined rating agencies used similar approaches to rating RMBS bonds. They employed three primary models: probability of default, loss severity and the cash flow model. The first two models estimate default probabilities and loss severity given default, respectively, on a loan-byloan basis. Historical loan performance data is used to estimate the conditional relationships between loan and borrower characteristics and the default probability and the loss severity given default. The parameters from the estimation are then applied to the loans in the RMBS portfolio based on the loan and borrower characteristics specific to each loan. The parameters are re-estimated periodically using updated loan performance data.

Relying on the materials described above, the OEA Staff understands the ratings agencies used the following approaches. One rating agency used hazard rates to predict time to default, simultaneously predicting time to prepayment and using Monte Carlo simulations of macroeconomic variables to create a loss distribution. Another rating agency used a logistic regression instead of a hazard rate model, to estimate probability of default, and similarly used Monte Carlo simulation of macroeconomic variables to create a loss distribution.[65] The Monte Carlo method simulates a time series of macroeconomic variables in a stochastic (random) process.[66] A third rating agency used several different types of models to determine the effect of a factor on the probability of default, with the form of the model depending on the relationship between the factor and default probability. Some examples of factors employed are FICO scores, documentation and loan type. This rating agency's model is a static model.[67]

From its conversations with the ratings agencies, OEA Staff understands that prior to 2007, one rating agency did not appear to rely upon a specific subprime model, and used a combination of the output from the model used to rate prime home mortgage RMBS and credit enhancement level benchmarks of previously issued deals by the same originator. Adjustments have been described as having been made based on the perceived relative risk of the pool as compared to the previously issued pools; however, no loan-by-loan analysis was done. RMBS pools are comprised of thousands of loans whose quality could change significantly over time.[68]

Risk Variables

The default probability and loss severity models incorporate loan and borrower characteristics as well as macroeconomic variables.[69] Loan characteristics include information about the loan term, the interest rate and whether the loan is for the purchase of the home as a residence or for investment purposes. Examples of borrower characteristics include FICO score, debt-to-income ratio and income documentation levels.

Each rating agency stated to the OEA Staff that it typically made explicit adjustments for the quality of the loan servicer since each perceived that the servicer can affect the probability that the borrower will continue to make regular and full payments on the loan. The three examined rating agencies described a process where they evaluated the originator and its underwriting practices less formally. This evaluation has been described to potentially include visits to an individual originator, perceived differences in performance of loan pools created by different originators, or other anecdotal experiences with the originator. As long as the originator was determined to be of sufficient quality, no other adjustment was made.[70]

Studies indicate that there was a steady deterioration in the performance of subprime mortgages between 2001 and mid-year 2006, even controlling for the factors included in the agencies models.[71] At least one study attributes the deterioration in loan performance to be due in large part to the deterioration in the lending standards of originators.[72]

2. Use of Historical Data

According to the ratings agencies, credit raters relied upon historical data in order to predict future behavior. As discussed above, the performance history of the types of subprime mortgages that dominated many of the RMBS portfolios, for example, 2/28 ARMS and zero-downs with second liens, has been very short. Further, the performance history that did exist occurred under very benign economic conditions. These conditions included: consistent high economic growth, interest rates at historic lows, very low volatility in interest rates and a period where housing prices increased consistently year over year. Based on discussions with the rating agencies examined and documents provided by them, it appears that the parameters of the models were re-estimated by executing the model with new data infrequently.

3. Surveillance of Ratings

The ratings agencies stated publicly and to the OEA Staff that they maintained surveillance procedures to monitor for the accuracy of their ratings. The rating agencies examined did not appear to use loan-level data as part of the surveillance process. Rather, they relied upon pool level triggers to determine whether there had been significant deterioration in the credit quality of the assets used to collateralize securities. These triggers typically were based upon factors such as the amount of remaining overcollateralization after defaults. The rating agencies examined told the OEA Staff that analysts relied upon over-collateralization levels to ensure sufficient loss coverage for the various bonds. As long as a pool of assets contained collateral in excess of that necessary to meet the RMBS's obligations, the pool was deemed unimpaired.

As described to the OEA Staff, the over-collateralization test used by the ratings agencies typically relied upon the total amount of losses on the underlying loan pool measured against the total dollar value of credit enhancements.

C. Factual Summary of the Ratings Process for CDOs

The OEA Staff reviewed publications by the ratings agencies describing their methods, as well as discussions with the ratings agencies and other studies. Based on these materials, the OEA Staff observes that the process used to rate CDOs by the rating agencies examined is fundamentally similar to that used for rating RMBS. But while RMBS default probability and loss severity (recovery rate) models required 50 to 60 inputs, CDO models required only five inputs: current credit rating, maturity, asset type, country and industry. These five inputs were used to determine the three assumptions that went into the loss model: default probability, recovery rate and asset correlation. These are described below.

The OEA Staff further observes that the default probability assumption was determined by the current credit rating and the maturity of the individual RMBS included in the pool. The rating agencies examined typically used their own rating on the underlying asset, where available. These ratings were translated into default probabilities based on the maturity of the asset. Until very recently, the rating agencies maintained that the default probabilities were consistent across asset classes; thus, the historical corporate bond rating performance was used as the probability of default for the securities in the CDO pool. Based on significant differences in the performance history of RMBS and CDOs (when compared to similarly rated corporate bonds) the rating agencies have more recently developed asset-specific default probability tables.

The rating agencies described the recovery rate assumption as determined by the asset type and country of origin. Each rating agency employed different recovery rate assumptions for subprime RMBS. These assets were assumed to have a lower recovery rate than similarly rated corporate bonds.

Asset correlations were employed to determine the likelihood that an asset would default given that another asset in the pool has already defaulted. If they are uncorrelated, then there is no predictive power of one asset default leading to the other. Correlation does not necessarily affect the expected loss on the portfolio but it does create higher probabilities of extremely high or extremely low portfolio losses.

Once estimated, default probability, recovery rate and asset correlation were generally entered into a Monte Carlo simulation along with macroeconomic variables to simulate thousands of scenarios for defaults and recoveries. An expected loss curve was generated to determine the default hurdle rate and loss recovery for each ratings level.

The CDO modeling techniques used required few factors but with very precise measurement. For instance, the default probability was a function of the current rating on the underlying RMBS. As discussed above, recently the agencies developed asset- specific default probability tables. Finally, because the rating agencies reassessed the ratings every 12 to 18 months, if the current ratings on the underlying assets were biased upward or downward, the predicted probability of default for the portfolio would also be biased in the same direction.

Variables typically used to estimate asset correlations were trading prices, ratings migration,[73] and defaults; however there is little history of subprime RMBS bonds.[74] To estimate RMBS asset correlations, the rating agencies generally used a combination of historical corporate bond correlations and an assumption that RMBS securities are likely to have a higher correlation than corporate bonds.

All three rating agencies examined have recently stated publicly that they increased the assumed correlation among subprime RMBS bonds used in their CDO ratings models. As discussed above, correlation increases the probability of extremely high or low portfolio losses. Underestimate of this correlation is a loss to senior bondholders but a benefit to equity holders.

VI. Conclusion

As described in this report, while the various rating agencies had differing practices and, as to each, the Staff identified a range of issues to be addressed, each of the examined firms can take steps to improve their practices, policies and procedures with respect to rating RMBS and CDOs, and other structured finance securities. Each credit rating agency was cooperative in the course of these examinations and has committed to taking remedial measures to address the issues identified.

References

[1] This is a report of the Commission's Staff and does not include findings or conclusions by the Commission. This report also includes a description of the examinations conducted and current regulatory requirements for NRSROs (in Section II) and a description of the ratings process (in Section III).

[2] Prior to being registered as NRSROs, Fitch, Moody's and S&P were designated as NRSROs pursuant to No-Action Letters issued by the Staff of the Division of Trading and Markets. *See* Release No. 34-55857 (June 18, 2007).

[3] In conducting these examinations, the Commission was expressly prohibited from regulating "the substance of the credit ratings or the procedures and methodologies" by which any NRSRO determines credit ratings. 15 U.S.C. §78o-7(c)(2).

[4] Over 50 Commission Staff participated in these examinations.

[5] *Proposed Rules for Nationally Recognized Statistical Rating Organizations*, June 16, 2008, http://www.sec.gov/rules/proposed/2008/34-57967.pdf. The comment period for the proposed rules extends through July 25, 2008.

[6] Because Commission Staff examinations of specific firms are non-public in nature, this public report provides a summary of the issues found. It does not, however, identify any particular rating agency. Firm identifications are made only with respect to information that is already public. The Staff provided each rating agency examined with the opportunity to explain or clarify its internal documents, including emails (and in particular, the emails cited in this report). In some instances, a rating agency may disagree with the Staff's characterization of the emails or other documents referred to in this report.

[7] For example, documents in a deal file state, regarding an issue related to the collateral manager: "We didn't ha [sic] time to discuss this in detail at the committee, so they dropped the issue for this deal due to timing. We will need to revisit in the future." Another document describes an outstanding issue as "poorly addressed – needs to be checked in the next deal" and addresses the question of weighted average recovery rate by writing "(WARR- don't ask ☺)." (Deal File Documents 1 & 2).

[8] Email No. 1: Analytical Staff to Analytical Staff (Apr. 5, 2007, 3:56 PM). In another email, an analytical manager in the same rating agency's CDO group wrote to a senior analytical manager that the rating agencies continue to create an "even bigger monster – the CDO market. Let's hope we are all wealthy and retired by the time this house of cards falters.;o)." Email No. 2: Analytical Manager to Senior Analytical Manager (Dec. 15, 2006, 8:31 PM).

[9] Email No. 3: Senior Business Manager to Senior Business Manager (Apr. 27, 2007, 1:13 PM).

[10] Email No. 4: Senior Business Manager to External Consultant (May 3, 2006, 10:20 AM).

[11] Email No. 5: Analytical Manager to Senior Analytical Manager (Dec. 3, 2004, 11:10 AM).

[12] Prior to being registered as NRSROs, the rating agencies did not have a regulatory requirement to disclose their methodologies.

[13] Email No. 11: Analytical Manager to Issuer/Banker (Aug. 31, 2006, 12:04 PM).

[14] Email No. 13: Senior Analytical Manager to Senior Analytical Manager (Mar. 14, 2007, 6:45 PM).

[15] Email No. 14: Analytical Manager to Analytical Manager (Nov. 29, 2007, 20:08 GMT). Also email No. 15: Senior Business Manager to Senior Analytical Manager (Apr. 24, 2007, 18:50 GMT). Also email No. 16: Analytical Manager to Senior Analytical Manager (Feb. 7, 2007, 20:54 GMT). Also email No. 17: Analytical Staff to Analytical Staff (Nov. 15, 2006, 19:10 GMT).

[16] Email No. 18: Analytical Staff to Senior Analytical Manager (Sept. 24, 2007, 18:26 GMT).

[17] Section 1 5E(a)(1)(B)(ii) of the Exchange Act. 15 U.S.C. 78o-7(a)(1)(B)(ii).

[18] Specifically, the instructions require an NRSRO to provide descriptions of the following areas (as applicable): policies for determining whether to initiate a credit rating; a description of the public and non-public sources of information used in determining credit ratings, including information and analysis provided by third-party

vendors; the quantitative and qualitative models and metrics used to determine credit ratings; the methodologies by which credit ratings of other credit rating agencies are treated to determine credit ratings for securities or money market instruments issued by an asset pool or as part of any asset-backed or mortgaged-backed securities transaction; the procedures for interacting with the management of a rated obligor or issuer of rated securities or money market instruments; the structure and voting process of committees that review or approve credit ratings; procedures for informing rated obligors or issuers of rated securities or money market instruments about credit rating decisions and for appeals of final or pending credit rating decisions; procedures for monitoring, reviewing, and updating credit ratings; and procedures to withdraw, or suspend the maintenance of, a credit rating.

[19] *Proposed Rules for Nationally Recognized Statistical Rating Organizations*, June 16, 2008, http://www.sec.gov/rules/proposed/2008/34-57967.pdf.

[20] Rule 1 7g-2 under the Exchange Act. 17 CFR 240. 17g-2.

[21] Rule 1 7g-2 under the Exchange Act. 17 CFR 240.1 7g-2. The rule also prescribes the time periods and manner in which all these records must be retained.

[22] Rule 1 7g-2 under the Exchange Act. 17 CFR 240.1 7g-2(a)(6).

[23] The same rating agency conducted an internal review of 45 loan files and reported that it found the appearance of fraud or misrepresentation in almost every file.

[24] http://www.oag.state.ny.us/press/2008/june/june5a 08.html.

[25] Proposed Rules for Nationally Recognized Statistical Rating Organizations, June 16, 2008, http://www.sec.gov/rules/proposed/2008/34-57967.pdf.

[26] Rule 17g-2 of the Exchange Act. 17 CFR 240.17g-2. The rule also prescribes the time periods and manner in which these records must be retained.

[27] Rule 17g-2 of the Exchange Act. 17 CFR 240.17g-2(a)(2).

[28] *Proposed Rules for Nationally Recognized Statistical Rating Organizations*, June 16, 2008, http://www.sec.gov/rules/proposed/2008/34-57967.pdf.

[29] Email No. 20: Analytical Manager to Senior Analytical Manager (July 11, 2005, 8:09 PM). A similar email from the Senior Analytical Manager of RMBS Surveillance noted similar issues: "He asked me to begin discussing taking rating actions earlier on the poor performing deals. I have been thinking about this for much of the night. We do not have the resources to support what we are doing now." "I am seeing evidence that I really need to add to the staff to keep up with what is going on with sub prime and mortgage performance in general, NOW." Email No. 21: Senior Analytical Manager to Senior Analytical Manager (Feb. 3, 2007, 12:02 PM).

[30] Email No. 22: Senior Analytical Manager to Analytical Manager (June 15, 2007, 9:05 AM).

[31] "If I were the S.E.C. I would ask why can [sic] you go back and run the report for each of the months using the same assumptions? In theory we should be able to do this." Email No. 22: Senior Analytical Manager to Analytical Manager (June 15, 2007, 9:05 AM).

[32] Section 1 5E(d) of the Exchange Act.

[33] *Proposed Rules for Nationally Recognized Statistical Rating Organizations*, June 16, 2008, http://www.sec.gov/rules/proposed/2008/34-57967.pdf.

[34] Exchange Act Rule 17g-5(b)(1).

[35] Section 1 5E(h) of the Exchange Act .

[36] *See* Release No. 34-55857 and Exchange Act Rule 17g-5.
[37] Proposed Rules for Nationally Recognized Statistical Rating Organizations, June 16, 2008, http://www.sec.gov/rules/proposed/2008/34-57967.pdf.
[38] In one instance, a Senior Analytical Manager in the RMBS group distributed a negotiated fee schedule and a large percentage of the recipients were analytical staff. Email No. 23: Senior Analytical Manager to Analytical Manager (Dec. 29, 2005, 5:29 PM). In another instance, analytical staff is copied on an email communication to an issuer containing a letter confirming the fees for a transaction. Email No. 24: Research Staff to Issuer/Banker copying Analytical Staff (Mar. 27, 2007, 4:02 PM). Also email No. 25: Senior Analytical Manager to Analytical Manager (Dec. 19, 2005, 1:08 PM).
[39] An email communication from a senior analytical manager to at least one analyst requests that the recipient(s): "Please confirm status codes as soon as possible on the below mentioned deals. Additionally, any fees that are blank should be filled in. All issuer/bankers should be called for confirmation." In the same email chain, this request is reinforced by a senior Analytical Manager who states "It is imperative that deals are labeled as to Flow or Pending, etc as accurately and timely as possible. These codes along with the fee and closing date, drive our weekly revenue projections . . .." Email No. 26: Senior Analytical Manager to Senior Analytical Manager (Aug. 24, 2005, 3:53 PM).
[40] Email No. 28: Analytical Staff to Senior Analytical Manager (May 7, 2006, 13:38 GMT).
[41] Email No. 29: Business Manager to Analytical Manager (Jan. 31, 2007, 9:33 AM).
[42] Email No. 30: Analytical Staff to Business Manager (Aug. 23, 2007, 23:10 GMT). Email No. 31: Analytical Staff to Analytical Staff (Mar. 15, 2007, 1:37 PM).
[43] Email No. 32: Senior Analytical Manager to Senior Business Manager (Nov. 9, 2004, 12:11 PM).
[44] Email No. 33: Senior Business Manager to Senior Business Manager (Aug. 17, 2004, 6:14 PM).
[45] Email No. 34: Senior Analytical Manager to Analytical Manager (Sept. 25, 2006, 6:50 PM).
[46] Email No. 35: Senior Business Manager to Senior Business Manager (May 25, 2004, 12:08 PM).
[47] The affected securities, while structured products, were not RMBS or CDOs.
[48] Section 1 5E(h)(1) of the Exchange Act. 15 U.S.C. 78o-7(h)(1).
[49] 15 U.S.C. 78o-7(h)(1).
[50] 17 CFR 240.17g-5(b)(1).
[51] Proposed Rules for Nationally Recognized Statistical Rating Organizations, June 16, 2008, http://www.sec.gov/rules/proposed/2008/34-57967.pdf.
[52] One of these rating agencies is currently reviewing this policy.
[53] Section 1 5E(h)(1) of the Exchange Act. 15 U.S.C. 78o-7(h)(1).
[54] Rule 1 7g-5 of the Exchange Act and Section 1 5E(h)(1) of the Exchange Act. 17 CFR 240.1 7g-5(b)(6) and 15 U.S.C. 78o-7(h)(1).
[55] Rule 17g-5 of the Exchange Act. 17 CFR 240.17g-5(b)(6).
[56] Rule 17g-5 of the Exchange Act. 17 CFR 240.17g-5(c)(2). In adopting the rule, the Commission stated that the prohibition applied to "direct" ownership of securities and,

therefore, would not apply to indirect ownership interests, for example, through mutual funds or blind trusts. *See* Adopting Release, 72 FR at 33598.

[57] Rule 1 7g-2(b)(5) under the Exchange Act.

[58] Section 15E(c)(2) of the Exchange Act.

[59] For a sample of 650 subprime RMBS deals issued with a par value of $650 billion and 375 CDOs of RMBS issued with a par value of $310 billion during 2006 and 2007.

[60] As some rating agencies are either private firms or parts of conglomerates, it is difficult to evaluate their rate of return. White, "*The Credit Ratings Industry: An Industrial Organization Analysis*," in Levich, Majnoni, and Reinhart, ed, *Ratings, Rating Agencies, and the Global Financial System* (2002) at 49 cites data that indicates that one rating agency had an average rate of return of slightly over 42% from 1995 to 2000. The Economist, "*Measuring the Measurers,*" May 31, 2007 reports a rating agency's operating margin at 54% for 2006.

[61] http://research.stlouisfed.org/publications/review/06/01/ChomPennCross.pdf

[62] Adam Ashcraft and Til Schuermann, "Understanding the Securitization of Subprime Mortgage *Credit,*" Federal Reserve Bank of New York working paper, 2008.

[63] Ibid.

[64] A 2/28 ARM is a type of mortgage that has an initial two-year fixed rate that subsequently adjusts (is reset) to a variable rate for the remaining 28 years. The fixed rate typically is lower than a comparable 30-year fixed rate; however, the reset rate is higher.

[65] A logistic regression is a model used for prediction of the probability of occurrence of an event by fitting data to a logistic curve.

[66] Monte Carlo Simulation is an analytical technique in which a large number of simulations are run using random quantities for uncertain variables and looking at the distribution of results to infer which values are most likely.

[67] According to the rating agency, the static models used a limited number of values to represent a variable over time.

[68] In fact, evidence suggests that pool characteristics did deteriorate over time in the 2001-2006 period, with certain originators allowing greater slippage in pool quality than others. Yuliya Demyanyk and Otto Van Hemert, 2008, "*Understanding the Subprime Mortgage Crisis,*" Federal Reserve Bank of St. Louis and New York University working paper.

[69] Based on information provided to the Staff by the ratings agencies, the loan and borrower characteristics as well as other deal information are typically provided to the NRSRO by the arranger.

[70] One credit rating agency began making adjustments for originator quality in December 2006.

[71] Op. cit. Demyanyk and Van Hemert (2008).

[72] Ibid.

[73] Ratings migration approximates the changing credit quality of a security measured as the path-dependent change in the ratings over the life of the security.

[74] In the corporate bond markets, there are decades of high quality data that are used to estimate asset correlations.

In: Credit Rating Agency Reform
Editors: John De Luca and Paul Russo, pp. 129-206
ISBN: 978-1-60692-192-0

Chapter 3

FEDERAL RESERVE BANK OF NEW YORK STAFF REPORTS: UNDERSTANDING THE SECURITIZATION OF SUBPRIME MORTGAGE CREDIT*

Adam B. Ashcraft* and Til Schuermann*

ABSTRACT

In this paper, we provide an overview of the subprime mortgage securitization process and the seven key informational frictions that arise. We discuss the ways that market participants work to minimize these frictions and speculate on how this process broke down. We continue with a complete picture of the subprime borrower and the subprime loan, discussing both predatory borrowing and predatory lending. We present the key structural features of a typical subprime securitization, document how rating agencies assign credit ratings to mortgage-backed securities, and outline how these agencies monitor the performance of mortgage pools over time. Throughout the paper, we draw upon the example of a mortgage pool securitized by New Century Financial during 2006.

Keywords: subprime mortgage credit, securitization, rating agencies, principal agent, moral hazard.

EXECUTIVE SUMMARY

Section numbers containing more detail are provided in [square] brackets.

---

* Excerpted from Staff Report no. 318, dated March 2008.

* Ashcraft: Federal Reserve Bank of New York (e-mail: adam.ashcraft@ny.frb.org). Schuermann: Federal Reserve Bank of New York (e-mail: til.schuermann@ny.frb.org). The authors would like to thank Mike Holscher, Josh Frost, Alex LaTorre, Kevin Stiroh, and especially Beverly Hirtle for their valuable comments and contributions. The views expressed in this paper are those of the authors and do not necessarily reflect the position of the Federal Reserve Bank of New York or the Federal Reserve System.

- Until very recently, the origination of mortgages and issuance of mortgage-backed securities (MBS) was dominated by loans to prime borrowers conforming to underwriting standards set by the Government Sponsored Agencies (GSEs) [2]
    - By 2006, non-agency origination of $1 .480 trillion was more than 45% larger than agency origination, and non-agency issuance of $1.033 trillion was 14% larger than agency issuance of $905 billion.
- The securitization process is subject to seven key frictions.

1. Fictions between the mortgagor and the originator: predatory lending [2.1.1]

- Subprime borrowers can be financially unsophisticated
- Resolution: federal, state, and local laws prohibiting certain lending practices, as well as the recent regulatory guidance on subprime lending

2. Frictions between the originator and the arranger: Predatory borrowing and lending [2.1.2]

- The originator has an information advantage over the arranger with regard to the quality of the borrower.
- Resolution: due diligence of the arranger. Also the originator typically makes a number of representations and warranties (R&W) about the borrower and the underwriting process. When these are violated, the originator generally must repurchase the problem loans.

3. Frictions between the arranger and third-parties: Adverse selection [2.1.3]

- The arranger has more information about the quality of the mortgage loans which creates an adverse selection problem: the arranger can securitize bad loans (the lemons) and keep the good ones. This third friction in the securitization of subprime loans affects the relationship that the arranger has with the warehouse lender, the credit rating agency (CRA), and the asset manager.
- Resolution: haircuts on the collateral imposed by the warehouse lender. Due diligence conducted by the portfolio manager on the arranger and originator. CRAs have access to some private information; they have a franchise value to protect.

4. Frictions between the servicer and the mortgagor: Moral hazard [2.1.4]

- In order to maintain the value of the underlying asset (the house), the mortgagor (borrower) has to pay insurance and taxes on and generally maintain the property. In the approach to and during delinquency, the mortgagor has little incentive to do all that.
- Resolution: Require the mortgagor to regularly escrow funds for both insurance and property taxes. When the borrower fails to advance these funds, the servicer is typically required to make these payments on behalf of the investor. However,

limited effort on the part of the mortgagor to maintain the property has no resolution, and creates incentives for quick foreclosure.

5. Frictions between the servicer and third-parties: Moral hazard [2.1.5]

- The income of the servicer is increasing in the amount of time that the loan is serviced. Thus the servicer would prefer to keep the loan on its books for as long as possible and therefore has a strong preference to modify the terms of a delinquent loan and to delay foreclosure.
- In the event of delinquency, the servicer has a natural incentive to inflate expenses for which it is reimbursed by the investors, especially in good times when recovery rates on foreclosed property are high.
- Resolution: servicer quality ratings and a master servicer. Moody's estimates that servicer quality can affect the realized level of losses by plus or minus 10 percent. The master servicer is responsible for monitoring the performance of the servicer under the pooling and servicing agreement.

6. Frictions between the asset manager and investor: Principal-agent [2.1.6]

- The investor provides the funding for the MBS purchase but is typically not financially sophisticated enough to formulate an investment strategy, conduct due diligence on potential investments, and find the best price for trades. This service is provided by an asset manager (agent) who may not invest sufficient effort on behalf of the investor (principal).
- Resolution: investment mandates and the evaluation of manager performance relative to a peer group or benchmark

7. Frictions between the investor and the credit rating agencies: Model error [2.1.7]

- The rating agencies are paid by the arranger and not investors for their opinion, which creates a potential conflict of interest. The opinion is arrived at in part through the use of models (about which the rating agency naturally knows more than the investor) which are susceptible to both honest and dishonest errors.
- Resolution: the reputation of the rating agencies and the public disclosure of ratings and downgrade criteria.

- Five frictions caused the subprime crisis [2.2]

  - Friction #1: Many products offered to sub-prime borrowers are very complex and subject to mis-understanding and/or mis-representation.
  - Friction #6: Existing investment mandates do not adequately distinguish between structured and corporate ratings. Asset managers had an incentive to reach for yield by

purchasing structured debt issues with the same credit rating but higher coupons as corporate debt issues.[1]

- o Friction #3: Without due diligence of the asset manager, the arranger's incentives to conduct its own due diligence are reduced. Moreover, as the market for credit derivatives developed, including but not limited to the ABX, the arranger was able to limit its funded exposure to securitizations of risky loans.
- o Friction #2: Together, frictions 1, 2 and 6 worsened the friction between the originator and arranger, opening the door for predatory borrowing and lending.
- o Friction #7: Credit ratings were assigned to subprime MBS with significant error. Even though the rating agencies publicly disclosed their rating criteria for subprime, investors lacked the ability to evaluate the efficacy of these models.
- o We suggest some improvements to the existing process, though it is not clear that any additional regulation is warranted as the market is already taking remedial steps in the right direction.

- An overview of subprime mortgage credit [3] and subprime MBS [4]
- Credit rating agencies (CRAs) play an important role by helping to resolve many of the frictions in the securitization process

- o A credit rating by a CRA represents an overall assessment and opinion of a debt obligor's creditworthiness and is thus meant to reflect only credit or default risk. It is meant to be directly comparable across countries and instruments. Credit ratings typically represent an unconditional view, sometimes called "cycle-neutral" or "through-the-cycle." [5.1]
- o Especially for investment grade ratings, it is very difficult to tell the difference between a "bad" credit rating and bad luck [5.3]
- o The subprime credit rating process can be split into two steps: (1) estimation of a loss distribution, and (2) simulation of the cash flows. With a loss distribution in hand, it is straightforward to measure the amount of credit enhancement necessary for a tranche to attain a given credit rating. [5.4]
- o There seem to be substantial differences between corporate and asset backed securities (ABS) credit ratings (an MBS is just a special case of an ABS – the assets are mortgages) [5.5]
- o Corporate bond (obligor) ratings are largely based on firm-specific risk characteristics. Since ABS structures represent claims on cash flows from a *portfolio* of underlying assets, the rating of a structured credit product must take into account systematic risk.
- o ABS ratings refer to the performance of a static pool instead of a dynamic corporation.
- o ABS ratings rely heavily on quantitative models while corporate debt ratings rely heavily on analyst judgment.
- o Unlike corporate credit ratings, ABS ratings rely explicitly on a forecast of (macro)economic conditions.

---

[1] The fact that the market demands a higher yield for similarly rated structured products than for straight corporate bonds ought to provide a clue to the potential of higher risk.

- While an ABS credit rating for a particular rating grade should have similar expected loss to corporate credit rating of the same grade, the volatility of loss (i.e. the *un*expected loss) can be quite different across asset classes.
- Rating agency must respond to shifts in the loss distribution by increasing the amount of needed credit enhancement to keep ratings stable as economic conditions deteriorate. It follows that the stabilizing of ratings through the cycle is associated with pro-cyclical credit enhancement: as the housing market improves, credit enhancement falls; as the housing market slows down, credit enhancement increases which has the potential to amplify the housing cycle. [5.6]
- An important part of the rating process involves simulating the cash flows of the structure in order to determine how much credit excess spread will receive towards meeting the required credit enhancement. This is very complicated, with results that can be rather sensitive to underlying model assumptions. [5.7]

1. INTRODUCTION

How does one securitize a pool of mortgages, especially subprime mortgages? What is the process from origination of the loan or mortgage to the selling of debt instruments backed by a pool of those mortgages? What problems creep up in this process, and what are the mechanisms in place to mitigate those problems? This paper seeks to answer all of these questions. Along the way we provide an overview of the market and some of the key players, and provide an extensive discussion of the important role played by the credit rating agencies.

In Section 2, we provide a broad description of the securitization process and pay special attention to seven key frictions that need to be resolved. Several of these frictions involve moral hazard, adverse selection and principal-agent problems. We show how each of these frictions is worked out, though as evidenced by the recent problems in the subprime mortgage market, some of those solutions are imperfect. In Section 3, we provide an overview of subprime mortgage credit; our focus here is on the subprime borrower and the subprime loan. We offer, as an example a pool of subprime mortgages New Century securitized in June 2006. We discuss how predatory lending and predatory borrowing (i.e. mortgage fraud) fit into the picture. Moreover, we examine subprime loan performance within this pool and the industry, speculate on the impact of payment reset, and explore the ABX and the role it plays. In Section 4, we examine subprime mortgage-backed securities, discuss the key structural features of a typical securitization, and, once again illustrate how this works with reference to the New Century securitization. We finish with an examination of the credit rating and rating monitoring process in Section 5. Along the way we reflect on differences between corporate and structured credit ratings, the potential for pro-cyclical credit enhancement to amplify the housing cycle, and document the performance of subprime ratings. Finally, in Section 6, we review the extent to which investors rely upon on credit rating agencies views, and take as a typical example of an investor: the Ohio Police & Fire Pension Fund.

We reiterate that the views presented here are our own and not those of the Federal Reserve Bank of New York or the Federal Reserve System. And, while the paper focuses on subprime mortgage credit, note that there is little qualitative difference between the securitization and ratings process for Alt-A and home equity loans. Clearly, recent problems in mortgage markets are not confined to the subprime sector.

2. OVERVIEW OF SUBPRIME MORTGAGE CREDIT SECURITIZATION

Until very recently, the origination of mortgages and issuance of mortgage-backed securities (MBS) was dominated by loans to prime borrowers conforming to underwriting standards set by the Government Sponsored Agencies (GSEs). Outside of conforming loans are non-agency asset classes that include Jumbo, Alt-A, and Subprime. Loosely speaking, the Jumbo asset class includes loans to prime borrowers with an original principal balance larger than the conforming limits imposed on the agencies by Congress;[2] the Alt-A asset class involves loans to borrowers with good credit but include more aggressive underwriting than the conforming or Jumbo classes (i.e. no documentation of income, high leverage); and the Subprime asset class involves loans to borrowers with poor credit history.

Table 1 documents origination and issuance since 2001 in each of four asset classes. In 2001, banks originated $1.433 trillion in conforming mortgage loans and issued $1.087 trillion in mortgage-backed securities secured by those mortgages, shown in the "Agency" columns of Table 1. In contrast, the non-agency sector originated $680 billion ($190 billion subprime + $60 billion Alt-A + $430 billion jumbo) and issued $240 billion ($87.1 billion subprime + $11.4 Alt-A + $142.2 billion jumbo), and most of these were in the Jumbo sector. The Alt-A and Subprime sectors were relatively small, together comprising $250 billion of $2.1 trillion (12 percent) in total origination during 2001.

A reduction in long-term interest rates through the end of 2003 was associated with a sharp increase in origination and issuance across all asset classes. While the conforming markets peaked in 2003, the non-agency markets continued rapid growth through 2005, eventually eclipsing activity in the conforming market. In 2006, non-agency production of $1 .480 trillion was more than 45 percent larger than agency production, and non-agency issuance of $1.033 trillion was larger than agency issuance of $905 billion.

Interestingly, the increase in Subprime and Alt-A origination was associated with a significant increase in the ratio of issuance to origination, which is a reasonable proxy for the fraction of loans sold. In particular, the ratio of subprime MBS issuance to subprime mortgage origination was close to 75 percent in both 2005 and 2006. While there is typically a one-quarter lag between origination and issuance, the data document that a large and increasing fraction of both subprime and Alt-A loans are sold to investors, and very little is retained on the balance sheets of the institutions who originate them. The process through which loans are removed from the balance sheet of lenders and transformed into debt securities purchased by investors is called securitization.

---

[2] This limit is currently $417,000.

Table 1. Origination and Issue of Non-Agency Mortgage Loans

	Sub-prime			Alt-A			Jumbo			Agency		
Year	Origination	Issuance	Ratio	Origination	Issuance	Ratio	Origination	Issuance	Ratio	Origination	Issuance	Ratio
2001	$ 190.00	$ 87.10	46%	$ 60.00	$ 11.40	19%	$ 430.00	$ 142.20	33%	$ 1,433.00	$ 1,087.60	76%
2002	$ 231.00	$ 122.70	53%	$ 68.00	$ 53.50	79%	$ 576.00	$ 171.50	30%	$ 1,898.00	$ 1,442.60	76%
2003	$ 335.00	$ 195.00	58%	$ 85.00	$ 74.10	87%	$ 655.00	$ 237.50	36%	$ 2,690.00	$ 2,130.90	79%
2004	$ 540.00	$ 362.63	67%	$ 200.00	$ 158.60	79%	$ 515.00	$ 233.40	45%	$ 1,345.00	$ 1,018.60	76%
2005	$ 625.00	$ 465.00	74%	$ 380.00	$ 332.30	87%	$ 570.00	$ 280.70	49%	$ 1,180.00	$ 964.80	82%
2006	$ 600.00	$ 448.60	75%	$ 400.00	$ 365.70	91%	$ 480.00	$ 219.00	46%	$ 1,040.00	$ 904.60	87%

Source: Inside Mortgage Finance (2007).

Notes: Jumbo origination includes non-agency prime. Agency origination includes conventional/conforming and FHA/VA loans. Agency issuance GNMA, FHLMC, and FNMA. Figures are in billions of USD.

2.1. The Seven Key Frictions

The securitization of mortgage loans is a complex process that involves a number of different players. Figure 1 provides an overview of the players, their responsibilities, the important frictions that exist between the players, and the mechanisms used in order to mitigate these frictions. An overarching friction which plagues every step in the process is asymmetric information: usually one party has more information about the asset than another. We think that understanding these frictions and evaluating the mechanisms designed to mitigate their importance is essential to understanding how the securitization of subprime loans could generate bad outcomes.[3]

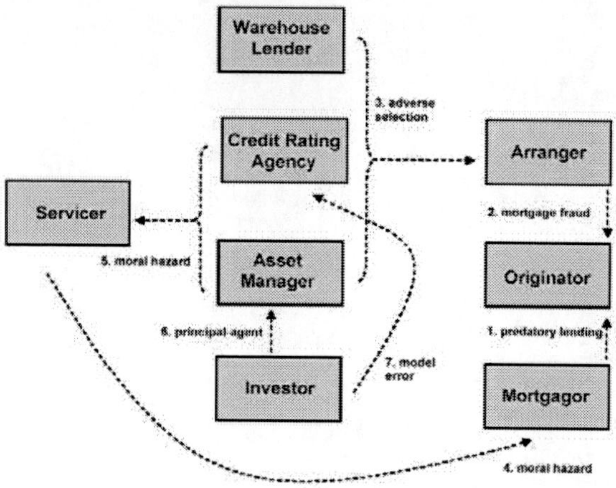

Figure 1. Key Players and Frictions in Subprime Mortgage Credit Securitization.

Table 2. Top Subprime Mortgage Originators

		2006		2005	
Rank	Lender	Volume ($b)	Share (%)	Volume ($b)	%Change
1	HSBC	$52.8	8.8%	$58.6	-9.9%
2	New Century Financial	$51.6	8.6%	$52.7	-2.1%
3	Countrywide	$40.6	6.8%	$44.6	-9.1%
4	CitiGroup	$38.0	6.3%	$20.5	85.5%
5	WMC Mortgage	$33.2	5.5%	$31.8	4.3%
6	Fremont	$32.3	5.4%	$36.2	-10.9%
7	Ameriquest Mortgage	$29.5	4.9%	$75.6	-61.0%
8	Option One	$28.8	4.8%	$40.3	-28.6%
9	Wells Fargo	$27.9	4.6%	$30.3	-8.1%
10	First Franklin	$27.7	4.6%	$29.3	-5.7%
	Top 25	$543.2	90.5%	$604.9	-10.2%
	Total	$600.0	100.0%	$664.0	-9.8%

Source: Inside Mortgage Finance (2007).

[3] A recent piece in *The Economist* (September 20, 2007) provides a nice description of some of the frictions described here.

Table 3. Top Subprime MBS Issuers

		2006		2005	
Rank	Lender	Volume ($b)	Share (%)	Volume ($b)	%Change
1	Countrywide	$38.5	8.6%	$38.1	1.1%
2	New Century	$33.9	7.6%	$32.4	4.8%
3	Option One	$31.3	7.0%	$27.2	15.1%
4	Fremont	$29.8	6.6%	$19.4	53.9%
5	Washington Mutual	$28.8	6.4%	$18.5	65.1%
6	First Franklin	$28.3	6.3%	$19.4	45.7%
7	Residential Funding Corp	$25.9	5.8%	$28.7	-9.5%
8	Lehman Brothers	$24.4	5.4%	$35.3	-30.7%
9	WMC Mortgage	$21.6	4.8%	$19.6	10.5%
10	Ameriquest	$21.4	4.8%	$54.2	-60.5%
	Top 25	$427.6	95.3%	$417.6	2.4%
	Total	$448.6	100.0%	$508.0	-11.7%

Source: Inside Mortgage Finance (2007).

Table 4. Top Subprime Mortgage Servicers

		2006		2005	
Rank	Lender	Volume ($b)	Share (%)	Volume ($b)	%Change
1	Countrywide	$119.1	9.6%	$120.6	-1.3%
2	JP MorganChase	$83.8	6.8%	$67.8	23.6%
3	CitiGroup	$80.1	6.5%	$47.3	39.8%
4	Option One	$69.0	5.6%	$79.5	-13.2%
5	Ameriquest	$60.0	4.8%	$75.4	-20.4%
6	Ocwen Financial Corp	$52.2	4.2%	$42.0	24.2%
7	Wells Fargo	$51.3	4.1%	$44.7	14.8%
8	Homecomings Financial	$49.5	4.0%	$55.2	-10.4%
9	HSBC	$49..5	4.0%	$43.8	13.0%
10	Litton Loan Servicing	$47.0	4.0%	$42.0	16.7%
	Top 30	$1,105.7	89.2%	$1,057.8	4.5%
	Total	$1,240	100.0%	$1,200	3.3%

Source: Inside Mortgage Finance (2007).

2.1.1. Frictions between the Mortgagor and Originator: Predatory Lending

The process starts with the mortgagor or borrower, who applies for a mortgage in order to purchase a property or to refinance and existing mortgage. The originator, possibly through a broker (yet another intermediary in this process), underwrites and initially funds and services the mortgage loans. Table 2 documents the top 10 subprime originators in 2006, which are a healthy mix of commercial banks and non-depository specialized mono-line lenders. The originator is compensated through fees paid by the borrower (points and closing costs), and by the proceeds of the sale of the mortgage loans. For example, the originator might sell a portfolio of loans with an initial principal balance of $100 million for $102 million, corresponding to a gain on sale of $2 million. The buyer is willing to pay this premium because of anticipated interest payments on the principal.

The first friction in securitization is between the borrower and the originator. In particular, subprime borrowers can be financially unsophisticated. For example, a borrower might be unaware of all of the financial options available to him. Moreover, even if these options are known, the borrower might be unable to make a choice between different financial options that is in his own best interest. This friction leads to the possibility of predatory lending, defined by Morgan (2005) as the welfare-reducing provision of credit. The main safeguards against these practices are federal, state, and local laws prohibiting certain lending practices, as well as the recent regulatory guidance on subprime lending. See Appendix 1 for further discussion of these issues.

2.1.2. Frictions between the Originator and the Arranger: Predatory Lending and Borrowing

The pool of mortgage loans is typically purchased from the originator by an institution known as the arranger or issuer. The first responsibility of the arranger is to conduct due diligence on the originator. This review includes but is not limited to financial statements, underwriting guidelines, discussions with senior management, and background checks. The arranger is responsible for bringing together all the elements for the deal to close. In particular, the arranger creates a bankruptcy-remote trust that will purchase the mortgage loans, consults with the credit rating agencies in order to finalize the details about deal structure, makes necessary filings with the SEC, and underwrites the issuance of securities by the trust to investors. Table 3 documents the list of the top 10 subprime MBS issuers in 2006. In addition to institutions which both originate and issue on their own, the list of issuers also includes investment banks that purchase mortgages from originators and issue their own securities. The arranger is typically compensated through fees charged to investors and through any premium that investors pay on the issued securities over their par value.

The second friction in the process of securitization involves an information problem between the originator and arranger. In particular, the originator has an information advantage over the arranger with regard to the quality of the borrower. Without adequate safeguards in place, an originator can have the incentive to collaborate with a borrower in order to make significant misrepresentations on the loan application, which, depending on the situation, could be either construed as predatory lending (the lender convinces the borrower to borrow "too much) or predatory borrowing (the borrower convinces the lender to lend "too much"). See Appendix 2 on predatory borrowing for further discussion.

There are several important checks designed to prevent mortgage fraud, the first being the due diligence of the arranger. In addition, the originator typically makes a number of representations and warranties (R&W) about the borrower and the underwriting process. When these are violated, the originator generally must repurchase the problem loans. However, in order for these promises to have a meaningful impact on the friction, the originator must have adequate capital to buy back those problem loans. Moreover, when an arranger does not conduct or routinely ignores its own due diligence, as suggested in a recent Reuters piece by Rucker (1 Aug 2007), there is little to stop the originator from committing widespread mortgage fraud.

2.1.3. Frictions between the Arranger and Third-Parties: Adverse Selection

There is an important information asymmetry between the arranger and third-parties concerning the quality of mortgage loans. In particular, the fact that the arranger has more information about the quality of the mortgage loans creates an adverse selection problem:

the arranger can securitize bad loans (the lemons) and keep the good ones (or securitize them elsewhere). This third friction in the securitization of subprime loans affects the relationship that the arranger has with the warehouse lender, the credit rating agency (CRA), and the asset manager. We discuss how each of these parties responds to this classic lemons problem.

Adverse Selection and the Warehouse Lender

The arranger is responsible for funding the mortgage loans until all of the details of the securitization deal can be finalized. When the arranger is a depository institution, this can be done easily with internal funds. However, mono-line arrangers typically require funding from a third-party lender for loans kept in the "warehouse" until they can be sold. Since the lender is uncertain about the value of the mortgage loans, it must take steps to protect itself against overvaluing their worth as collateral. This is accomplished through due diligence by the lender, haircuts to the value of collateral, and credit spreads. The use of haircuts to the value of collateral imply that the bank loan is over-collateralized (o/c) – it might extend a $9 million loan against collateral of $10 million of underlying mortgages –, forcing the arranger to assume a funded equity position – in this case $1 million – in the loans while they remain on its balance sheet.

We emphasize this friction because an adverse change in the warehouse lender's views of the value of the underlying loans can bring an originator to its knees. The failure of dozens of mono-line originators in the first half of 2007 can be explained in large part by the inability of these firms to respond to increased demands for collateral by warehouse lenders (Wei, 2007; Sichelman, 2007).

Adverse Selection and the Asset Manager

The pool of mortgage loans is sold by the arranger to a bankruptcy-remote trust, which is a special-purpose vehicle that issues debt to investors. This trust is an essential component of credit risk transfer, as it protects investors from bankruptcy of the originator or arranger. Moreover, the sale of loans to the trust protects both the originator and arranger from losses on the mortgage loans, provided that there have been no breaches of representations and warranties made by the originator.

The arranger underwrites the sale of securities secured by the pool of subprime mortgage loans to an asset manager, who is an agent for the ultimate investor. However, the information advantage of the arranger creates a standard lemons problem. This problem is mitigated by the market through the following means: reputation of the arranger, the arranger providing a credit enhancement to the securities with its own funding, and any due diligence conducted by the portfolio manager on the arranger and originator.

Adverse Selection and Credit Rating Agencies

The rating agencies assign credit ratings on mortgage-backed securities issued by the trust. These opinions about credit quality are determined using publicly available rating criteria which map the characteristics of the pool of mortgage loans into an estimated loss distribution. From this loss distribution, the rating agencies calculate the amount of credit enhancement that a security requires in order for it to attain a given credit rating. The opinion of the rating agencies is vulnerable to the lemons problem (the arranger likely still knows more) because they only conduct limited due diligence on the arranger and originator.

2.1.4. Frictions between the Servicer and the Mortgagor: Moral Hazard

The trust employs a servicer who is responsible for collection and remittance of loan payments, making advances of unpaid interest by borrowers to the trust, accounting for principal and interest, customer service to the mortgagors, holding escrow or impounding funds related to payment of taxes and insurance, contacting delinquent borrowers, and supervising foreclosures and property dispositions. The servicer is compensated through a periodic fee by paid the trust. Table 4 documents the top 10 subprime servicers in 2006, which is a mix of depository institutions and specialty non-depository mono-line servicing companies.

Moral hazard refers to changes in behavior in response to redistribution of risk, e.g., insurance may induce risk-taking behavior if the insured does not bear the full consequences of bad outcomes. Here we have a problem where one party (the mortgagor) has unobserved costly effort that affects the distribution over cash flows which are shared with another party (the servicer), and the first party has limited liability (it does not share in downside risk). In managing delinquent loans, the servicer is faced with a standard moral hazard problem vis-à-vis the mortgagor. When a servicer has the incentive to work in investors' best interest, it will manage delinquent loans in a fashion to minimize losses. A mortgagor struggling to make a mortgage payment is also likely struggling to keep hazard insurance and property tax bills current, as well as conduct adequate maintenance on the property. The failure to pay property taxes could result in costly liens on the property that increase the costs to investors of ultimately foreclosing on the property. The failure to pay hazard insurance premiums could result in a lapse in coverage, exposing investors to the risk of significant loss. And the failure to maintain the property will increase expenses to investors in marketing the property after foreclosure and possibly reduce the sale price. The mortgagor has little incentive to expend effort or resources to maintain a property close to foreclosure.

In order to prevent these potential problems from surfacing, it is standard practice to require the mortgagor to regularly escrow funds for both insurance and property taxes. When the borrower fails to advance these funds, the servicer is typically required to make these payments on behalf of the investor. In order to prevent lapses in maintenance from creating losses, the servicer is encouraged to foreclose promptly on the property once it is deemed uncollectible. An important constraint in resolving this latter issue is that the ability of a servicer to collect on a delinquent debt is generally restricted under the Real Estate Settlement Procedures Act, Fair Debt Collection Practices Act and state deceptive trade practices statutes. In a recent court case, a plaintiff in Texas alleging unlawful collection activities against Ocwen Financial was awarded $12.5 million in actual and punitive damages.

2.1.5. Frictions between the Servicer and Third-Parties: Moral Hazard

The servicer can have a significantly positive or negative effect on the losses realized from the mortgage pool. Moody's estimates that servicer quality can affect the realized level of losses by plus or minus 10 percent. This impact of servicer quality on losses has important implications for both investors and credit rating agencies. In particular, investors want to minimize losses while credit rating agencies want to minimize the uncertainty about losses in order to make accurate opinions. In each case articulated below we have a similar problem as in the fourth friction, namely where one party (here the servicer) has unobserved costly effort that affects the distribution over cash flows which are shared with other parties, and the first party has limited liability (it does not share in downside risk).

Moral Hazard between the Servicer and the Asset Manager[4]

The servicing fee is a flat percentage of the outstanding principal balance of mortgage loans. The servicer is paid first out of receipts each month before any funds are advanced to investors. Since mortgage payments are generally received at the beginning of the month and investors receive their distributions near the end of the month, the servicer benefits from being able to earn interest on float.[5]

There are two key points of tension between investors and the servicer: (a) reasonable reimbursable expenses, and (b) the decision to modify and foreclose. We discuss each of these in turn.

In the event of a delinquency, the servicer must advance unpaid interest (and sometimes principal) to the trust as long as it is deemed collectable, which typically means that the loan is less than 90 days delinquent. In addition to advancing unpaid interest, the servicer must also keep paying property taxes and insurance premiums as long as it has a mortgage on the property. In the event of foreclosure, the servicer must pay all expenses out of pocket until the property is liquidated, at which point it is reimbursed for advances and expenses. The servicer has a natural incentive to inflate expenses, especially in good times when recovery rates on foreclosed property are high.

Note that the un-reimbursable expenses of the servicer are largely fixed and front-loaded: registering the loan in the servicing system, getting the initial notices out, doing the initial escrow analysis and tax setups, etc. At the same time, the income of the servicer is increasing in the amount of time that the loan is serviced. It follows that the servicer would prefer to keep the loan on its books for as long as possible. This means it has a strong preference to modify the terms of a delinquent loan and to delay foreclosure.

Resolving each of these problems involves a delicate balance. On the one hand, one can put hard rules into the pooling and servicing agreement limiting loan modifications, and an investor can invest effort into actively monitoring the servicer's expenses. On the other hand, the investor wants to give the servicer flexibility to act in the investor's best interest and does not want to incur too much expense in monitoring. This latter point is especially true since other investors will free-ride off of any one investor's effort. It is not surprising that the credit rating agencies play an important role in resolving this collective action problem through servicer quality ratings.

In addition to monitoring effort by investors, servicer quality ratings, and rules about loan modifications, there are two other important ways to mitigate this friction: servicer reputation and the master servicer. As the servicing business is an important counter-cyclical source of income for banks, one would think that these institutions would work hard on their own to minimize this friction. The master servicer is responsible for monitoring the performance of the servicer under the pooling and servicing agreement. It validates data reported by the

---

[4] Several points raised in this section were first raised in a 20 February 2007 post on the blog http://calculatedrisk.blogspot.com/ entitled "Mortgage Servicing for Ubernerds."

[5] In addition to the monthly fee, the servicer generally gets to keep late fees. This can tempt a servicer to post payments in a tardy fashion or not make collection calls until late fees are assessed.

servicer, reviews the servicing of defaulted loans, and enforces remedies of servicer default on behalf of the trust.

Moral Hazard between the Servicer and the Credit Rating Agency

Given the impact of servicer quality on losses, the accuracy of the credit rating placed on securities issued by the trust is vulnerable to the use of a low quality servicer. In order to minimize the impact of this friction, the rating agencies conduct due diligence on the servicer, use the results of this analysis in the rating of mortgage-backed securities, and release their findings to the public for use by investors.

Servicer quality ratings are intended to be an unbiased benchmark of a loan servicer's ability to prevent or mitigate pool losses across changing market conditions. This evaluation includes an assessment of collections/customer service, loss mitigation, foreclosure timeline management, management, staffing & training, financial stability, technology and disaster recovery, legal compliance and oversight and financial strength. In constructing these quality ratings, the rating agency attempts to break out the actual historical loss experience of the servicer into an amount attributable to the underlying credit risk of the loans and an amount attributable to the servicer's collection and default management ability.

2.1.6. Frictions between the Asset Manager and Investor: Principal-Agent

The investor provides the funding for the purchase of the mortgage-backed security. As the investor is typically financially unsophisticated, an agent is employed to formulate an investment strategy, conduct due diligence on potential investments, and find the best price for trades. Given differences in the degree of financial sophistication between the investor and an asset manager, there is an obvious information problem between the investor and portfolio manger that gives rise to the sixth friction.

In particular, the investor will not fully understand the investment strategy of the manager, has uncertainty about the manager's ability, and does not observe any effort that the manager makes to conduct due diligence. This principal (investor)-agent (manager) problem is mitigated through the use of investment mandates, and the evaluation of manager performance relative to a peer benchmark or its peers.

As one example, a public pension might restrict the investments of an asset manager to debt securities with an investment grade credit rating and evaluate the performance of an asset manager relative to a benchmark index. However, there are other relevant examples. The FDIC, which is an implicit investor in commercial banks through the provision of deposit insurance, prevents insured banks from investing in speculative-grade securities or enforces risk-based capital requirements that use credit ratings to assess risk-weights. An actively-managed collateralized debt obligation (CDO) imposes covenants on the weighted average rating of securities in an actively-managed portfolio as well as the fraction of securities with a low credit rating.

As investment mandates typically involve credit ratings, it should be clear that this is another point where the credit rating agencies play an important role in the securitization process. By presenting an opinion on the riskiness of offered securities, the rating agencies help resolve the information frictions that exist between the investor and the portfolio manager. Credit ratings are intended to capture the expectations about the long-run or through-the-cycle performance of a debt security. A credit rating is fundamentally a statement about the suitability of an instrument to be included in a risk class, but importantly, it is an opinion only about credit risk; we discuss credit ratings in more detail in Section 5.1. It follows that the opinion of credit rating agencies is a crucial part of securitization, because in the end the rating is the means through which much of the funding by investors finds its way into the deal.

2.1.7. Frictions between the Investor and the Credit Rating Agencies: Model Error

The rating agencies are paid by the arranger and not investors for their opinion, which creates a potential conflict of interest. Since an investor is not able to assess the efficacy of rating agency models, they are susceptible to both honest and dishonest errors on the agencies' part. The information asymmetry between investors and the credit rating agencies is the seventh and final friction in the securitization process. Honest errors are a natural byproduct of rapid financial innovation and complexity. On the other hand, dishonest errors could be driven by the dependence of rating agencies on fees paid by the arranger (the conflict of interest).

Some critics claim that the rating agencies are unable to objectively rate structured products due to conflicts of interest created by issuer-paid fees. Moody's, for example, made 44 per cent of its revenue last year from structured finance deals (Tomlinson and Evans, 2007). Such assessments also command more than double the fee rates of simpler corporate ratings, helping keep Moody's operating margins above 50 per cent (Economist, 2007).

Beales, Scholtes and Tett (15 May 2007) write in the *Financial Times*:

> The potential for conflicts of interest in the agencies' "issuer pays" model has drawn fire before, but the scale of their dependence on investment banks for structured finance business gives them a significant incentive to look kindly on the products they are rating, critics say. From his office in Paris, the head of the Autorité des Marchés Financiers, the main French financial regulator, is raising fresh questions over their role and objectivity. Mr Prada sees the possibility for conflicts of interest similar to those that emerged in the audit profession when it drifted into consulting. Here, the integrity of the auditing work was threatened by the demands of winning and retaining clients in the more lucrative consultancy business, a conflict that ultimately helped bring down accountants Arthur Andersen in the wake of Enron's collapse. "I do hope that it does not take another Enron for everyone to look at the issue of rating agencies," he says.

This friction is minimized through two devices: the reputation of the rating agencies and the public disclosure of ratings and downgrade criteria. For the rating agencies, their business is their reputation, so it is difficult – though not impossible – to imagine that they would risk deliberately inflating credit ratings in order to earn structuring fees, thus jeopardizing their franchise. Moreover, with public rating and downgrade criteria, any deviations in credit ratings from their models are easily observed by the public.[6]

---

[6] We think that there are two ways these errors could emerge. One, the rating agency builds its model honestly, but then applies judgment in a fashion consistent with its economic interest. The average deal is structured appropriately, but the agency gives certain issuers better terms. Two, the model itself is knowingly aggressive. The average deal is structured inadequately.

2.2. Five Frictions that Caused the Subprime Crisis

We believe that five of the seven frictions discussed above help to explain the breakdown in the subprime mortgage market.

The problem starts with friction #1: many products offered to sub-prime borrowers are very complex and subject to mis-understanding and/or mis-representation. This opened the possibility of both excessive borrowing (predatory borrowing) and excessive lending (predatory lending.

At the other end of the process we have the principal-agent problem between the investor and asset manager (friction #6). In particular, it seems that investment mandates do not adequately distinguish between structured and corporate credit ratings. This is a problem because asset manager performance is evaluated relative to peers or relative to a benchmark index. It follows that asset managers have an incentive to reach for yield by purchasing structured debt issues with the same credit rating but higher coupons as corporate debt issues.[7]

Initially, this portfolio shift was likely led by asset managers with the ability to conduct their own due diligence, recognizing value in the wide pricing of subprime mortgage-backed securities. However, once the other asset managers started to under-perform their peers, they likely made similar portfolio shifts, but did not invest the same effort into due diligence of the arranger and originator.

This phenomenon worsened the friction between the arranger and the asset manager (friction #3). In particular, without due diligence by the asset manager, the arranger's incentives to conduct its own due diligence are reduced. Moreover, as the market for credit derivatives developed, including but not limited to the ABX, the arranger was able to limit its funded exposure to securitizations of risky loans. Together, these considerations worsened the friction between the originator and arranger, opening the door for predatory borrowing and provides incentives for predatory lending (friction #2). In the end, the only constraint on underwriting standards was the opinion of the rating agencies. With limited capital backing representations and warranties, an originator could easily arbitrage rating agency models, exploiting the weak historical relationship between aggressive underwriting and losses in the data used to calibrate required credit enhancement.

The inability of the rating agencies to recognize this arbitrage by originators and respond appropriately meant that credit ratings were assigned to subprime mortgage-backed securities with significant error. The friction between investors and the rating agencies is the final nail in the coffin (friction #7). Even though the rating agencies publicly disclosed their rating criteria for subprime, investors lacked the ability to evaluate the efficacy of these models.

While we have identified seven frictions in the mortgage securitization process, there are mechanisms in place to mitigate or even resolve each of these frictions, including for example anti-predatory lending laws and regulations. As we have seen, some of these mechanisms have failed to deliver as promised. Is it hard to fix this process? We believe not, and we think the solution might start with investment mandates. Investors should realize the incentives of asset managers to push for yield. Investments in structured products should be compared to a benchmark index of investments in the same asset class. When investors or asset managers are

---

[7] The fact that the market demands a higher yield for similarly rated structured products than for straight corporate bonds ought to provide a clue to the potential of higher risk.

forced to conduct their own due diligence in order to outperform the index, the incentives of the arranger and originator are restored. Moreover, investors should demand that either the arranger or originator – or even both – retain the first-loss or equity tranche of every securitization, and disclose all hedges of this position. At the end of the production chain, originators need to be adequately capitalized so that their representations and warranties have value. Finally, the rating agencies could evaluate originators with the same rigor that they evaluate servicers, including perhaps the designation of originator ratings.

It is not clear to us that any of these solutions require additional regulation, and note that the market is already taking steps in the right direction. For example, the credit rating agencies have already responded with greater transparency and have announced significant changes in the rating process. In addition, the demand for structured credit products generally and subprime mortgage securitizations in particular has declined significantly as investors have started to re-assess their own views of the risk in these products. Along these lines, it may be advisable for policymakers to give the market a chance to self-correct.

3. An Overview of Subprime Mortgage Credit

In this section, we shed some light on the subprime mortgagor, work through the details of a typical subprime mortgage loan, and review the historical performance of subprime mortgage credit.

The Motivating Example

In order to keep the discussion from becoming too abstract, we find it useful to frame many of these issues in the context of a real-life example which will be used throughout the paper. In particular, we focus on a securitization of 3,949 subprime loans with aggregate principal balance of $881 million originated by New Century Financial in the second quarter of 2006.[8]

Our view is that this particular securitization is interesting because illustrates how typical subprime loans from what proved to be the worst-performing vintage came to be originated, structured, and ultimately sold to investors. In each of the years 2004 to 2006, New Century Financial was the second largest subprime lender, originating $51.6 billion in mortgage loans during 2006 (Inside Mortgage Finance, 2007). Volume grew at a compound annual growth rate of 59% between 2000 and 2004. The backbone of this growth was an automated internet-based loan submission and pre-approval system called *FastQual*. The performance of New Century loans closely tracked that of the industry through the 2005 vintage (Moody's, 2005b).

However, the company struggled with early payment defaults in early 2007, failed to meet a call for more collateral on its warehouse lines of credit on 2 March 2007 and ultimately filed for bankruptcy protection on 2 April 2007. The junior tranches of this

---

[8] The details of this transaction are taken from the prospectus filed with the SEC and with monthly remittance reports filed with the Trustee. The former is available on-line using the Edgar database at http://www.sec.gov/edgar/searchedgar/companysearch.html with the company name GSAMP Trust 2006-NC2 while the latter is available with free registration from http://www.absnet.net/.

securitization were part of the historical downgrade action by the rating agencies during the week of 9 July 2007 that affected almost half of first-lien home equity ABS deals issued in 2006.

As illustrated in Figure 2, these loans were initially purchased by a subsidiary of Goldman Sachs, who in turn sold the loans to a bankruptcy-remote special purpose vehicle named GSAMP TRUST 2006-NC2. The trust funded the purchase of these loans through the issue of asset-backed securities, which required the filing of a prospectus with the SEC detailing the transaction. New Century serviced the loans initially, but upon creation of the trust, this business was transferred to Ocwen Loan Servicing, LLC in August 2006, who receives a fee of 50 basis points (or $4.4 million) per year on a monthly basis. The master servicer and securities administrator is Wells Fargo, who receives a fee of 1 basis point (or $88 1K) per year on a monthly basis. The prospectus includes a list of 26 reps and warranties made by the originator. Some of the items include: the absence of any delinquencies or defaults in the pool; compliance of the mortgages with federal, state, and local laws; the presence of title and hazard insurance; disclosure of fees and points to the borrower; statement that the lender did not encourage or require the borrower to select a higher cost loan product intended for less creditworthy borrowers when they qualified for a more standard loan product.

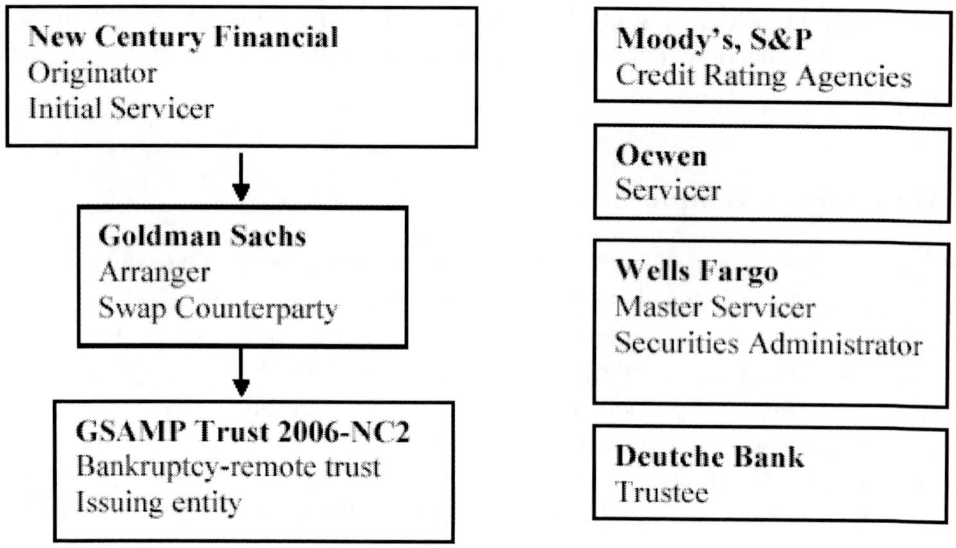

Figure 2. Key Institutions Surrounding GSAMP Trust 2006-NC2.

3.1. Who Is the Subprime Mortgagor?

The 2001 *Interagency Expanded Guidance for Subprime Lending Programs* defines the subprime borrower as one who generally displays a range of credit risk characteristics, including one or more of the following:

- Two or more 30-day delinquencies in the last 12 months, or one or more 60-day delinquencies in the last 24 months;

- Judgment, foreclosure, repossession, or charge-off in the prior 24 months;
- Bankruptcy in the last 5 years;
- Relatively high default probability as evidenced by, for example, a credit bureau risk score (FICO) of 660 or below (depending on the product/collateral), or other bureau or proprietary scores with an equivalent default probability likelihood; and/or,
- Debt service-to-income ratio of 50 percent or greater; or, otherwise limited ability to cover family living expenses after deducting total debt-service requirements from monthly income.

The Motivating Example

The pool of mortgage loans used as collateral in the New Century securitization can be summarized as follows:

- 98.7% of the mortgage loans are first-lien. The rest are second-lien home equity loans.
- 43.3% are purchase loans, meaning that the mortgagor's stated purpose for the loan was to purchase a property. The remaining loans' stated purpose are cash-out refinance of existing mortgage loans.
- 90.7% of the mortgagors claim to occupy the property as their primary residence. The remaining mortgagors claim to be investors or purchasing second homes.
- 73.4% of the mortgaged properties are single-family homes. The remaining properties are split between multi-family dwellings or condos.
- 38.0% and 10.5% are secured by residences in California and Florida, respectively, the two dominant states in this securitization.
- The average borrower in the pool has a FICO score of 626. Note that 31.4% have a FICO score below 600, 5 1.9% between 600 and 660, and 16.7% above 660.
- The combined loan-to value ratio is sum of the original principal balance of all loans secured by the property to its appraised value. The average mortgage loan in the pool has a CLTV of 80.34%. However, 62.1% have a CLTV of 80% or lower, 28.6% between 80% and 90%, and 9.3% between 90% and 100%.
- The ratio of total debt service of the borrower (including the mortgage, property taxes and insurance, and other monthly debt payments) to gross income (income before taxes) is 41.78%.

It is worth pausing here to make a few observations. First, the stated purpose of the majority of these loans is not to purchase a home, but rather to refinance an existing mortgage loan. Second, 90 percent of the borrowers in this portfolio have at least 10 percent equity in their homes. Third, while it might be surprising to find borrowers with a FICO score above 660 in the pool, these loans are much more aggressively underwritten than the loans to the lower FICO-score borrowers. In particular, while not reported in the figures above, loans to borrowers with high FICO scores tend to be much larger, have a higher CLTV, are less likely to use full-documentation, and are less likely to be owner-occupied. The combination of good credit with aggressive underwriting suggests that many of these borrowers could be investors looking to take advantage of rapid home price appreciation in order to re-sell houses for profit. Finally, while the average loan size in the pool is $223,221, much of the aggregate principal balance of the pool is made up of large loans. In particular, 24% of the total number of loans are in excess of $300,000 and make up about 45% of the principal balance of the pool.

Industry Trends

Table 5 documents average borrower characteristics for loans contained in Alt-A and Subprime MBS pools in panel (a) and (b), respectively, broken out by year of origination. The most dramatic difference between the two panels is the credit score, as the average Alt-A borrower has a FICO score that is 85 points higher than the average Subprime borrower in 2006 (703 versus 623). Subprime borrowers typically have a higher CLTV, but are more likely to document income and are less likely to purchase a home. Alt-A borrowers are more likely to be investors and are more likely to have silent 2nd liens on the property. Together, these summary statistics suggest that the example securitization discussed seems to be representative of the industry, at least with respect to stated borrower characteristics.

The industry data is also useful to better understand trends in the subprime market that one would not observe by focusing on one deal from 2006. In particular, the CLTV of a subprime loan has been increasing since 1999, as has the fraction of loans with silent second liens. A silent second is a second mortgage that was not disclosed to the first mortgage lender at the time of origination. Moreover, the table illustrates that borrowers have become less likely to document their income over time, and that the fraction of borrowers using the loan to purchase a property has increased significantly since the start of the decade. Together, these data suggest that the average subprime borrower has become significantly more risky in the last two years.

Table 5. Underwriting Characteristics of Loans in MBS Pools

	CLTV	Full Doc	Purchase	Investor	No Prepayment Penalty	FICO	Silent 2nd lien
A. Alt-A Loans							
1999	77.5	38.4	51.8	18.6	79.4	696	0.1
2000	80.2	35.4	68.0	13.8	79.0	697	0.2
2001	77.7	34.8	50.4	8.2	78.8	703	1.4
2002	76.5	36.0	47.4	12.5	70.1	708	2.4
2003	74.9	33.0	39.4	18.5	71.2	711	12.4
2004	79.5	32.4	53.9	17.0	64.8	708	28.6
2005	79.0	27.4	49.4	14.8	56.9	713	32.4
2006	80.6	16.4	45.7	12.9	47.9	708	38.9
B. Subprime Loans							
1999	78.8	68.7	30.1	5.3	28.7	605	0.5
2000	79.5	73.4	36.2	5.5	25.4	596	1.3
2001	80.3	71.5	31.3	5.3	21.0	605	2.8
2002	80.7	65.9	29.9	5.4	20.3	614	2.9
2003	82.4	63.9	30.2	5.6	23.2	624	7.3
2004	83.9	62.2	35.7	5.6	24.6	624	15.8
2005	85.3	58.3	40.5	5.5	26.8	627	24.6
2006	85.5	57.7	42.1	5.6	28.9	623	27.5

All entries are in percentage points except FICO.
Source: LoanPerformance (2007).

3.2. What Is a Subprime Loan?

The Motivating Example

Table 6 documents that only 8.98% of the loans by dollar-value in the New Century pool are traditional 30-year fixed-rate mortgages (FRMs). The pool also includes a small fraction – 2.81% -- of fixed-rate mortgages which amortize over 40 years, but mature in 30 years, and consequently have a balloon payment after 30 years. Note that 88.2% of the mortgage loans by dollar value are adjustable-rate loans (ARMs), and that each of these loans is a variation on the 2/28 and 3/27 hybrid ARM. These loans are known as hybrids because they have both fixed- and adjustable-rate features to them. In particular, the initial monthly payment is based on a "teaser" interest rate that is fixed for the first two (for the 2/28) or three (for the 3/27) years, and is lower than what a borrower would pay for a 30-year fixed rate mortgage (FRM). The table documents that the average initial interest rate for a vanilla 2/28 loan in the first row is 8.64%. However, after this initial period, the monthly payment is based on a higher interest rate, equal to the value of an interest rate index (i.e. 6-month LIBOR) measured at the time of adjustment, plus a margin that is fixed for the life of the loan. Focusing again on the first 2/28, the margin is 6.22% and LIBOR at the time of origination is 5.3 1%. This interest rate is updated every six months for the life of the loan, and is subject to limits called adjustment caps on the amount that it can increase: the cap on the first adjustment is called the initial cap; the cap on each subsequent adjustment is called the period cap; the cap on the interest rate over the life of the loan is called the lifetime cap; and the floor on the interest rate is called the floor. In our example of a simple 2/28 ARM, these caps are equal to 1.49%, 1.50%, 15.62%, and 8.62% for the average loan. More than half of the dollar value of the loans in this pool are a 2/28 ARM with a 40-year amortization schedule in order to calculate monthly payments. A substantial fraction are a 2/28 ARM with a five-year interest-only option. This loan permits the borrower to only pay interest for the first sixty months of the loan, but then must make payments in order to repay the loan in the final 25 years. While not noted in the table, the prospectus indicates that none of the mortgage loans carry mortgage insurance. Moreover, approximately 72.5% of the loans include prepayment penalties which expire after one to three years.

These ARMs are rather complex financial instruments with payout features often found in interest rate derivatives. In contrast to a FRM, the mortgagor retains most of the interest rate risk, subject to a collar (a floor and a cap). Note that most mortgagors are not in a position to easily hedge away this interest rate risk.

Table 7 illustrates the monthly payment across loan type, using the average terms for each loan type, a principal balance of $225,000, and making the assumption that six-month LIBOR remains constant. The payment for the 30-year mortgage amortized over 40 years is lower due to the longer amortization period and a lower average interest rate. The latter loan is more risky from a lender's point of view because the borrower's equity builds more slowly and the borrower will likely have to refinance after 30 years or have cash equal to 84 monthly payments. The monthly payment for the 2/28 ARM is documented in the third column. When the index interest rate remains constant, the payment increases by 14% in the month 25 at initial adjustment and by another 12% in month 31. When amortized over 40 years, as in the fourth column, the payment shock is more severe as the loan balance is much higher in every month compared to the 30-year amortization. In particular, the payment increases by 18% in month 25 and another 14% in month 31.

However, when the 2/28 is combined with an interest- only option, the payment shock is even more severe since the principal balance does not decline at all over time when the borrower makes the minimum monthly payment. In this case, the payment increases by 19% in month 25, another 26% in month 31, and another 11% in month 61 when the interest-only option expires. The 3/27 ARMs exhibit similar patterns in monthly payments over time.

In order to better understand the severity of payment shock, Table 8 illustrates the impact of changes in the mortgage payment on the ratio of debt (service) to gross income. The table is constructed under the assumption that the borrower has no other debt than mortgage debt, and imposes an initial debt-to-income ratio of 40 percent, similar to that found in the mortgage pool. The third column documents that the debt-to-income ratio increases in month 31 to 50.45% for the simple 2/28 ARM, to 52.86% for the 2/28 ARM amortized over 40 years, and to 58.14% for the 2/28 ARM with an interest-only option. Without significant income growth over the first two years of the loan, it seems reasonable to expect that borrowers will struggle to make these higher payments. It begs the question why such a loan was made in the first place.

The likely answer is that lenders expected that the borrower would be able to refinance before payment reset.

Industry Trends

Table 9 documents the average terms of loans securitized in the Alt-A and subprime markets over the last eight years. Subprime loans are more likely than Alt-A loans to be ARMs, and are largely dominated by the 2/28 and 3/27 hybrid ARMs. Subprime loans are less likely to have an interest-only option or permit negative amortization (i.e. option ARM), but are more likely to have a 40-year amortization instead of a 30-year amortization. The table also documents that hybrid ARMs have become more important over time for both Alt-A and subprime borrowers, as have interest only options and the 40-year amortization term. In the end, the mortgage pool referenced in our motivating example does not appear to be very different from the average loan securitized by the industry in 2006.

The immediate concern from the industry data is obviously the widespread dependency of subprime borrowers on what amounts to short-term funding, leaving them vulnerable to adverse shifts in the supply of subprime credit. Figure 3 documents the timing ARM resets over the next six years, as of January 2007. Given the dominance of the 2/28 ARM, it should not be surprising that the majority of loans that will be resetting over the next two years are subprime loans. The main source of uncertainty about the future performance of these loans is driven by uncertainty over the ability of these borrowers to refinance. This uncertainty has been highlighted by rapidly changing attitudes of investors towards subprime loans (see the box below on the ABX for the details). Regulators have released guidance on subprime loans that forces a lender to qualify a borrower on a fully-indexed and -amortizing interest rate and discourages the use of state-income loans. Moreover, recent changes in structuring criteria by the rating agencies have prompted several subprime lenders to stop originating hybrid ARMs. Finally, activity in the housing market has slowed down considerably, as the median price of existing homes has declined for the first time in decades while historical levels of inventory and vacant homes.

Table 6. Loan Type in the GSAMP 2006-NC2 Mortgage Loan Pool

Loan Type	Gross Rate	Margin	Initial Cap	Periodic Cap	Lifetime Cap	Floor	IO Period	Notional ($m)	% Total
FIXED	8.18	X	X	X	X	X	X	$ 79.12	8.98 %
FIXED 40-year Balloon	7.58	X	X	X	X	X	X	$ 24.80	2.81%
2/28 ARM	8.64	6.22	1.49	1.49	15.62	8.62	X	$ 221.09	25.08%
2/28 ARM 40-year Balloon	8.31	6.24	1.5	1.5	15.31	8.31	X	$ 452.15	51.29%
2/28 ARM IO	7.75	6.13	1.5	1.5	14.75	7.75	60	$ 101.18	11.48%
3/27 ARM	7.48	6.06	1.5	1.5	14.48	7.48	X	$ 1.71	0.19%
3/27 ARM 40-year Balloon	7.61	6.11	1.5	1.5	14.61	7.61	X	$ 1.46	0.17%
Total	8.29	X	X	X	X	X		$ 881.50	100.00%

Note: LIBOR is 5.31% at the time of issue. Notional amount is reported in millions of dollars.
Source: SEC filings, Author's calculations.

Table 7. Monthly Payment Across Mortgage Loan Type

Monthly Payment Across Mortgage Loan Type							
Month	30-year fixed	30-year fixed	2/28 ARM	2/28 ARM	2/28 ARM IO	3/27 ARM	3/27 ARM
1	$1,633.87	$ 1,546.04	$ 1,701.37	$ 1,566.17	$ 1,404.01	$ 1,533.12	$ 1,437.35
24	1.00	1.00	1.00	1.00	1.00	1.00	1.00
25	1.00	1.00	1.14	1.18	1.19	1.00	1.00
30	1.00	1.00	1.14	1.18	1.19	1.00	1.00
31	1.00	1.00	1.26	1.32	1.45	1.00	1.00
36	1.00	1.00	1.26	1.32	1.45	1.00	1.00
37	1.00	1.00	1.26	1.32	1.45	1.13	1.18
42	1.00	1.00	1.26	1.32	1.45	1.13	1.18
43	1.00	1.00	1.26	1.32	1.45	1.27	1.34
48	1.00	1.00	1.26	1.32	1.45	1.27	1.34
49	1.00	1.00	1.26	1.32	1.45	1.27	1.43
60	1.00	1.00	1.26	1.32	1.45	1.27	1.43
61	1.00	1.00	1.26	1.32	1.56	1.27	1.43
359	1.00	1.00	1.26	1.32	1.56	1.27	1.43
360	1.00	83.81	1.26	100.72	1.56	1.27	105.60
Amortization	30 years	40 years	30 years	40 years	30 years	30 years	40 years

Note: The first line documents the average initial monthly payment for each loan type. The subsequent rows document the ratio of the future to the initial monthly payment under an assumption that LIBOR remains at 5.3 1% through the life of the loan.
Source: SEC filing, Author's Calculations.

Table 8. Ratio of Debt to Income Across Mortgage Loan Type

Ratio of Debt to Income Across Mortgage Loan Type							
Month	30-year fixed	30-year fixed	2/28 ARM	2/28 ARM	2/28 ARM IO	3/27 ARM	3/27 ARM
1	40.00%	40.00%	40.00%	40.00%	40.00%	40.00%	40.00%
24	40.00%	40.00%	40.00%	40.00%	40.00%	40.00%	40.00%
25	40.00%	40.00%	45.46%	47.28%	47.44%	40.00%	40.00%
30	40.00%	40.00%	45.46%	47.28%	47.44%	40.00%	40.00%
31	40.00%	40.00%	50.35%	52.86%	58.14%	40.00%	40.00%
36	40.00%	40.00%	50.35%	52.86%	58.14%	40.00%	40.00%
37	40.00%	40.00%	50.45%	52.86%	58.14%	45.36%	47.04%
42	40.00%	40.00%	50.45%	52.86%	58.14%	45.36%	47.04%
43	40.00%	40.00%	50.45%	52.86%	58.14%	50.83%	53.53%
48	40.00%	40.00%	50.45%	52.86%	58.14%	50.83%	53.53%
49	40.00%	40.00%	50.45%	52.86%	58.14%	50.83%	57.08%
60	40.00%	40.00%	50.45%	52.86%	58.14%	50.83%	57.08%
61	40.00%	40.00%	50.45%	52.86%	62.29%	50.83%	57.08%
359	40.00%	40.00%	50.45%	52.86%	62.29%	50.83%	57.08%
360	40.00%	3352.60	50.45%	4028.64%	62.29%	50.83%	4223.92%
Amortization	30 years	40 years	30 years	40 years	30 years	30 years	40 years

Note: The table documents the path of the debt-to-income ratio over the life of each loan type under an assumption that LIBOR remains at 5.31% through the life of the loan. The calculation assumes that all debt is mortgage debt.

Source: SEC filing, Author's Calculations.

Table 9. Terms of Mortgage Loans in MBS Pools

Year	ARM	2/28 ARM	3/27 ARM	5/25 ARM	IO	Option ARM	40-year
Alt-A							
1999	6.3	2.6	0.9	1.9	0.8	0.0	0.0
2000	12.8	4.7	1.7	3.4	1.1	1.1	0.1
2001	20.0	4.9	2.3	8.8	3.9	0.0	0.0
2002	28.0	3.7	2.8	10.9	7.7	0.4	0.0
2003	34.0	4.8	5.3	16.7	19.6	1.7	0.1
2004	68.7	8.9	16.7	24.0	46.4	10.3	0.5
2005	69.7	4.0	6.3	15.6	38.6	34.2	2.7
2006	69.8	1.8	1.7	15.8	35.6	42.3	11.0
Subprime							
1999	51.0	31.0	16.2	0.6	0.1	0.0	0.0
2000	64.5	45.5	16.6	0.6	0.0	0.1	0.0
2001	66.0	52.1	12.4	0.8	0.0	0.0	0.0
2002	71.6	57.4	12.1	1.4	0.7	0.0	0.0
2003	67.2	54.5	10.6	1.5	3.6	0.0	0.0
2004	78.0	61.3	14.7	1.6	15.3	0.0	0.0
2005	83.5	66.7	13.3	1.5	27.7	0.0	5.0
2006	81.7	68.7	10.0	2.5	18.1	0.0	26.9

Source: LoanPerformance (2007).

Exhibit 42: **Adjustable Rate Mortgage Reset Schedule**

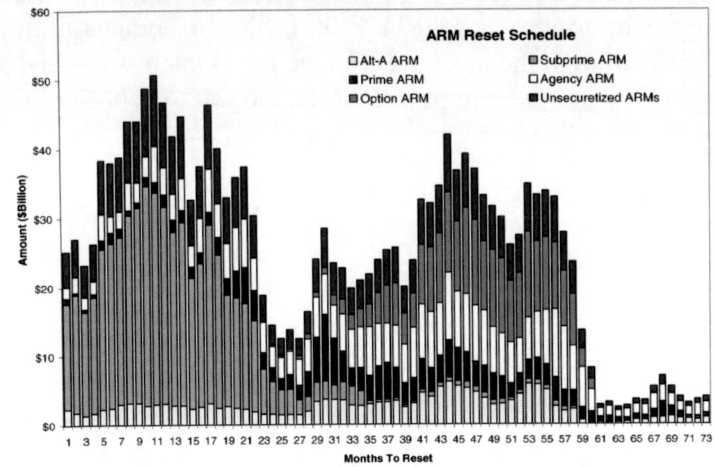

Note: Data as of January 2007.

Source: Credit Suisse Fixed Income U.S. Mortgage Strategy.

Figure 3. ARM reset schedule.

The Impact of Payment Reset on Foreclosure

The most important issue facing the sub-prime credit market is obviously the impact of payment reset on the ability of borrowers to continue making monthly payments. Given that over three-fourths of the subprime-loans underwritten over 2004 to 2006 were hybrid ARMS, it is not difficult to understand the magnitude of the problem. But what is the likely outcome? The answer depends on a number of factors, including but not limited to: the amount of equity that these borrowers have in their homes at the time of reset (which itself is a function of CLTV at origination and the severity of the decline in home prices), the severity of payment reset (which depends not only on the loan but also on the six-month LIBOR interest rate), and of course conditions in the labor market.

A recent study by Cagan (2007) of mortgage payment reset tries to estimate what fraction of resetting loans will end up in foreclosure. The author presents evidence suggesting that in an environment of zero home price appreciation and full employment, 12 percent of subprime loans will default due to reset. We review the key elements of this analysis.[9]

Table 10 documents the amount of loans issued over 2004-2006 that were still outstanding as of March 2007, broken out by initial interest rate group and payment reset size group. The data includes all outstanding securitized mortgage loans with a future payment reset date. Each row corresponds to a different initial interest rate bucket: RED corresponding to loans with initial rates between 1 and 3.9 percent; YELLOW corresponding to an initial interest rate of 4.0 to 6.49 percent; and ORANGE with an initial interest rate of 6.5 to 12 percent. Subprime loans can be easily identified by the high original interest rate in the third row (ORANGE). Each column corresponds to a different payment reset size group under an assumption of no change in the 6-month LIBOR interest rate: A to payments which increase between 0 and 25 percent; B to payments which increase between 26 and 50 percent; C to payments which increase between 51 and 99 percent; and D to payments which increase by at least 100 percent. Note that almost all of subprime payment reset is in either the 0-25% or the 26-50% groups, with a little more than $300 billion in loans sitting in each group. There is a clear correlation in the table between the initial interest rate and the average size of the payment reset. The most severe payment resets appear to be the problem of Alt-A and Jumbo borrowers.

Table 10. Distribution of Loans by First Reset Size

	Reset size ($ billions)				
Initial interest rate	A (0-25%)	B (26-50%)	C (51-99%)	D (100%+)	Total
RED (1.0-3.9%)	$0	$0	$61	$460	$521
YELLOW (4.0-6.49%)	$545	$477	$102	$0	$1,124
ORANGE (6.5-12%)	$366	$316	$49	$0	$631
Total	$811	$793	$212	$460	$2,276

Source: Cagan (2007); data refer to all ARMs originated 2004-2006.

Cagan helpfully provides estimates of the distribution of updated equity across the initial interest rate group in Table 11. The author uses an automated appraisal system in order to estimate the value of each property, and then constructs an updated value of the equity for each borrower. The table reports the cumulative distribution of equity for each initial interest rate bucket reported in the table above. Note that 22.4 percent of subprime borrowers (ORANGE) are estimated to have no equity in their homes, about half have no more than 10 percent, and two-thirds have less than 20 percent. Disturbingly, the table suggests that a national price decline of 10 percent could put half of all subprime borrowers underwater.

Table 11 Cumulative distribution of equity by initial interest rate

	Initial Rate Group		
Equity	Red	Yellow	Orange
<-20%	2.2%	1.5%	2.7%
<-15%	3.2	2.0	4.0
<-10%	4.9	2.9	6.2
<-5%	8.2	4.8	11.6
<0%	14.1	8.6	22.4
<5%	23.9	15.5	36.0
<10%	36.7	24.5	47.7
<15%	49.7	34.7	57.9
<20%	62.4	45.4	67.3
<25%	73.3	56.8	76.8
<30%	81.3	67.5	84.6

Source: Cagan (2007); data refer to all ARMs originated 2004-2006.

In order to transform this raw data into estimates of foreclosure due to reset, the author makes assumptions in Table 12 about the amount of equity or the size of payment

[9] The author is a PhD economist at First American, a credit union which owns LoanPerformance.

reset and the probability of foreclosures.[10] A borrower will only default given difficulty with payment reset and difficulty in refinancing. For example, 70% of borrowers with equity between -5% and 5% are assumed to face difficulty refinancing, while only 30% of borrowers with equity between 15% and 25% have difficulty. At the same time, the author assumes that only 10 percent of borrowers with payment reset 0-25% will face difficulty with the higher payment, while 70 percent with a payment reset of 51-99% will be unable to make the higher payment.

Table 12. Assumed probability of default by reset size and equity risk group

		Reset Size Group			
		A	B	C	D
		25% or less	26-50%	51-99%	100% or more
Equity	Pr(difficulty)	10%	40%	70%	100%
>25%	10%	1%	4%	7%	10%
15-25%	30%	3	12	21	30
5-15%	50%	5	20	35	50
-5-5%	70%	7	28	49	70
<-5%	90%	9	36	63	90

Source: Cagan (2007).

Estimates of foreclosure due to reset in an environment of constant home prices are documented in Table 13. The author estimates that foreclosures due to reset will be 3.5% (= 106.2/3033.1) for the 0-25% reset group and 13.5% (= 446.4/3282.8) for the 26-50% group.

Given the greater equity risk of subprime mortgages documented in Table 11, a back-of-the-envelope calculation suggests that these numbers would be 4.5% and 18.6% for subprime mortgages.

Table 13. Summary of foreclosure estimates under 0% home price appreciation

Reset Size	Reset Risk	Equity Risk	Pr(loss)	Loans (t)	Foreclosures (t)
A (25% or less)	10%	35%	3.5%	3033.1	106.2
B (26-50%)	40%	34%	13.6%	3282.8	446.4
C (51-99%)	70%	31%	21.7%	839.2	182.1
D (100% or more)	100%	36%	36.0%	1,216.7	438.0
			Total	8,371.9	1,172.7
			Percent foreclosures		14.0%

Source: Cagan (2007).

The author also investigates a scenario where home prices fall by 10 percent in Table 14, and estimates foreclosures due to reset for the two payment reset size groups to be 5.5% and 21.6%, respectively. Note that the revised July 2007 economic forecast for Moody's called for this exact scenario by the end of 2008.

---

[10] The author offers no rationale for these figures, but the analysis here should be transparent enough that one

Table 14. Summary of foreclosure estimates under 10% national home price decline

Reset Size	Reset Risk	Equity Risk	Pr(loss)	Loans (t)	Foreclosures (t)
A (25% or less)	10%	55%	5.5%	3033.1	166.8
B (26-50%)	40%	54%	21.6%	3282.8	709.1
C (51-99%)	70%	51%	35.7%	839.2	299.6
D (100% or more)	100%	56%	56.0%	1,216.7	681.3
			Total	8,371.9	1856.8
			Percent foreclosures		22.2%

Source: Cagan (2007).

Market conditions have deteriorated dramatically since this study was published, as the origination of both sub-prime and Alt-A mortgage loans has all but disappeared, making the author's assumptions about equity risk even in the stress scenario for home prices look optimistic. Moreover, the author's original assumption that reset risk is constant across the credit spectrum is likely to be optimistic. In particular, sub-prime borrowers are less likely to be able to handle payment reset, resulting with estimates of foreclosures that are quite modest relative to those in the research reports of investment banks.

3.3. How Have Subprime Loans Performed?

Motivating Example

Table 15 documents how the GSAMP 2006-NC2 deal has performed through August 2007. The first three columns report mortgage loans still in the pool that are 30-days, 60-days, and 90-days past due. The fourth column reports loans that are in foreclosure. The fifth column reports loans where the bank has title to the property. The sixth column reports actual cumulative losses. The last column documents the fraction of original loans that remain in the pool.

Table 15. Performance of GSAMP 2006-NC2

Date	30 day	60 day	90 day	Foreclosure	Bankruptcy	REO	Cum Loss	CPR	Principal
Aug-07	6.32%	3.39%	1.70%	7.60%	0.90%	3.66%	0.25%	20.35%	72.48%
Jul-07	5.77%	3.47%	1.31%	7.31%	1.03%	3.15%	0.20%	20.77%	73.90%
Jun-07	5.61%	3.09%	1.43%	6.92%	0.70%	2.63%	0.10%	25.26%	75.38%
May-	4.91%	3.34%	1.38%	6.48%	0.78%	1.83%	0.08%	19.18%	77.26%
Apr-07	4.68%	3.38%	1.16%	6.77%	0.50%	0.72%	0.04%	15.71%	78.68%
Mar-07	4.74%	2.77%	1.12%	6.76%	0.38%	0.21%	0.02%	19.03%	79.84%
Feb-07	4.79%	2.59%	0.96%	6.00%	0.37%	0.03%	0.00%	23.08%	81.29%
Jan-07	4.58%	2.85%	0.88%	5.04%	0.36%	0.00%	0.00%	28.54%	83.12%

Source: ABSNet.

What do these numbers imply for the expected performance of the mortgage pool. UBS (June 2007) outlines an approach to use actual deal performance in order to estimate lifetime losses. Using historical data on loans in an environment of low home

could use different inputs to construct their own alternative scenarios.

price appreciation (less than 5 percent), the author documents that approximately 70 percent of loans in the 60-day, 90-day, and bankruptcy categories eventually default, defined as the event of foreclosure. Interestingly, only about 60-70 percent of loans in bankruptcy are actually delinquent. Moreover, these transitions into foreclosure take about 4 months.

The amount of default "in the pipeline" for remaining loans in the next four months is constructed as follows:

Pipeline default = 0.7 × (60-day + 90-day + bankruptcy) + (foreclosure + real-estate owned)

For GSAMP 2006-NC2, the pipeline default from the August report is 15.45%, suggesting that this fraction of loans remaining in the pool are likely to default in the next four months.

Total default is constructed by combining this measure with the fraction of loans remaining in the pool, actual cumulative losses to date, and an assumption about the severity of loss. In the UBS study, the author assumes a loss given default of 37%.

Total default = pipeline default × (fraction of loans remaining) + (Cum loss)/(loss severity)

For the GSAMP 2006-NC2, this number is 11.88%, which suggests that this fraction of the original pool will have defaulted in four months.

Finally, the paper uses historical data in order to estimate the fraction of total defaults over the life of deal. In particular, a mapping is constructed between weighted-average loan age and the fraction of lifetime default that a deal typically realizes. For example, the typical deal realizes 33% of its defaults by month 13, 59% by month 23, 75% by month 35, and 100% by month 60.

Projected cumulative default = Total default/Default timing factor

The New Century pool was originated in May 2006, implying that the average loan is about 16 months old at the end of August 2007. The default timing factor for 20 months, which must be used since defaults were predicted through four months in the future, is 51.2%, suggesting that projected cumulative default on this mortgage pool is 23.19%. Using a loss severity of 37% results in expected lifetime loss on this mortgage pool of 8.58%.

There are several potential weaknesses of this approach, the foremost being the fact that it is backward-looking and essentially ignores the elephant in the room, payment reset. In particular, in the fact of payment reset, losses are likely to be more back-loaded than the historical curve used above, implying the fraction of lifetime losses which have been observed to date is likely to be too small, resulting in lifetime loss estimates which are too low. In order to address this problem, UBS (23 October 2007) has developed a shut-down model to take into account the inability of borrowers to refinance their way out of payment resets. In that article, the authors estimate the lower prepayment speeds associate with refinancing stress will increase losses by an average of 50 percent. Moreover, the authors also speculate that loss severities will be higher than the 37 percent used above, and incorporate an assumption of 45 percent. Together, these assumptions imply that a more conservative view on losses would be to scale those from the loss projection model above by a factor of two, implying a lifetime loss rate of 17.16% on the example pool.

Industry

UBS (June 2007) applies this methodology to home equity ABS deals that constitute three vintages of the ABX: 06-1, 06-2, and 07-1. In order to understand the jargon, note that deals in 06-1 refer mortgages that were largely originated in the second half of 2005, while deals in 06- 2 refer to mortgages that were largely underwritten in the first half of 2006.

Figure 4 illustrates estimates of the probability distribution of estimated losses as of the June remittance reports across the 20 different deals for each of the three vintages of loans. The mean loss rate of the 06-1 vintage is 5.6%, while the mean of the 06-2 and 07-1 vintages are 9.2% and 11.7%, respectively. From the figure, it is clear that not only the mean but also the variance of the distribution of losses at the deal level has increased considerably over the last year. Moreover, expected lifetime losses from the New Century securitization studied in the example are a little lower than the average deal in the ABX from 06-2.

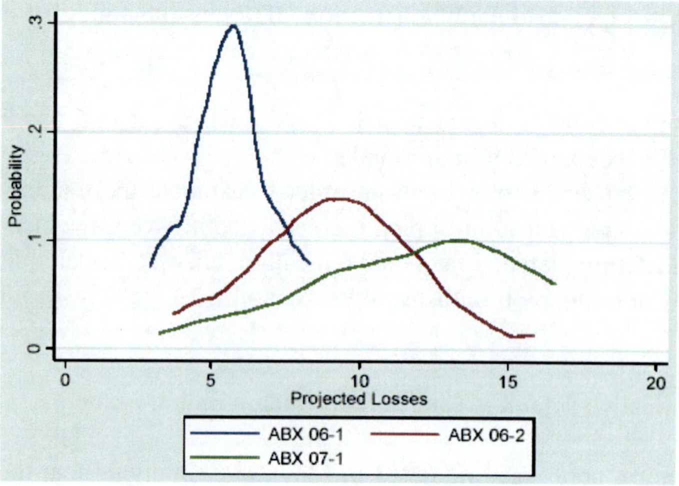

Figure 4. Subprime Projected Losses by Vintage.

3.4. How Are Subprime Loans Valued?

In January 2006, Markit launched the ABX, which is a series of indices that track the price of credit default insurance on a standardized basket of home equity ABS obligations.[11] The ABX actually has five indices, differentiated by credit rating: AAA, AA, A, BBB, and BBB-. Each of these indices is an equally-weighted average of the price of credit insurance at a maturity of 30-years across similarly-rated tranches from 20 different home equity ABS

---

[11] In the jargon, first-lien sub-prime mortgage loans as well as second- lien home equity loans and home equity lines of credit (HELCOs) are all part of what is called the Home Equity ABS sector. First- lien Alt-A and Jumbo loans are part of what is called the Residential Mortgage-backed Securities (RMBS) sector.

deals. For example, the BBB index tracks the average price of credit default insurance on the BBB-rated tranche.

Every six months, a new set of 20 home equity deals is chosen from the largest dealer shelves in the previous half year. In order to ensure proper diversification in the portfolio, the same originator is limited to no more than four deals and the same master servicer is limited to no more than six deals. Each reference obligation must be rated by both Moody's and S&P and have a weighted-average remaining life of 4-6 years.

In a typical transaction, a protection buyer pays the protection seller a fixed coupon at a monthly rate on an amount determined by the buyer. For example, Table 16 documents that the price of protection on the AAA tranche of the most recent vintage (07-2) is a coupon rate of 76 basis points per year. Note the significant increase in coupons on all tranches between 07-1 and 07-2, which reflects a significant change in investor sentiment from January to Jul 2007.

When a credit event occurs, the protection seller makes a payment to the protection buyer in an amount equal to the loss. Credit events include the shortfall of interest or principal (i.e. the servicer fails to forward a payment when it is due) as well as the write-down of the tranche due to losses on underlying mortgage loans. In the event that these losses are later reimbursed, the protection buyer must reimburse the protection seller.

For example, if one tranche of a securitization referenced in the index is written down by an amount of 1%, and the current balance of the tranche is 70% of its original balance, an institution which has sold $10 million in protection must make a payment of $583,333 [= $10m × 70% × (1/20)] to the protection buyer. Moreover, the future protection fee will be based on a principal balance that is 0.20% [= 1% × (1/20)] lower than before the write-down of the tranche.

Changes in investor views about the risk of the mortgage loans over time will affect the price at which investors are willing to buy or sell credit protection. However, the terms of the insurance contract (i.e. coupon, maturity, pool of deals) are fixed. The ABX tracks the amount that one party has to pay the other at the onset of the contract in order for both parties to accept the terms. For example, when investors think the underlying loans have become more risky since the index was created, a protection buyer will have to pay an up-front fee to the protection seller in order to only pay a coupon of 76 basis points per year. On 24 July, the ABX.AAA.07 was at 98.04, suggesting that a protection buyer would have to pay the seller a fee of 1.96% upfront. Using an estimate of 5.19 from UBS of this tranche's estimated duration, it is possible to write the implied spread on the tranche as 114 basis points per year [= 100 × (100 - 98.04)/5.19 + 76].

Figure 5 documents the behavior of the BBB-rated 06-2 vintage of the ABX over the first six and a half months of 2007. Note from Table 16 that the initial coupon on this tranche was 133 basis points. However, the first two months of the year marked a significant adverse change in investor sentiment against the home equity sector. In particular, the BBB-rated index fell from 95 to below 75 by the end of February. Using an estimated duration of 3.3, the implied spread increased from just under 300 basis points to almost 900 basis points. Through the end of May, this index fluctuated between 80 and 85, consistent with an implied spread of about 650 basis points. However, the market responded adversely to a further deterioration in performance following the May remittance report, and at the time of this writing, the index has dropped to about 54, consistent with an implied spread of approximately 1800 basis points.

While it is not clear what exactly triggered the sell-off in the first two months of January, there were some notable events that occurred over this period. There were early concerns about the vintage in the form of early payment defaults resulting in originators being forced to repurchase loans from securitizations. These repurchase requests put pressure on the liquidity of originators. Moreover, warehouse lenders began to ask for more collateral, putting further liquidity pressure on originators.

Table 16. Overview of the ABX Index

Vintage	Credit Rating	Coupon Rate	Index Price	Estimated Duration	Implied Spread
07-2	AAA	76	98.04	5.19	114
07-2	AA	192	95.36	3.85	313
07-2	A	369	78.05	3.47	1002
07-2	BBB	500	54.43	3.31	1877
07-2	BBB-	500	47.31	3.30	2097
07-1	AAA	9	95.05	5.07	107
07-1	AA	15	88.36	3.7	330
07-1	A	64	65.5	3.44	1067
07-1	BBB	224	44.55	3.02	2060
07-1	BBB-	389	41.79	2.75	2506
06-2	AAA	11	96.45	4.68	87
06-2	AA	17	92.79	3.21	242
06-2	A	44	74.45	3.05	882
06-2	BBB	133	53.57	2.77	1809
06-2	BBB-	242	46.75	2.53	2347
06-1	AAA	18	99.04	4.27	40
06-1	AA	32	97.82	2.89	107
06-1	A	54	85.04	2.74	600
06-1	BBB	154	74.79	2.57	1135
06-1	BBB-	267	66.93	2.42	1634

Source: Coupon and Price: Markit (24 July 2007); duration: UBS; Implied spread is author's calculation as follows: implied spread = 100*[100-price]/duration + coupon rate.

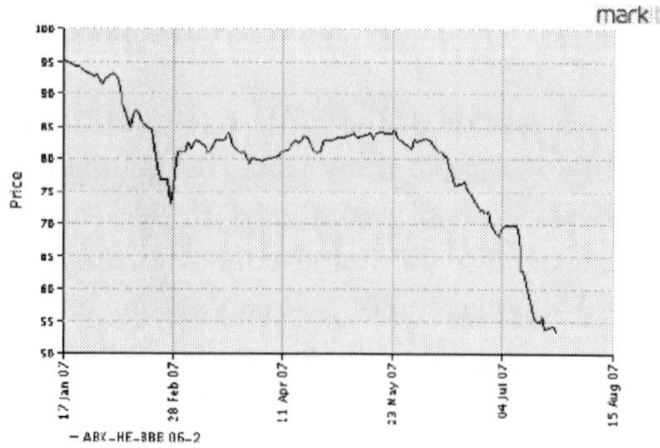

Source: Markit.

Figure 5. ABX.BBB 06-2.

4. Overview of Subprime MBS

The typical subprime trust has the following structural features designed to protect investors from losses on the underlying mortgage loans:

- Subordination
- Excess spread
- Shifting interest
- Performance triggers
- Interest rate swap

We discuss each of these forms of credit enhancement in turn.

4.1. Subordination

The distribution of losses on the mortgage pool is typically tranched into different classes. In particular, losses on the mortgage loan pool are applied first to the most junior class of investors until the principal balance of that class is completely exhausted. At that point, losses are allocated to the most junior class remaining, and so on.

The most junior class of a securitization is referred to as the equity tranche. In the case of subprime mortgage loans, the equity tranche is typically created through over-collateralization (o/c), which means that the principal balance of the mortgage loans exceeds the principal balance of all the debt issued by the trust. This is an important form of credit enhancement that is funded by the arranger in part through the premium it receives on offered securities. O/C is used to reduce the exposure of debt investors to loss on the pool mortgage loans.

A small part of the capital structure of the trust is made up of the mezzanine class of debt securities, which are next in line to absorb losses once the o/c is exhausted. This class of securities typically has several tranches with credit ratings that vary between AA and B. With greater risk comes greater return, as these securities pay the highest interest rates to investors. The lion's share of the capital structure is always funded by the senior class of debt securities, which are last in line to absorb losses. Senior securities are protected not only by o/c, but also by the width of the mezzanine class. In general, the sum of o/c and the width of all tranches junior is referred to as subordination. Senior securities generally have the highest rating, and since they are last in line (to absorb losses), pay the lowest interest rates to investors.

The capital structure of GSAMP 2006-NC1 is illustrated in Table 17. First, note that the o/c is the class X, which represents 1.4% of the principal balance of the mortgages. There are two B classes of securities not offered in the prospectus. The mezzanine class benefits from a total of 3.10% of subordination created by the o/c and the class B securities. However, note that the mezzanine class is split up into 9 different classes, M- 1 to M- 10, which class M-2 being junior to class M-1, etc. For example, the M-8 class tranche, which has an investment grade-rating of BBB, has subordination of 3.9% and pays a coupon of 100 basis points. Investors receive 1/12 of this amount on the distribution date, which is the 25th of each month. The senior class benefits from 20.65% of total subordination, including the width of the mezzanine class (19.25%).

Table 17. Capital structure of GSAMP Trust 2006-NC2

Tranche description				Credit Ratings		Coupon Rate	
Class	Notional	Width	Subordination	S&P	Moody's	(1)	(2)
A-1	$239,618,000	27.18%	72.82%	AAA	Aaa	0.15%	0.30%
A-2A	$214,090,000	24.29%	48.53%	AAA	Aaa	0.07%	0.14%
A-2B	$102,864,000	11.67%	36.86%	AAA	Aaa	0.09%	0.18%
A-2C	$99,900,000	11.33%	25.53%	AAA	Aaa	0.15%	0.30%
A-2D	$42,998,000	4.88%	20.65%	AAA	Aaa	0.24%	0.48%
M-1	$35,700,000	4.05%	16.60%	AA+	Aa1	0.30%	0.45%
M-2	$28,649,000	3.25%	13.35%	AA	Aa2	0.31%	0.47%
M-3	$16,748,000	1.90%	11.45%	AA-	Aa3	0.32%	0.48%
M-4	$14,986,000	1.70%	9.75%	A+	A1	0.35%	0.53%
M-5	$14,545,000	1.65%	8.10%	A	A2	0.37%	0.56%
M-6	$13,663,000	1.55%	6.55%	A-	A3	0.46%	0.69%
M-7	$12,341,000	1.40%	5.15%	BBB+	Baa1	0.90%	1.35%
M-8	$11,019,000	1.25%	3.90%	BBB	Baa2	1.00%	1.50%
M-9	$7,052,000	0.80%	3.10%	BBB-	Baa3	2.05%	3.08%
B-1	$6,170,000	0.70%	2.40%	BB+	Ba1	2.50%	3.75%
B-2	$8,815,000	1.00%	1.40%	BB	Ba2	2.50%	3.75%
X	$12,340,995	1.40%	0.00%	NR	NR	N/A	N/A

Source: Prospectus filed with the SEC of GSAMP 2006-NC2.

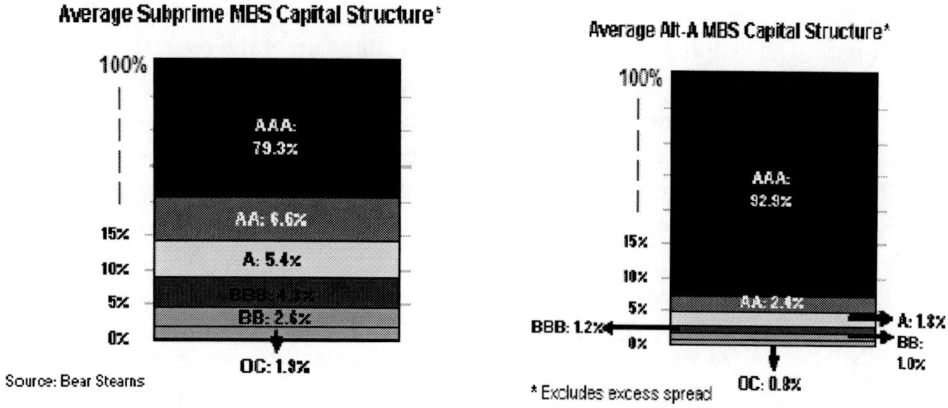

Figure 6. Typical Capital Structure of Subprime and Alt-A MBS.

Note that the New Century structure is broken into two groups of Class A securities, corresponding to two sub-pools of the mortgage loans. In Group I loans, every mortgage has original principal balance lower than the GSE-conforming loan limits. This feature permits the GSEs to purchase these Class A-1 securities. However, in the Group II loans, there is a mixture of mortgage loans with original principal balance above and below the GSE-conforming loan limit.

The table does not mention either the class P or class C certificates, which have no face value and are not entitled to distributions of principal or interest. The class P securities are the sole beneficiary of all future prepayment penalties. Since the arranger will be paid for these rights, it reduces the premium needed on other offered securities for the deal to work. The class C securities contain a clean-up option which permits the trust to call the offered securities should the principal balance of the mortgage pool fall to a sufficiently low level.[12] In our example deal, the offered debt securities are rated by both S&P and Moody's. Note that Table 17 documents that there is no disagreement between the agencies in their opinion of the appropriate credit rating for each tranche.

4.2. Excess Spread

Subordination is not the only protection that senior and mezzanine tranche investors have against loss. As an example, the weighted average coupon from the mortgage loan will typically be larger than fees to the servicers, net payments to the swap counterparty, and the weighted average coupon on debt securities issued by the trust. This difference is referred to as excess spread, which is used to absorb credit losses on the mortgage loans, with the remainder distributed each month to the owners of the Class X securities. Note that this is the first line of defense for investors for credit losses, as the principal of no tranche is reduced by any amount until credit losses reduce excess spread to a negative number. The amount of credit enhancement provided by excess spread depends on both the severity as well as the timing of losses.

In the New Century deal, the weighted average coupon on the tranches at origination is LIBOR plus 23 basis points. With LIBOR at 5.32% at the time of issue, this implies an interest cost of 5.55%. In addition to this cost, the trust pays 51 basis points in servicing fees and initially pays 13 basis points to the swap counterparty (see below). As the weighted average interest rate on collateral at the time of issue is 8.30%, the initial excess spread on this mortgage pool is 2.11%.

More generally, the amount of excess spread varies by deal, but averaged about 2.5 percent during 2006. Dealers estimate that loss rates must reach 9 percent before the average BBB minus bond sustains its first dollar of principal loss, about twice its initial subordination of 4.5 percent in Figure 6 above.

4.3. Shifting Interest

Senior investors are also protected by the practice of shifting interest, which requires that all principal payments to be applied to senior notes over a specified period of time (usually the first 36 months) before being paid to mezzanine bondholders. During this time, known as the "lockout period," mezzanine bondholders receive only the coupon on their notes. As the

---

[12] The figure also omits discussion of certain "residual certificates" that are not entitled to distributions of interest but appear to be related to residual ownership interests in assets of the trust.

principal of senior notes is paid down, the ratio of the senior class to the balance of the entire deal (senior interest) decreases during the first couple years, hence the term "shifting interest". The amount of subordination (alternatively, credit enhancement) for the senior class increases over time because the amount of senior bonds outstanding is smaller relative to the amount outstanding for mezzanine bonds.

4.4. Performance Triggers

After the lockout period, subject to passing performance tests,[13] the o/c is released and principal is applied to mezzanine notes from the bottom of the capital structure up until target levels of subordination are reached (usually twice the initial subordination, as a percent of current balance). In addition to protecting senior note holders, the purpose of the shifting interest mechanism is to adjust subordination across the capital structure after sufficient seasoning. Also, the release of o/c and pay-down of mezzanine notes reduces the average life of these bonds and the interest costs of the securitization.

In our example securitization, o/c is specified to be 1.4% of the principal balance of the mortgage loans as of the cutoff-date, at least until the step-down date. The step-down date is the earlier of the date on which the principal balance of the senior class has been reduced to zero and the later to occur of 36 months or subordination of the senior class being greater than or equal to 41.3% of the aggregate principal balance of remaining mortgage loans. The trigger event is defined as a distribution date when one of the following two conditions is met:

- The rolling three-month average of 60-days or more delinquent (including those in foreclosure, REO properties, or mortgage loans in bankruptcy) divided by the remaining principal balance of the mortgage loans is larger than 3 8.70% of the subordination of the senior class from the previous month; or,
- The amount of cumulative realized losses incurred over the life of the deal as a fraction of the original principal balance of the mortgage loans exceeds the thresholds in Figure 7.

If the trigger event does not occur, the deal is 36 months old, and the subordination of the senior class is larger than 41.3%, then the deal will step-down. In this case, o/c is specified to be 2.8 percent of the principal balance of the mortgage loans in the previous month, subject to a floor equal to 0.5% of the principal balance of the mortgage loans as of the cut-off date. At this time, any excess o/c is released to holders of the Class X tranche. Note that the trigger event only affects whether or not o/c is released.

---

13 There are two types of performance tests in subprime deals, one testing the deal's cumulative losses against a loss schedule, and another test for 60+ day delinquencies.

4.5. Interest Rate Swap

While most of the loans are ARMs, as discussed above, the interest rates will not adjust for two to three years following origination. It follows that the trust is exposed to the risk that interest rates increase, so that the cost of funding increases faster than interest payments received on the mortgages. In order to mitigate this risk, the trust engages in an interest rate swap with a third-party named the swap counterparty. In particular, the third-party has agreed to accept a sequence of fixed payments in return for promising to send a sequence of adjustable-rate payments.

In our example, Goldman Sachs is the Swap counterparty, which has agreed to pay 1-month LIBOR and accept a fixed interest rate of 5.45% on a notional amount described in Figure 8 over a term of 60 months. Note that the notional amount hedged decreases over time, as the trust expects pre-payments of principal on the pool of mortgage loans to reduce the amount of debt securities outstanding.

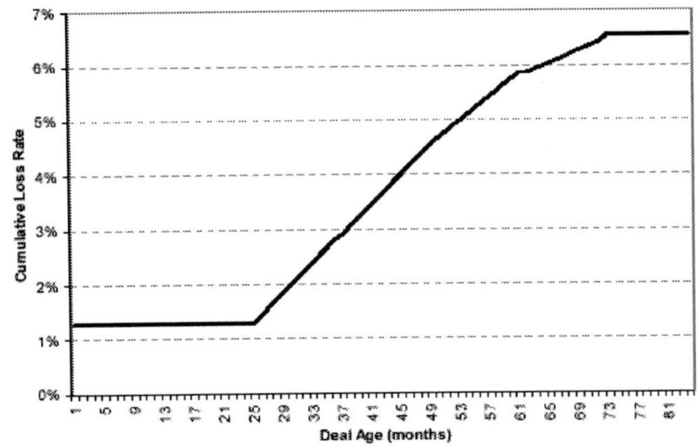

Source: SEC Prospectus for GSAMP Trust 2006-NC2.

Figure 7. Cumulative Loss Thresholds for GSAMP Trust 2006-NC2 Trigger Event.

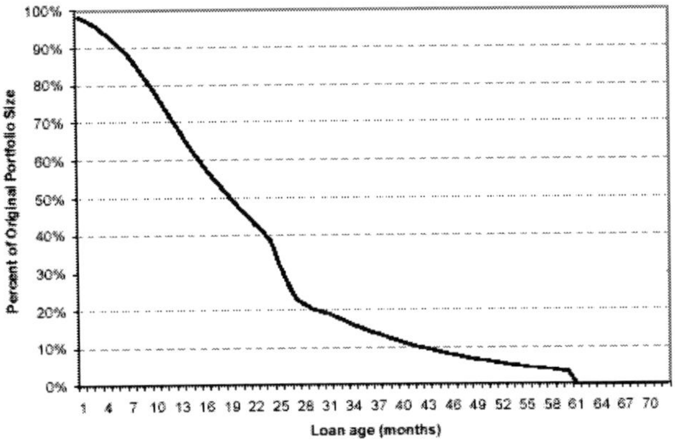

Source: SEC Prospectus for GSAMP Trust 2006-NC2.

Figure 8. Schedule of Interest Swap Notional for GSAMP Trust 2006-NC2.

4.6. Remittance Reports

The trustee makes monthly reports to investors known as remittance reports. In this section, we use data from these reports in order to document the performance of the New Century deal through August 2007.

Table 18 documents cash receipts of the trust. Scheduled principal and interest are collected from a borrower's monthly payment. Unscheduled principal is collected from borrowers who pay more than their required monthly payment, as well as borrowers who either pre-pay or default on their loans. The first three columns of the table report the remittance of scheduled and unscheduled principal as well as interest and pre-payment penalties. The fourth column reports advances of principal and interest made to the trust by the servicer to cover the nonpayment of these items by certain borrowers. The fifth column documents the repurchase of loans by New Century which have been determined to violate the originator's representations and warranties. Note that only one loan has been repurchased with a principal balance of $184,956 as of this writing. Finally, realized losses are reported in the sixth column.

Table 18. GSAMP Trust 2006-NC2 cash receipts

Date	Remittances of principal		Remittances of interest and prepayment penalties	Servicer Advances	Loan Repurchases	Realized losses	Deposits
	Scheduled	Unscheduled					
Jul-06	$329,304	$9,067,656	$5,860,567	$233,039	$0	$0	$15,561,090
Aug-06	$328,927	$11,818,842	$5,772,726	$483,778	$0	$0	$18,492,964
Sep-06	$328,005	$18,872,868	$5,099,068	$1,317,531	$0	$0	$25,783,064
Oct-06	$324,632	$21,123,948	$5,874,901	$1,230,848	$0	$0	$28,870,206
Nov-06	$320,165	$21,913,838	$5,669,909	$1,191,300	$0	$0	$29,496,641
Dec-06	$315,176	$42,949,370	$5,496,644	$1,174,086	$0	$0	$50,229,238
Jan-06	$303,981	$20,805,981	$4,992,533	$1,342,346	$0	$0	$27,717,274
Feb-06	$298,715	$15,842,586	$4,874,742	$1,293,706	$184,956	-$1,162	$22,738,857
Mar-06	$294,018	$12,488,956	$4,845,576	$1,346,264	$0	-$179,720	$18,945,495
Apr-06	$292,054	$9,947,596	$4,781,758	$1,369,108	$0	-$166,703	$16,351,873
May-06	$290,315	$12,190,508	$4,605,848	$1,493,314	$0	-$323,425	$18,459,415
Jun-06	$285,113	$16,320,384	$4,554,347	$1,577,756	$0	-$233,174	$22,742,178
Jul-06	$279,953	$12,764,719	$4,386,611	$1,712,117	$0	-$835,539	$18,504,802
Aug-06	$275,885	$12,226,786	$4,425,290	$1,720,552	$0	-$459,357	$18,380,129

Source: remittance reports through ABSNet.

Table 19 documents the cash expenses of the trust. The net swap payments are reported in the first column. Recall that the trust pays Goldman Sachs a fixed interest rate of 5.45 percent and receives an amount equal to one-month LIBOR, each on the amount referenced by Table 18 above. The servicer fees are based on the outstanding principal balance of the mortgage loans at the end of the last month, with 50 basis points paid to the servicer (Owcen) and just under 1 basis point paid to the master servicer (Wells Fargo). All principal paid by the borrower is advanced to the holders of Class A certificates. Each tranche is paid the stated coupon from Table 18 above based on the amount outstanding at the end of the previous month. Prepayment penalties are paid to the owners of the Class P tranche.

The residual is denoted excess spread, and is paid to the owners of the Class X tranche each month.

The face value of the Class X tranche is $12.3 million. To date, this tranche has been paid excess spread in the amount of $16.1 million. Note that the amount paid to this tranche has decreased over time as credit losses have reduced excess spread. Interestingly, even if the owners of this class are not paid another dollar of interest, they will have received an amount equal to 130.9% of par.[14]

Table 19. Trust cash outlays

Date	Net Swap payments	Servicing fees	Servicer advance reimbursements	LIBOR certificate		Prepayment penalties	Excess Spread
				Principal	Interest		
Jul-06	$62,518	$374,270	$0	$9,396,455	$3,503,784	$70,524	$2,153,539
Aug-06	$47,927	$370,280	$233,039	$12,147,768	$4,159,454	$88,691	$1,445,805
Sep-06	$91,323	$365,123	$483,778	$19,200,881	$4,058,029	$165,593	$1,418,337
Oct-06	$82,957	$356,970	$1,317,531	$21,448,581	$3,844,241	$315,875	$1,504,051
Nov-06	$96,794	$347,863	$1,230,848	$22,234,002	$4,114,629	$401,429	$1,071,070
Dec-06	$82,988	$338,423	$1,191,300	$43,264,545	$3,518,752	$293,963	$1,539,266
Jan-06	$64,178	$320,054	$1,174,086	$21,109,962	$3,463,517	$272,433	$1,313,044
Feb-06	$86,137	$311,091	$1,342,346	$16,141,301	$3,573,069	$245,315	$1,039,598
Mar-06	$72,641	$304,238	$1,293,706	$12,782,974	$3,058,328	$150,401	$1,283,208
Apr-06	$74,677	$298,810	$1,346,264	$10,239,650	$3,219,019	$128,060	$1,045,393
May-06	$71,316	$294,463	$1,369,108	$12,480,823	$3,172,768	$202,855	$868,082
Jun-06	$70,108	$289,163	$1,493,314	$16,605,497	$3,220,305	$237,753	$826,037
Jul-06	$64,543	$282,113	$1,577,756	$13,044,672	$3,041,335	$196,941	$297,443
	$67,536	$276,574	$1,712,117	$12,502,671	$3,280,603	$190,972	$349,654

Source: remittance reports from ABSNet.

There are two trigger events which prevent the release of over-collateralization at the step- down date, as shown in Table 20. The trigger amount in the third column for the 3-month moving average of 60-day delinquencies is 38.7 percent of the previous month's senior enhancement percentage reported in the fourth column. Recall that the trigger amount for the cumulative losses is constant at 1.3 percent over the first two years of the deal. While losses to date remain lower than the loss trigger amount, the 3-month moving average of 60-day delinquencies has been larger than the threshold amount since the April 2007 remittance report.

The remittance report also discloses loan modifications performed by the servicer each month. Note that through the August remittance report, there have been no modifications of any mortgage loan in the pool. This is not surprising as the first payment reset date for these 2/28 ARMs will not be until spring 2008.

Finally, the remittance report also discloses information that permits a calculation of loss severity. At the time of this writing, the trust has incurred a loss of $2.1 99 million on 44 mortgage loans with principal balance of $5.042 million, for a loss severity of 43.6 percent. This number is only modestly higher than the assumption used in forecasting the lifetime performance of the deal using the UBS methodology.

---

[14] Note given the amount of cash being paid out to equity tranche investors in such a bad state of nature, it is likely that these investors have paid a premium over par for these securities, so this should not be interpreted as a return.

Table 20. Key triggers

Date	LIBOR 1-month	Moving Average 60d Delinquency		Senior Enhancement		Cumulative Loss	
		Amount	Trigger	Amount	Specified	Amount	Trigger
Jul-06	5.35%	0.04%	7.99%	20.87%	41.30%	0.00%	1.30%
Aug-06	5.38%	0.02%	8.08%	21.17%	41.30%	0.00%	1.30%
Sep-06	5.32%	0.78%	8.19%	21.65%	41.30%	0.00%	1.30%
Oct-06	5.33%	2.32%	8.38%	22.22%	41.30%	0.00%	1.30%
Nov-06	5.32%	4.84%	8.60%	22.84%	41.30%	0.00%	1.30%
Dec-06	5.32%	6.42%	8.84%	24.18%	41.30%	0.00%	1.30%
Jan-06	5.35%	7.97%	9.35%	24.84%	41.30%	0.00%	1.30%
	5.32%	9.12%	9.61%	25.40%	41.30%	0.00%	1.30%
Feb-06	5.32%	4.47%	9.83%	25.86%	41.30%	0.02%	1.30%
Mar-06	5.32%	12.62%	10.10%	26.25%	41.30%	0.04%	1.30%
Apr-06	5.32%	14.32%	10.16%	26.73%	41.30%	0.08%	1.30%
May-06	5.32%	16.07%	10.34%	27.40%	41.30%	0.10%	1.30%
Jun-06	5.32%	17.83%	10.60%	27.94%	41.30%	0.19%	1.30%
Jul-06	5.32%	19.66%	10.81%	28.49%	41.30%	0.24%	1.30%

Source: remittance reports from ABSnet.

5. AN OVERVIEW OF SUBPRIME MBS RATINGS

This section is intended to provide an overview of how the rating agencies assign credit ratings on tranches of a securitization. We start with a general discussion of credit ratings before moving into the details on the rating process. We continue with an overview of the process through which the credit rating agencies monitor performance of securitization deals over time, and review performance of credit ratings on securities secured by subprime mortgages. In this section there are a number of asides to complement the analysis: conceptual differences between corporate and structured credit ratings; a note on how through-the-cycle structured credit ratings can amplify the housing cycle; an explanation of the timing of recent downgrades.

5.1. What Is a Credit Rating?

A credit rating by a CRA represents an overall assessment and opinion of a debt obligor's creditworthiness and is thus meant to reflect only credit or default risk. To be sure, it is not the obligor but the instrument issued by the obligor which receives a credit rating. The distinction is not that relevant for corporate bonds, where the obligor rating is commensurate with the rating on a senior unsecured instrument, but is quite relevant for structured credit products such as asset-backed securities (ABS). Nonetheless, in the words of a Moody's presentation (Moody's 2004), "[t]he comparability of these opinions holds regardless of the country of the issuer, is industry, asset class, or type of fixed-income debt." A recent S&P document states "[o]ur ratings represent a uniform measure of credit quality globally and across all types of debt instruments. In other words, an 'AAA' rated corporate bond should exhibit the same degree of credit quality as an 'AAA' rated securitized issue." (S&P 2007, p.4).

This stated intent implies that an investor can assume that, say, a double-A rated instrument is the same in the U.S. as in Belgium or Singapore, regardless whether that instrument is a standard corporate bond or a structured product such as a tranche on a collateralized debt obligation (CDO); see also Mason and Rosner (2007). The actual behavior of rated obligors or instruments may turn out to have more heterogeneity across countries, industries, and product types, and there is substantial supporting evidence. See Nickell, Perraudin, and Varvotto (2000) for evidence across countries of domicile and industries for corporate bond ratings, and CGFS (2005) for differences between corporate bonds and structured products.

The rating agencies differ about what exactly is assessed. Whereas Fitch and S&P evaluate an obligor's overall capacity to meet its financial obligation, and hence is best through of as an estimate of probability of default, Moody's assessment incorporates some judgment of recovery in the event of loss. In the argot of credit risk management, S&P measures PD (probability of default) while Moody's measure is somewhat closer to EL (expected loss) (BCBS, 2000).[15] Interestingly, these differences seem to remain for structured products. In describing their ratings criteria and methodology for structured products, S&P states: "[w]e base our ratings framework on the likelihood of default rather than expected loss or loss given default. In other words, our ratings at the rated instrument level don't incorporate any analysis or opinion on post-default recovery prospects." (S&P, 2007, p. 3) By contrast, Fitch incorporates some measure of expected recovery into their structured product ratings.[16]

Credit ratings issued by the agencies typically represent an unconditional view, sometimes called "cycle-neutral" or "through-the-cycle:" the rating agency's own description of their rating methodology broadly supports this view.

> (Moody's 1999, p. 6-7) "...[O]ne of Moody's goals is to achieve stable *expected* [italics in original] default rates across rating categories and time ... Moody's believes that giving only modest weight to cyclical conditions serves the interests of the bulk of investors."

> (S&P 2001, p. 41): "Standard & Poor's credit ratings are meant to be forward-looking; ... Accordingly, the anticipated ups and downs of business cycles – whether industry specific or related to the general economy – should be factored into the credit rating all along ... The ideal is to rate 'through the cycle'".

This unconditional or firm-specific view of credit risk stands in contrast to risk measures such as EDFs (expected default frequency) from Moody's KMV. An EDF has two principal inputs: firm leverage and asset volatility, where the latter is derived from equity (stock price) volatility. As a result EDFs can change frequently and significantly since they reflect the stock market's view of risk for that firm at a given point in time, a view which incorporates both systematic and idiosyncratic risk.

Unfortunately there is substantial evidence that credit rating changes, including changes to default, exhibit pro-cyclical or systematic variation (Nickell, Perraudin, and Varotto, 2000;

---

15 Specifically, EL = PD×LGD, where LGD is loss given default. However, given the paucity of LGD data, little variation in EL exists at the obligor (as opposed to instrument) level can be attributed to variation in LGD making the distinction between the agencies modest at best.

16 See http://www.fitchratings.com/corporate/fitchResources.cfm?detail=1&rd file=intro#r tng actn.

Bangia et. al, 2002; Lando and Skodeberg, 2002), especially for speculative grades (Hanson and Schuermann, 2006).

5.2. How Does One Become a Rating Agency?[17]

Credit ratings have a long history of playing a role in the regulatory process going back to the 1930s in the U.S. (Sylla, 2002). Asset managers such as pension funds and insurers often have strict asset allocation guidelines which are ratings driven, such as, for instance, a ceiling on the amount that can be invested in speculative grade debt.[18] With the introduction of the Basel 2 standards, ratings have entered bank capital regulation. But whose ratings can be used is left up to the host country supervisor.[19] In the U.S. we use the SEC designation of a "Nationally Recognized Statistical Rating Organization," NRSRO, introduced in 1975. All three main rating agencies at the time – Moody's, S&P and Fitch – received this designation (White, 2002). It was not until 1997 that the SEC laid out formal criteria for becoming an NRSRO (Levich, Majnoni and Reinhart, 2002). Only with the Credit Rating Agency Reform Act of 2006 did the SEC officially obtain authority to regulate and supervise CRAs that have been designated NRSROs.[20]

Under the Reform Act, in order to qualify as an NRSRO, a credit agency must register with the SEC and it must have been in business as a credit rating agency for at least three consecutive years proceeding the date of its application.[21] The application must contain, among other things, information regarding the applicant's credit ratings performance measurement statistics over short-term, mid-term, and long-term periods; the procedures and methodologies that the applicant uses in determining credit ratings; policies or procedures adopted and implemented to prevent misuse of material, nonpublic information; and any conflict of interest relating to the issuance of credit ratings by the applicant.[22] All documentation submitted by the applicant must be made publicly available on its website,[23] and the information must be kept up to date and current.[24]

Since the early 1970s (1970 for Moody's and Fitch, S&P a few years later), issuers rather than investors are charged for obtaining a rating. These ratings are costly: $25,000 for issues up to $500 million, 1/2 bp for issues greater than $500 million (Kliger and Sarig, 2000). Treacy and Carey (2000) report that the usual fee charged by S&P is 3.25 bp of the face amount, though it may be up to 4.25 bp (Tomlinson and Evans, 2007); Fitch charges 3-7 bp (Tomlinson and Evans, 2007). The fees charged for rating structured credit products are higher: up to 12 bp by S&P and 7-8 bp by Fitch (Tomlinson and Evans, 2007). Moody's does not publish its pricing schedule.

---

[17] We are indebted to Michelle Meertens for help with this section.

[18] ERISA, the Employee Retirement Income Security Act of 1974, is one such example.

[19] European guidelines can be found in "Committee of European Banking Supervisors, Guidelines on the Recognition of External Credit Assessment Institutions (Jan 20, 2006); available at http://www.bundesbank.de/download/bankenaufsicht/pdf/cebs/GL07.pdf.

[20] The final rule did not come out until June 2007 (http://www.sec.gov/rules/final/2007/34-55857fr.pdf).

[21] 15 U.S.C. 78c(a)(62).

[22] 15 U.S.C. 78o-7(a)(1)(B).

[23] 15 U.S.C. 78o-7(a)(3).

[24] 15 U.S.C. 78o-7(b)(1).

5.3. When Is a Credit Rating Wrong? How Could We Tell?

Highly rated firms default quite rarely. For example, Moody's reports that the one-year investment grade default rate over the period 1983-2006 was 0.073% or 7.3 bp. This is an average over four letter grade ratings: Aaa through Baa. Thus in a pool of 10,000 investment grade obligors or instruments we would expect seven to default over the course of one year. What if only three default? What about eleven? Higher than expect default could be the result of either a bad draw (bad luck) or an indicator that the rating is wrong, and it is very hard to distinguish between the two, especially for small probabilities (see also Lopez and Saidenberg, 2000). Indeed the use of the regulatory color scheme, which is behind the 1996 Market Risk Amendment to the Basel I, was motivated precisely by this recognition, and in that case the probability to be validated is comparatively large 1% (for 99% VaR) (BCBS, 1996) with daily data.

There are other approaches. Although rating agencies insist that their ratings scale reflects an ordinal ranking of credit risk, they also publish default rates for different horizons by rating. Thus we would expect default rates or probabilities to be monotonically increasing as one descends the credit spectrum. Using ratings histories from S&P, Hanson and Schuermann (2006) show formally that monotonicity is violated frequently for most notch-level investment grade one-year estimated default probabilities. The precision of the probability of default (PD) point estimates is quite low; see Appendix 3 for further discussion. Indeed there have been no defaults over one year for triple-A or AA+ (Aa1) rated firms, yet surely we do not believe that the one-year probability of default is identically equal to zero.

Although the one-year horizon is typical in credit analysis (and is also the horizon used in Basel 2), most traded credit instruments have longer maturity. For example, the typical CDS contract is five years, and over that horizon there are positive empirical default rates for Aaa and Aa1 which Moody's reports to be 7.8bp and 14.9bp respectively (Moody's, 2007c).

"We perform a very significant but extremely limited role in the credit markets. We issue reasoned, forward-looking opinions about credit risk," says Fran Laserson, vice president of corporate communications at Moody's. "Our opinions are objective and not tied to any recommendations to buy and sell."

5.4. The Subprime Credit Rating Process

The rating process can be split into two steps: (1) estimation of a loss distribution, and (2) simulation of the cash flows. With a loss distribution in hand, it is straightforward to measure the amount of credit enhancement necessary for a tranche to attain a given credit rating. Credit enhancement (CE) is simply the amount of loss on underlying collateral that can be absorbed before the tranche absorbs any loss. When a credit rating is associated with the probability of default, the amount of credit enhancement is simply the level of loss CE such that the probability that loss is higher than CE is equal to the probability of default.

Figure 9 below illustrates how one can use the portfolio loss distribution in order map the PD associated with a credit rating on a particular tranche to a level of credit enhancement required for that tranche. For example, given a PD associated with a AAA credit rating, the credit enhancement is quite high at CE(AAA). However, given a higher PD associated with a

BBB credit rating, the required credit enhancement is much lower at CE(BBB). A better credit rating is achieved through greater credit enhancement.

In a typical subprime structure, credit enhancement comes from two sources: subordination and excess spread. Subordination refers to the par value of tranches with claims junior to the tranche in question relative to the par value of collateral. It represents the maximum level of loss that could occur immediately without investors in the tranche losing one dollar of interest or principal. Excess spread refers to the difference between the income and expenses of the structure. On the income side, the trust receives interest payments and prepayment penalties from borrowers. On the expense side, the trust pays interest on tranches to investors, pays a fee to the servicer, and might have other payments to make related to derivatives like interest rate swaps. In most structures, excess spread is captured for the first three to five years of the life of the deal, which increases the amount of subordination for each rated tranche over time. Determining how much credit excess spread can be given to meet the required credit enhancement is a dynamic problem that involves simulating cash flows over time, and is the second step of the rating process. We now discuss each of these two steps in greater detail.

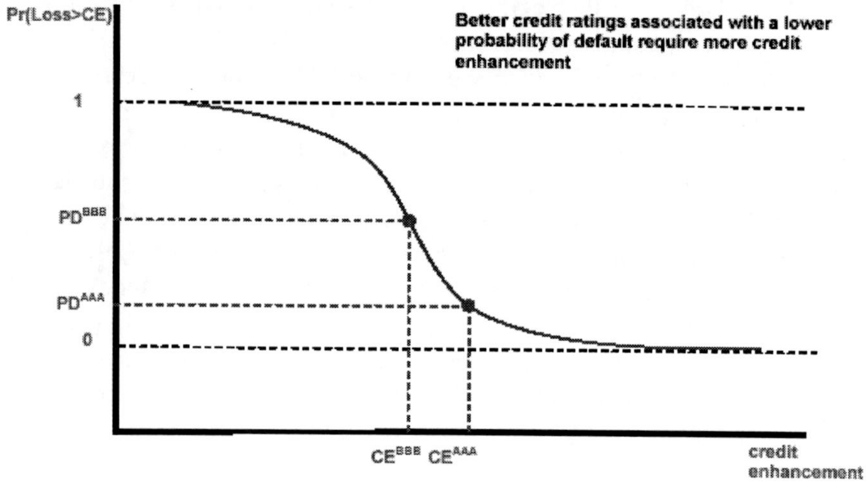

Figure 9. Mapping the Loss Distribution to Required Credit Enhancement.

5.4.1. Credit Enhancement

In the first step of the rating process, the rating agency estimates the loss distribution associated with a given pool of collateral. The mean of the loss distribution is measured through the construction of a baseline frequency of foreclosure and loss severity for each loan that depends on the characteristics of the loan and local area economic conditions. The distribution of losses is constructed by estimating the sensitivity of losses to local area economic conditions for each mortgage loan, and then simulating future paths of local area economic conditions.

In order to construct the baseline, the rating agency uses historical data in order to estimate the likely sensitivity of the frequency of foreclosure and severity of loss to underwriting characteristics of the loan, the experience of the originator and servicer, and local area and national economic conditions. Most of the agencies claim to rely in part on loan-level data from *LoanPerformance* over 1992-2000 in order to estimate these relationships.

The key loan underwriting characteristics include:

- cumulative loan-to-value ratio (CLTV)
- consumer credit score (FICO)
- loan maturity (15 years, 30 years, 40 years, etc)
- interest rate
- fixed-rate (FRM) vs. adjustable-rate (ARM)
- property type (single-family, townhouse, condo, multi-family)
- home value
- documentation of income and assets
- loan purpose (purchase, term refinance, cash-out refinance)
- owner occupancy (owner-occupied, investor)
- mortgage insurance
- asset class (Jumbo, Alt-A, Subprime)
- The key originator and servicer adjustments include:
- past performance of the originator's loans
- underwriting guidelines of the mortgage loans and adherence to them
- loan marketing practices
- credit checks made on borrowers
- appraisal standards
- experience in origination of mortgages
- collection practices
- loan modification and liquidation practices

Table 21 documents how the credit support (the product of the frequency of foreclosure and loss severity) for a pool of mortgage loans is sensitive to changes in loan attributes.

The Aaa credit enhancement for the base pools are illustrated in the first row. As Pool A has a higher LTV, lower FICO, and lower percentage of full documentation than Pool B, it has a higher level of credit support (3.17 percent versus 2.57 percent). Table 21 also illustrates the impact of changing one characteristic of the pool for all loans in the pool, holding all other characteristics constant. For example, if all loans in the pool were underwritten under an Alternative Documentation program, the credit support of Pool A would increase by 6 percent to 3.35 percent and Pool B would increase by 8 percent to 2.78 percent. Note that the change in support depends on both the sensitivity of support to the loan characteristic as well as the size of the change in the characteristic. Changes in leverage appear to have significant effects on credit support, as an increase of five percentage points is associated with an increase in credit support by more than one-third.[25]

---

[25] Note that Moody's have increased subordination levels in subprime RMBS by 30 percent over last three years, and this can be largely attributed to an increase in support required by a decline in underwriting standards.

Table 21. Sensitivity of Aaa Credit Enhancement Levels to Loan Attributes

	Sample Pool A		Sample Pool B	
	Aaa credit support	Change from Base	Aaa credit support	Change from Base
Base Pool	3.17		2.57	
LTV+5%	4.28	35%	3.52	37%
LTV-5%	2.32	-27%	1.85	-28%
FICO+20	3.02	-5%	2.49	-3%
FICO-20	3.42	8%	2.75	7%
All Cashout				
Appraisal Quality	4.68	48%	3.91	52%
All Purchase	2.62	-17%	2.15	-16%
All Investor	3.69	16%	2.99	16%
All 15-year term	2.42	-24%	1.93	-25%
All ARM	3.47	9%	2.81	9%
All Condo	3.31	4%	2.68	4%
All Alt Doc	3.35	6%	2.78	8%
Price > $300k, LTV constant	3.8	20%	3.10	21%

Source: Moody's Mortgage Metrics.

Pool A: LTV 67, FICO 732, CashOut 19%, Purch 21%, Single Fam 89%, Owner 98%, Fulldoc 75%, 30-year 98%, Fixed Rate 100% Pool B: LTV 65, FICO 744, CashOut 17%, Purch 21%, Single Fam 89%, Owner 96%, Fulldoc 95%, 30-year 98%, Fixed Rate 100%.

The rating agency will typically adjust this baseline for current local area economic conditions like the unemployment rate, interest rates, and home price appreciation. The agencies are quite opaque about this relationship, and for some reason do not illustrate the impact of changes in local area economic conditions on credit enhancement in their public rating criteria. For example, Fitch employs scaling factors developed by University Financial Associates which control for four different components of regional factors: macro factors like employment rates and construction activity, demographic factors like population growth; political/legal factors; and even topographic factors that might constrain the growth of housing markets. The multipliers typically range from 0.5 to 1.7 and are updated quarterly.

In order to simulate the loss distribution, the rating agency needs to estimate the sensitivity of losses to local area economic conditions. Fitch tackles this problem by breaking out actual losses on mortgage loans into independent national and state components for each quarter. The sensitivity of losses to each factor is equal to one by construction. The final step is to fix a distribution for each of these components, and then simulate the loss distribution of the mortgage pool using random draws from the distribution of state and national components of unexpected loss.[26]

[26] Note that Fitch actually simulates the frequency of foreclosure and loss severity separately, but the discussion here focuses on the product (expected loss) for simplicity. Each of the national and state components is likely transformed by subtracting the mean and dividing by the standard deviation, so that the distribution converges to a standard normal distribution. This permits the agency to use a two-factor copula model in order to simulate the loss distribution. Note that the sensitivity of losses to the normalized component would be equal to the inverse of the standard deviation of the actual component.

5.5. Conceptual Differences between Corporate and ABS Credit Ratings

Subprime ABS ratings differ from corporate debt ratings in a number of different dimensions:

- Corporate bond (obligor) ratings are largely based on firm-specific risk characteristics. Since ABS structures represent claims on cash flows from a *portfolio* of underlying assets, the rating of a structured credit product must take into account systematic risk. It is correlated losses which matter especially for the more senior (higher rated) tranches, and loss correlation arises through dependence on shared or common (or systematic) risk factors.[27] For ABS deals which have a large number of underlying assets, for instance MBS, the portfolio is large enough such that all idiosyncratic risk is diversified away leaving only systematic exposure to the risk factors particular to that product class (here, mortgages). By contrast, a substantial amount of idiosyncratic risk may remain in ABS transactions with smaller asset pools, for instance CDOs (CGFS, 2005; Amato and Remolona, 2005). Because these deals are portfolios, the effect of correlation is not the same for all tranches: equity tranches prefer higher correlation, senior tranches prefer lower correlation (tail losses are driven by loss correlation). As correlation increases, so does portfolio loss volatility. The payoff function for the equity tranche is, true to its name, like a call option. Indeed equity itself is a call option on the assets of the underlying firm, and the value of a call option is increasing in volatility. If the equity tranche is long a call option, the senior tranche is short a call option, so that their payoffs behave in an opposite manner. The impact of increased correlation on the value of mezzanine tranches is ambiguous and depends on the structure of a particular deal (Duffie, 2007). By contrast, correlation with systematic risk factors should not matter for corporate ratings. As a result of the portfolio nature of the rated products, the ratings migration behavior may also be different than for ordinary obligor ratings. Moody's (2007a) reports that rating changes are much more common for corporate bond than for structured product ratings, but the magnitude of changes (number of notches up- or downgraded) was nearly double for the structured products.
- Subprime ABS ratings refer to the performance of a static pool instead of a dynamic corporation. When a firm becomes distressed, it has the option to change its investment strategy and inject more capital. As long as a firm is deemed to be creditworthy during neutral economic conditions, it is reasonable to expect that the firm could take prompt corrective action in order to avoid defaulting on its debt during a transitory decline in aggregate or industry conditions. However, the pool of mortgages underlying subprime ABS is fixed, and investors do not expect an issuer to support a weakly-performing deal.
- Subprime ABS ratings rely heavily on quantitative models while corporate debt ratings rely heavily on analyst judgment. In particular, corporate credit ratings require the separation of a firm's long-run condition and competitiveness from the business cycle, the assessment of whether or not an industry downturn is cyclical or permanent,

[27] Note that correlation includes more than just economic conditions, as it includes (a) model risk by the agencies (b) originator and arranger effects (c) servicer effects.

and determination about whether or not a firm could actually survive a pro-longed transitory downturn.

- Unlike corporate credit ratings, ABS ratings rely heavily on a forecast of economic conditions. Note that a corporate credit rating is based on the agency's assessment that a firm will default during neutral economic conditions (i.e. full employment at the national and industry level). However, the rating agency is unable to focus on neutral economic conditions when assigning subprime ABS ratings, because in the model, uncertainty about the level of loss in the mortgage pool is driven completely by changes in economic conditions. If one were to fix the level of economic activity – for example at full employment – the level of losses is determined, and according to the model, the probability of default is either zero or one. It follows that the credit rating on an ABS tranche is the agency's assessment that economic conditions will deteriorate to the point where losses on the underlying mortgage pool will exceed the tranche's credit enhancement. In other words, it is largely based on a forecast of economic conditions combined with the agency's estimated sensitivity of losses to that forecast.
- Finally, while an ABS credit rating for a particular rating grade should have similar expected loss to corporate credit rating of the same grade, the volatility of loss can be quite different across asset classes.

5.6. How through-the-Cycle Rating Could Amplify the Housing Cycle

Like corporate credit ratings, the agencies seek to make subprime ABS credit ratings through the housing cycle. Stability means that one should not see upgrades concentrated during a housing boom and downgrades concentrated during a housing bust.

It is not difficult to understand that changes in economic conditions affect the distribution of losses on a mortgage pool. The unemployment rate and home price appreciation have obvious effects on the ability of a borrower to avoid default and the severity of loss in the event of default.

Consider a AAA-rated tranche issued during an environment of high home price appreciation (HPA). Figure 10 illustrates that the level of credit enhancement is determined using the probability associated with a AAA credit rating and the rating agency's estimate of the loss distribution (blue) in this economic environment. However, as the housing market slows down, the loss distribution shifts to the right, as any level of probability is now associated with a higher level of loss. If the rating agency does not respond to this new loss distribution and uses the same level of credit enhancement to structure new deals in a tough economic environment, the probability of default associated with these AAA-rated tranche will actually be closer to a AA than a AAA. It follows that keeping enhancement constant through the cycle will result in ratings instability, with upgrades during a boom and downgrades during a bust.

Rating agency must respond to shifts in the loss distribution by increasing the amount of needed credit enhancement to keep ratings stable as economic conditions deteriorate, as illustrated in the Figure. It follows that the stabilizing of ratings through the cycle is associated with pro-cyclical credit enhancement: as the housing market improves, credit enhancement falls; as the housing market slows down, credit enhancement increases.

This phenomenon has two important implications:

- Pro-cyclical credit enhancement has the potential to amplify the housing cycle, creating credit and asset price bubbles on the upside and contributing to severe credit crunches and on the downside. In order to understand this point, consider the hypothetical example in Figure 11. On the left is an aggressive structure based on strong housing market conditions. The AAA tranche is 80 percent of the funding, and the weighted- average cost of funds is LIBOR+92 bp. However, as the housing market slows down, the rating agency removes leverage from the structure, and increases the subordination of the AAA-rated tranche from 20 to 25 percent. By requiring a larger fraction of the deal to be financed by BBB-rated debt, the weighted-average cost of funds increases to LIBOR+100 bp. This higher cost of funds will require higher interest rates on subprime mortgage loans, or will require a significant tightening in underwriting standards on the underlying mortgage loans. Note that the de-leveraging the structure has a knock-on effect on economic activity by reducing the supply of credit. It is difficult at this point to assess the importance of this phenomenon to what appeared to be a bubble in housing credit and prices on the upside. One source of concern is that the ratio of upgrades to downgrades appeared to be fairly stable for home equity ABS over 2001-2006 (see the discussion on rating performance below). However, the impact on the downside is fairly certain. One week after a historical downgrade action by the agencies, leading subprime lenders discontinued offering the 2/28 and 3/27 hybrid ARM (see the discussion of ratings performance below).
- Investors in subprime ABS are vulnerable to the ability of the rating agency to predict turning points in the housing cycle and respond appropriately. One must be fair to note that the downturn in housing did not surprise the rating agencies, who had been warning investors about the possibility and the impact on performance for quite some time. However, it does not appear that the agencies appropriately measured the sensitivity of losses to economic activity or anticipated the severity of the downturn.

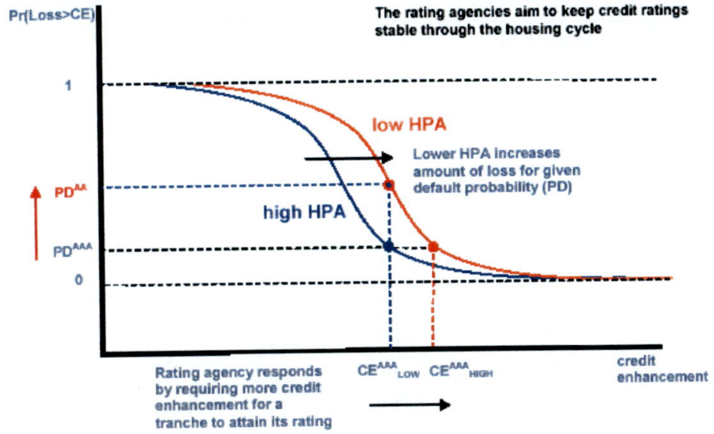

Figure 10. Credit enhancement and economic conditions.

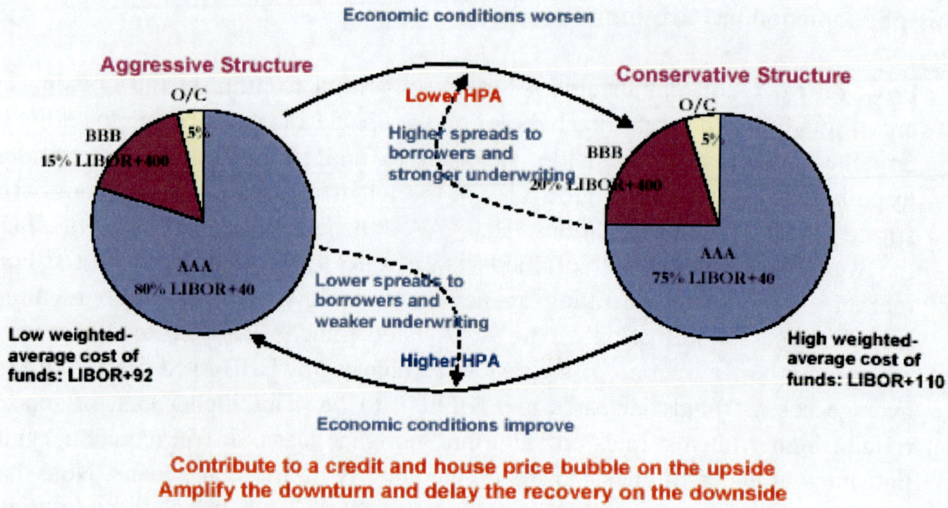

Figure 11. Procyclical credit enhancement.

5.7. Cash Flow Analytics for Excess Spread

The second part of the rating process involves simulating the cash flows of the structure in order to determine how much credit excess spread will receive towards meeting the required credit enhancement. As an example, in Table 22 we consider the credit enhancement corresponding to a hypothetical pool of subprime mortgage loans. In this example, the required credit enhancement for the Aaa tranche is 22.50%. A simulation of cash flows suggests that excess spread can contribute 9.2 5% to meet this requirement, suggesting that the amount of subordination for this tranche must be 13.25%. In this section, we briefly describe how the rating agencies measure this credit attributed to excess spread, focusing on subprime RMBS.

Table 22. Cash flow analytics

Tranche Rating	Required Credit Enhancement	Spread Credit	Subordination	Class Size
Aaa	22.50%	9.25%	13.25%	86.75%
Aa2	16.75%	9.25%	7.50%	5.75%
A2	12.25%	8.75%	3.50%	4.00%
Baa2	8.50%	8.50%	0.00%	3.50%
Total				100%

Source: Moody's.

The key inputs into the cash flow analysis involve:

- the credit enhancement for given credit rating
- the timing of these losses
- prepayment rates

- interest rates and index mismatches
- trigger events
- weighted average loan rate decrease
- prepayment penalties
- pre-funding accounts
- swaps, caps, and other derivatives.

The first input to the analysis is amount of losses on collateral that a tranche with a given rating would be able to withstand without sustaining a loss, which corresponds to the required credit enhancement implied from the loss distribution. Note that better credit ratings are associated with higher levels credit enhancement, and thus are associated with a higher level of expected loss on the underlying collateral.

The Timing of Losses

Table 23 illustrates Moody's assumption about the timing of losses, which is based on historical performance over 1993-1999. Note there are slight differences in the timing between fixed-rate and ARMs. Except for the first year, losses are assumed to be distributed evenly throughout the year. In the first year, losses are distributed evenly throughout the last six months. Adjustments to this assumption need to be made if the pool contains seasoned or delinquent loans.

Table 23. First-lien loss curve (as % of original pool balance)

Year	FRMs	ARMs
1	3%	3%
2	12%	17%
3	20%	25%
4	25%	25%
5	20%	20%
6	15%	10%
7	5%	0%
8	0%	0%
Total	100%	0%

Source: Moody's; based on historical performance over 1993-1999.

Note that an acceleration in the timing of losses implies a lower level of excess spread in later periods, which reduces the contribution that excess spread can make to meet the required credit enhancement. It follows that a conservative approach to rating involves front-loading the timing of losses. Moreover, given the importance of the timing, it is possible to understand how the existence of elevated early payment defaults observed in the 2006 vintages of RMBS will correspond to significant adverse effects on the ratings performance.

Prepayment Risk

Prepayments of principal include both the voluntary and involuntary (i.e. default) varieties. Note that the path of the dollar value of involuntary prepayments over time has been tied down by assumptions about the level and timing of losses. It follows that assumptions about the prepayment curve really just pin down the severity of loss on defaulted mortgages (in order to identify the number of involuntary prepayments) and the number of voluntary prepayments. Table 24 documents Moody's assumptions about prepayment rates for a Baa2-rated tranche secured by a portfolio of subprime loans. The standard measure of prepayment frequency is the Constant Prepayment Rate (CPR), defined as the annualized one-month prepayment rate of loans that remain in the pool.

Table 24. Pre-payment assumption for Baa2-rated tranches

Loan age (months)	FRMs	ARMs	2/28s	3/27s
1	6%	5.5%	5.5%	5.5%
2-18	↑ by 1.33%/mth	↑by 1.639%/mth	↑ by 1.639%/mth	↑by 1.639%/mth
19-24	30%	35%	33%	33%
25-30	30%	35%	55%	33%
31-36	30%	35%	33%	33%
37-42	30%	35%	33%	55%
43+	30%	35%	33%	33%

Source: Moody's.

For both fixed-rate (FRMs) and adjustable-rate mortgages (ARMs), the CPR increases every month until the 19th month, where it stays constant through the remaining life of the deal. However, for hybrid ARMs, which have a fixed interest rate for either 2 or 3 years and then revert to an ARM, there is a spike in the CPR in the six months following payment reset. Note that since prepayments include defaults, it is necessary to adjust the prepayment curve for the credit rating of the tranche under analysis. Recall that a better credit rating is associated with a higher level of loss on collateral, which means a higher frequency of involuntary prepayments. Table 25 documents adjustments that Moody's makes to the CPR by rating category. For example, the prepayment rate is 15 percent higher for a Aaa-rated tranche than a Baa2 -rated tranche in order to capture the higher frequency of involuntary prepayment (i.e. default) associated with the Aaa level of loss.

The assumptions made above identify the dollar value of involuntary prepayments and the total number of prepayments. In order to identify the number of involuntary prepayments (and consequently the number of voluntary prepayments), it is necessary to make an assumption about loss severity. Note that this assumption about severity is different from the one used in the determination of credit enhancement in the first step outlined above. Moody's makes the assumption that the fraction of involuntary prepayments in total prepayments increases with the severity of loss (i.e. as the credit rating improves). This phenomenon is described in Table 26.

Table 25. Adjustments by tranche credit rating to Baa2 pre-payment curves

Rating	FRM	ARM
Aaa	133%	115%
Aa1	126%	112.5%
Aa2	120%	110%
Aa3	117%	108.5%
A1	113%	106.5%
A2	110%	105%
A3	107%	103.5%
Baa1	103%	101.5%
Baa2	100%	100%
Baa3	97%	98.5%
Ba1	93%	96.5%
Ba2	90%	95%
Ba3	87%	93.5%
B1	83%	91.5%
B2	80%	90%
B3	77%	88.5%

Source: Moody's.

Table 26. Loss Severity Assumptions for 1st lien subprime mortgages

Aaa	60%
Aa	55%
A	50%
Baa	45%
Ba	42.5%
B	40%

Source: Moody's.

In the end, voluntary prepayments reduce principal and thus the benefit of excess spread. It follows that a conservative view toward rating will typically make high and front-loaded assumptions about the path of voluntary prepayments, as this reduces the contribution that excess spread makes towards credit enhancement.

Interest Rate Risk

The key remaining source of uncertainty in the analysis of cash flows is the behavior of interest rates. Note that the coupons on tranches typically have floating interest rates tied to the one- month LIBOR. Moreover, note that interest rates on some of the underlying loans are adjustable, which makes receipts from collateral vary with the level of interest rates. Interest rate risk is created by mis-matches between the sensitivity of collateral and tranches to interest rates. Some examples include:

- Fixed rate loans funded with floating rate certificates
- Prime rate index funded with LIBOR based certificates

- six-month LIBOR loans funded with one-month LIBOR certificates

Based on a number of factors, including the state of the economy, the forward-rate curve, and the current level of interest rates, interest rate stresses are determined.

Interest rate risk had an adverse impact on the performance of RMBS structures issued during the 2002 to 2004. In particular, throughout 2002 to mid-2004, the one-month LIBOR maintained a level to 1% - 1.8%. However, in June 2004, the one-month LIBOR began to increase quickly, reaching 5.3% in 2006. This increase in interest rates has an adverse impact through three channels. First, the coupons on ARM collateral adjust less quickly than the coupons on floating-rate certificates. Second, while rising rates will reduce the prepayment of fixed-rate loans, they also encourage a deterioration in the coupons on adjustable-rate loans as these obligors refinance out of high interest-rate loans, leaving a higher fraction of low- and fixed-interest rates in the pool. Finally, the increase in prepayment rates leads to quick return of principal to investors in senior tranches, where credit spreads are the smallest. Each of these factors leads to a compression of excess spread.

Many structures enter into an interest rate swap agreement which replaces the flexible-rate coupon paid to the tranches with a fixed-rate coupon in order to avoid this type of problem. However, note that this swap does not completely remove interest rate risk. For example, when pools contain ARM mortgages, the structure is vulnerable to a decline in interest rates which reduces the cash flows from collateral.

The approach of the rating agencies to interest rate risk is to construct a path of interest rate stresses in order to capture the worst likely movement in interest rates. Table 24 illustrates the interest rate stresses used by Fitch.

Table 27. Interest Rate Stresses

		Decreases from LIBOR				Increases from LIBOR		
Month	BBB	A	AA	AAA	BBB	A	AA	AAA
6	-1.06%	-1.24%	-1.42%	-1.68%	0.88%	1.40%	2.07%	3.10%
12	-1.81%	-2.09%	-2.37%	-2.76%	1.22%	2.02%	3.06%	4.66%
24	-2.28%	-2.68%	-3.08%	-3.64%	2.01%	3.15%	4.63%	6.90%
36	-2.52%	-2.95%	-3.39%	-4.00%	2.18%	3.43%	5.05%	7.53%
48	-2.52%	-2.97%	-3.43%	-4.09%	2.52%	3.85%	5.58%	8.24%
60	-2.52%	-2.98%	-3.45%	-4.12%	2.65%	4.02%	5.79%	8.52%

Source: Fitch (August 2007).

Note that these are changes (in percentage points) relative to the one-month LIBOR. The magnitude of the interest rate shocks is larger for better credit ratings and longer maturities.

Other Details

Cash flow analysis is performed incorporating step-down triggers. For each rating level, the triggers are analyzed for the probability that they will be breached. As the triggers are set at levels which protect the rated tranches, they typically will be breached in stress scenarios. It follows that one typically assumes that the transaction does not step down (i.e.

credit enhancement is not released) and that all tranches are paid sequentially for its life. Finally, mortgage loans with higher interest rates tend to prepay first, which reduces excess spread of the transaction over time. In order to capture this, Moody's assumes that the weighted average coupon (WAC) of the loans decreases by one basis point each month over the first three years of the deal.

Motivating Example

In order to better understand the cash flow analysis, we will illustrate using a structure similar to GSAMP Trust 2006-NC2. In particular, we focus on a hypothetical pool of 2/28 ARM mortgage loans with an initial interest rate of 8 percent, a margin of 6 percent, and interest rate caps of 1.5%. The servicer receives a fee of 50 bp and master servicer receives a fee of 1 bp, each per annum and senior to any distributions to investors. The trust enters into an interest rate swap with a counterparty paying a fixed rate of 5.45% and receiving LIBOR – initially at 5.32% --according to a swap notional schedule described in Figure 8. Each month, the net payment to the swap counterparty is senior to any distributions to investors. Table 28 documents that the capital structure is similar to that of the New Century deal, but with fewer tranches in order to simplify the analysis.

Table 28. Capital Structure

Tranche	Width	Spread
AAA	79.35%	0.25%
AA	9.20%	0.31%
A	4.90%	0.37%
BBB	3.45%	1.00%
BB	1.70%	2.50%
O/C	1.40%	

Note: spread over 1-month LIBOR.

We focus our analysis on the BBB-rated tranche. Our analysis starts with prepayment rates, which are illustrated in Figure 12. The total CPR is the fraction of remaining loans which prepay each month at an annualized rate, and is taken from Table 24 above for 2/28 ARMs. Notice the spike in prepayment rates shortly following payment rest at 24 months. The involuntary CPR is tied down by (a) the level of losses, assumed in this case to be 10% given the BBB rating; (b) the timing of losses documented in Table 23; (c) and the severity of losses from Table 26 in order to convert dollars of principal loss into an involuntary prepayment rate. Since the timing assumption precludes losses after 72 months, we only focus on the first six years of the deal life. As the capital structure of the deal is fixed, this exercise is essentially a test of whether or not the BBB-rated tranche as structured can receive a 6.9% credit (= 10% - 3.1%) from excess spread to meet the required credit enhancement.

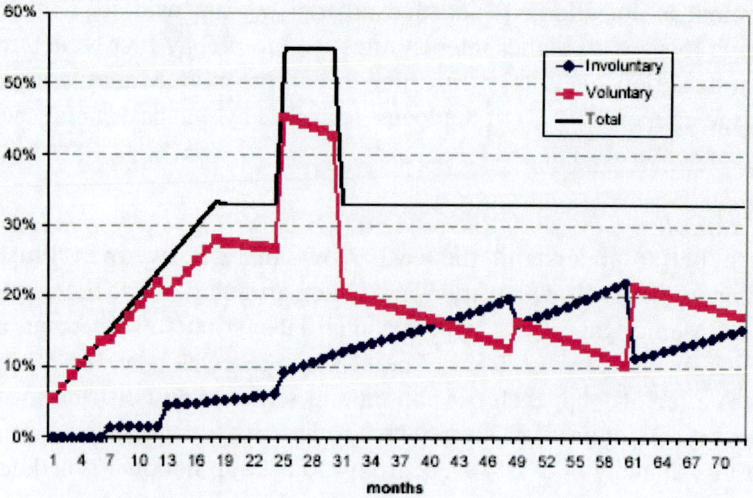

Figure 12. Decomposing Constant Prepayment Rates (CPRs).

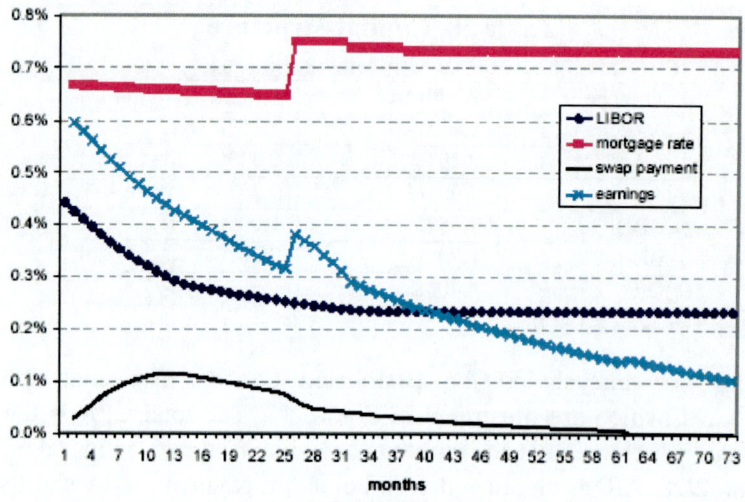

Note: the swap payment and earnings are each measured at a monthly rate and relative to original portfolio par. Earnings is defined as the difference between mortgage interest income, the net swap payment, and servicer fees of 51 basis points per annum.

Figure 13. LIBOR stress, trust earnings, and the net swap payment.

Given the path of pre-payments, one needs to use the interest rate stresses in order to simulate future cash flows. Since the structure is hedged, the most severe interest rate shock is a decline in interest rates. When the interest rate on mortgages declines but the interest rate on tranches is fixed there is pressure on earnings. Figure 13 documents that assumed path of LIBOR, taken from Table 27 above, but converted into a monthly interest rate. The slow decrease over the first 24 months in the mortgage income reflects adverse selection in prepayment (high interest rates pre-paying first). There is an obvious spike in the mortgage interest rate at 24 months once payments reset. As LIBOR is falling, there is a net payment made to the swap counterparty, but this declines over time as the amount of swap notional goes to zero over the five-year life of the contract. The earnings of the trust before distributions and loss falls over time as mortgages prepay and the interest rate on remaining mortgages falls.

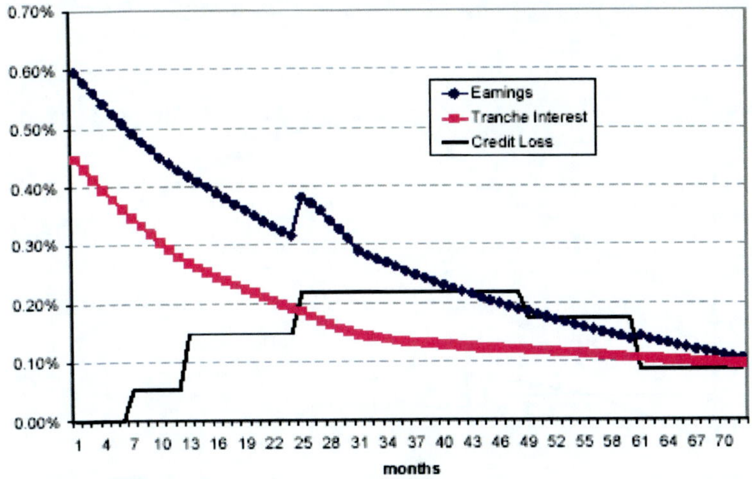

Note: Earnings, tranche interest, and credit loss are measured each at a monthly rate and relative to original portfolio par.

Figure 14. Earnings, Tranche Interest, and Credit Loss.

Figure 14 documents the path of trust earnings, tranche interest, and credit losses over time, each measured at a monthly rate and relative to portfolio par. Tranche interest declines over time as interest rates fall and as pre-payments reduce the principal value of the senior tranche. While earnings are adequate to cover tranche interest initially, after the first year credit losses are eating into over-collateralization. After 42 months, earnings no longer cover losses, and the structure is struggling greatly.

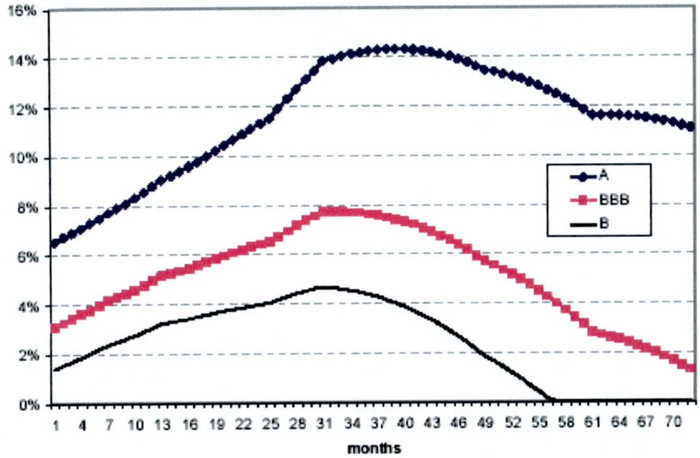

Figure 15. Dynamic subordination of mezzanine tranches (10% required enhancement).

Figure 15 documents that these losses reduce the subordination available to each tranche over time. At 56 months, over-collateralization has been exhausted and the BB-rated tranche defaults. However, the BBB-rate tranche is able to survive until 72 months, suggesting that this tranche could withstand a loss rate of 10 percent. It follows that the deal is structured adequately.

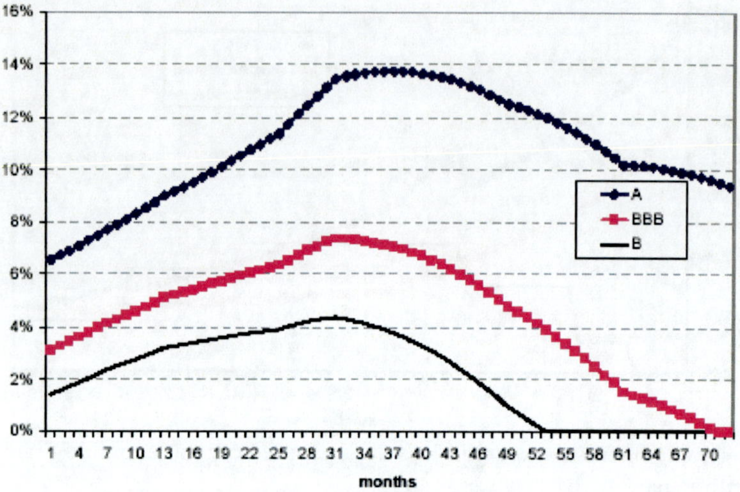

Figure 16. Dynamic subordination of mezzanine tranches (10.5% required enhancement).

Figure 16 documents the dynamic subordination of the same capital structure in the event that losses are only 50 basis points higher. In this case, the BBB rated tranche defaults in month 70. The actual losses to investors in this tranche would be quite low because there are no losses after 72 months. However, when losses on the pool increase to 14%, the investors in the BBB- rated tranche are completely wiped out and the A-rated tranche defaults.

5.8. Performance Monitoring

The rating agencies currently monitor the performance of approximately 10,000 pools of mortgage loan collateral. Deal performance is tracked using monthly remittance from Intex Solutions, Inc. Since there is no uniform reporting methodology, the first step is to ensure the integrity of the data.

The agencies use this performance data in order to identify which deals merit a detailed review, but do complete such a review for every deal at least once a year. The key performance metric is the loss coverage ratio (LCR), which is defined as the ratio of the current credit enhancement for a tranche relative to estimated unrealized losses. Note that losses are estimated using underwriting characteristics for unseasoned loans (less than 12 months), and actual performance for seasoned loans. When the loss coverage ratio falls below an acceptable level given the rating of the tranche, the agency will perform a detailed review of the transaction, and consider ratings action.

In the example subprime deal described in Table 29, which is taken from a Fitch (2007) and does not correspond to the New Century deal, the pipeline measure of loss is constructed by applying historical default rates to the fraction of loans in each delinquency status bucket, and applying a projected loss severity. For example, the rating agency assumes that 68 percent of loans 90 days past due will default, while only 11 percent of current loans will default.

Table 29. Example of Projected Loss as a Percentage of Current Pool Balance

Status	Delinquency Status Distribution	Projected Default As % of Bucket	Projected Default As % of Pool	Projected Loss Severity	Expected Loss as % of Pool
Current	83	11	9.1	35	3.2
30 Days	4.0	37	1.5	35	0.5
60 Days	2.6	54	1.4	35	0.5
90 Days	2.5	68	1.7	35	0.6
Bankruptcies	1.7	54	0.9	35	0.3
Foreclosure	3.8	76	2.9	35	1.0
REO	2.6	100	2.6	35	0.9
Total	100.0		20.0	35	7.1

Notes: The example transaction is 18 months seasoned, has 63% of the original pool remaining (called the pool factor), incurred 0.77% loss to date, and reports a 60+ day of 13.15% (=2.6+2.5+1.7+3.8+2.6). The delinquency bucket figures (with the exception of REO) have a 98% home price appreciation adjustment applied. The example deal's current three-month loss severity is 25%, and the projected lifetime loss severity is approximately 35%. The expected loss figures are as a percentage of the remaining pool balance. The expected loss as a percentage of original pool balance is 5.25% = (7.1%*63%+0.77%).

The current subordination of a tranche reflects excess spread that has been retained as well as any losses to date. In this example in Table 30 the M-1 tranche rated AA currently has subordination of 20.61 percent. However, due to expected future accumulation of excess spread, this class can withstand losses of 26.90 percent, corresponding to a loss coverage ratio of 3.8 (= 26.9/7.1). Note that the target loss coverage ratio for the AA rating is 2.82, suggesting that the original rating is sound. However, the B-2 class rated BBB- currently has subordination of 3 percent and a break-loss rate of 10.41 percent. Note that the target break- loss for this rating is 11.04 percent, and the target break-loss of 9.95 for the BB+ rating (not reported). In this case, the rating agency is using tolerance to prevent this tranche from being downgraded at this time. A conversation with a ratings analyst suggested that a tranche would not be downgraded until it failed the target break-loss level for one full rating-grade below the current level.

Table 30.Example of Ratings Analysis Using Break-Loss Figures

Class	Current Rating	Current Subordination (%)	Current Break-Loss (%)	Current Loss Coverage Ratio (%)	Target Break-Loss (%)	Target Loss Coverage Ratio (%)	Model Proposed After Tolerances
A	AAA	31.59	39.71	5.61	27.18	3.84	AAA
M-1	AA	20.61	26.90	3.80	19.95	2.82	AA
M-2	A	12.08	18.25	2.58	15.79	2.23	A
M-3	BBB+	7.50	15.62	2.21	13.32	1.88	BBB+
B-1	BBB	5.92	13.14	1.86	12.09	1.71	BBB
B-2	BBB-	3.00	10.41	1.47	11.04	1.56	BBB-

Notes: The example transaction is 18 months seasoned and has a projected loss as a percent of current balance of 7.1%. Based on the projected delinquency, the triggers will pass at the step-down date and toggle thereafter. The current annualized excess spread available to cover losses is 3.10% (including interest rate derivatives). Current break-loss: the amount of collateral loss that would call the class to default. This figure includes excess spread and triggers. Current loss coverage ratio (LCR): determined by dividing the bond's current break-loss amount by the current base-case projected loss of 7.1%. Model proposed: Considers the difference between the current LCR and the target LCR.

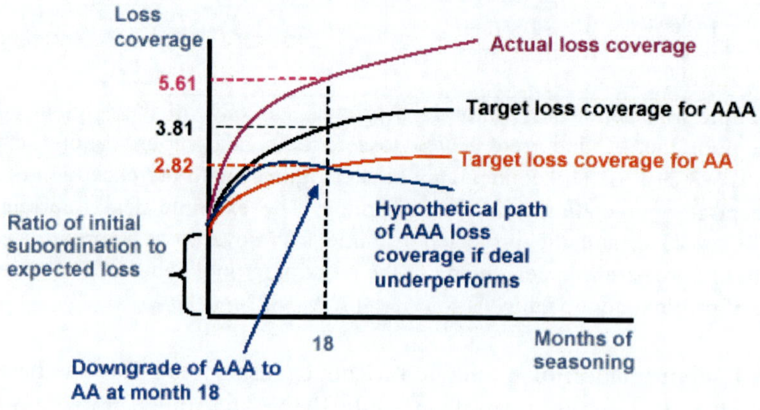

Figure 17. Anatomy of a downgrade.

It is worth taking the time to highlight how changes in rating criteria affect the ratings monitoring process. In particular, if the rating agencies become more conservative in structuring new deals, it is not clear that anything should change when it comes to making a decision to downgrade securities secured by seasoned loans. The numerator of the loss coverage ratio is the current subordination of the tranche, which is unaffected by any change in criteria. The denominator is the estimated unrealized loss. Unless the rating agency also changes its mapping from current loan performance to the probability of default, or updates its view on loss severity, the key input into the ratings monitoring process is unchanged. In this sense, there is no need to change the way the agency monitors existing transactions. If an existing transaction was structured with inadequate initial subordination, the normal ratings monitoring process will pick this up and downgrade appropriately. In this sense, there is no need to update existing transactions.

5.9. Home Equity ABS Rating Performance

Table 31 documents the performance of Moody's Subprime RMBS over the last five years.

The table documents downgrades in the top panel and upgrades in the bottom panel, broken out across first- and second-lien mortgage loans, as well as by origination year. Rating actions are measured by fraction of origination volume affected, the fraction of tranches affected, and the fraction of deals affected. The first observation to note is that by any measure, the rating agencies have appeared to struggle rating subprime deals throughout the period, as the ratio of downgrades to upgrades is larger than one. That being said, the recent performance of subprime RMBS ratings has been historically bad. The table documents that 92 percent of 1st- lien subprime deals originated in 2006 as well as 84.5 percent of 2nd-lien deals originated in 2005 and 91.8 percent of 2nd-lien deals originated in 2006 have been downgraded.

Note that half of all downgrades of tranches in the history of Home Equity ABS were made in the first seven months of 2007. About half of these were made during the week of 9 July, when Moody's downgraded 399 tranches. About two-thirds of these downgrades involved securitizations by four issuers who accounted for about one-third of 2006 issuance: New Century, WMC, Long Beach, and Fremont. Note that 86% of the downgraded tranches were originally rated Baa2 or worse, which meant that the notional amount downgraded was only about $9 billion. However, the ratings action affected just under 50 percent of 2006 1st-lien deals and almost two-thirds of 2005 2nd-lien deals, and the mean downgrade severity was 3.2 notches. Table 32 documents the ratings transition matrices for the 2005 and 2006 vintages across 1st and 2nd-lien status as of October 2007. It is clear from the table that ratings action has been concentrated in the mezzanine tranches, but there are some notable downgrades of Aaa-rated tranches in the 2006 vintage of 2nd-lien loans.

In addition to the ratings action, the rating agencies announced significant changes to rating criteria, and took a more pessimistic view on the housing market. At the time of the downgrade action, Moody's announced that it expected median existing family home prices to fall by 10 percent from the peak in 2005 to a trough at the end of 2008. The rating agency also significantly increased its loss expectations for certain flavors of sub-prime mortgages (hybrid ARMs, stated-income, high CLTV, first-time home-buyer), reduced the credit for excess spread, and adjusted its cash flow analysis to incorporate the likely impact of loan modifications.

In response to the historic rating action on subprime ABS during the week of 9 July 2007, the rating agencies were heavily criticized in the press about the timing. In particular, investors pointed to the fact that the ABX had been trading at very high implied spreads since February. Some examples of recent business press:

> "A lot of these should be downgraded sooner rather than later," said Jeff Given at John Hancock Advisors LLC in Boston, who oversees $3.5 billion of mortgage bonds. The ratings companies may be embarrassed to downgrade the bonds, he said. "It's easier to say two years from now that you were wrong on a rating than it is to say you were wrong five months after you rated it." [*Bloomberg*, 29 June 2007]
>
> "Standard & Poor's, Moody's Investors Service and Fitch Ratings are masking burgeoning losses in the market for subprime mortgage bonds by failing to cut the credit ratings on about $200 billion of securities backed by home loans...Almost 65 percent of the

bonds in indexes that track subprime mortgage debt don't meet the ratings criteria in place when they were sold, according to data compiled by Bloomberg." [ibid]

In response, the rating agencies counter that their actions are justified.

"People are surprised there haven't been more downgrades," Claire Robinson, a managing director at Moody's, said during an investor conference sponsored by the firm in New York on June 5. "What they don't understand about the rating process is that we don't change our ratings on speculation about what's going to happen." Bloomberg, 10 July 2007]

From the description of the ratings monitoring process above, it is clear that for unseasoned loans, the rating agencies weight their initial expectations of loss heavily in computing lifetime expected loss on the vintage. While the 2006 vintage did show some early signs of trouble with early payment defaults (EPDs), it was not clear if this just reflected the impact of lower home price appreciation on investors using subprime loans to flip properties, or foreshadowed more serious problems.

Figure 17 documents that the increase in serious delinquencies on a month-over-month basis on the ABX 06-1 and 06-2 vintages was actually slowing down through the remittance report released at the end of April. Figure 18 documents that implied spreads on the ABX tranches retreated from their February highs through the end of May. However, the remittance report at the end of May suggested a reversal of this trend, as serious delinquency accelerated. This pattern was confirmed with the report at the end of June, and the ratings action came approximately two weeks after the June 25 report.

While the aggregated data helps the rating agencies tell a reasonable story, it is certainly possible that aggregation hides a number of deals that were long overdue for downgrade. Given the public rating downgrade criteria, this is a quantitative question that we intend to address with future empirical work.[28]

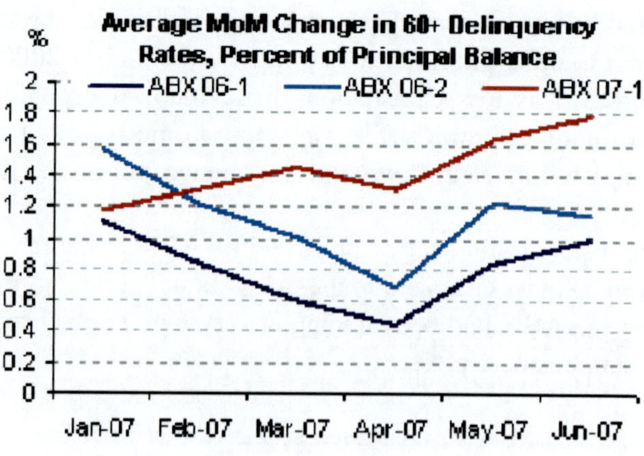

Source: Deutsche Bank, Remittance Reports.

Figure 18. Change in Serious Delinquency on Mortgages Referenced by the ABX.

[28] Note that the rating agencies took another wave of rating actions on RMBS in October.

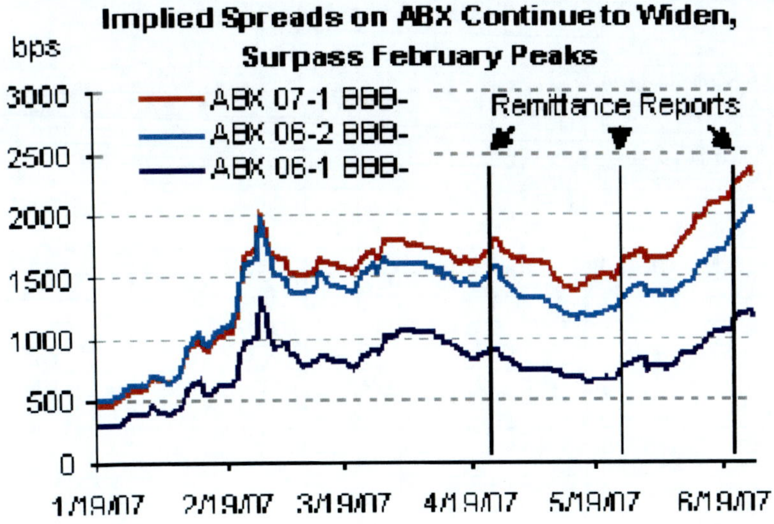

Source: JPMorgan.

Figure 19. ABX Implied Spreads and Remittance Reporting Dates.

Table 31. Rating Changes in RMBS and Home Equity ABS, by Year

Negative rating action									
	Subprime 1st lein			Subprime 2nd lein			Subprime all Lein		
Vintage	$	# tranche	# deals	$	# tranche	# deals	$	# tranche	# deals
2002	2.90%	13.80%	48.80%	1.50%	4.00%	9.10%	2.90%	13.20%	46.40%
2003	1.70%	10.10%	38.50%	0.70%	2.90%	11.10%	10.60%	9.60%	36.50%
2004	0.90%	6.20%	34.30%	1.70%	5.90%	44.00%	0.90%	6.20%	35.00%
2005	0.60%	3.60%	20.90%	3.30%	18.50%	85.40%	0.70%	4.90%	28.00%
2006	13.40%	48.00%	92.10%	60.00%	84.50%	91.80%	16.70%	52.30%	92.00%
Positive rating action									
	Subprime 1st lein			Subprime 2nd lein			Subprime all Lein		
Vintage	$	# tranche	# deals	$	# tranche	# deals	$	# tranche	# deals
2002	2.10%	6.40%	20.80%	6.70%	17.30%	63.60%	2.30%	7.00%	23.50%
2003	2.80%	8.60%	26.40%	9.20%	30.10%	83.30%	2.90%	10.00%	30.50%
2004	1.20%	3.30%	15.00%	7.20%	22.30%	56.00%	1.40%	4.30%	17.90%
2005	0.00%	0.00%	0.00%	5.30%	9.60%	39.60%	0.20%	0.90%	4.40%
2006	0.00%	0.00%	0.00%	0.00%	0.00%	0.00%	0.00%	0.00%	0.00%

Source: Moodys (26 October 2007).

Table 32. Rating Transition Matrices

Current Rating/Last Rating (1st lein)												
2005	Aaa	Aa	A	Baa	Ba	B	Caa	Ca	C	Total	Down	Up
Aaa	100.00%									2,058	0	0
Aa		100.00%								983	0	0
A			99.40%	0.60%						1,003	6	0
Baa				94.90%	3.50%	1.40%	0.20%			1,066	54	0
Ba					81.10%	14.50%	4.40%			318	60	0
Current Rating/Last Rating (2nd lein)												
2005	Aaa	Aa	A	Baa	Ba	B	Caa	Ca	C	Total	Down	Up
Aaa	100.00%									113	0	0
Aa	22.00%	78.00%								100	0	22
A	0.90%	14.70%	81.90%	1.70%	0.90%					116	3	18
Baa				81.50%	9.60%	6.80%	1.40%	0.007		146	27	0
Ba					21.20%	34.80%	0.30%	0.273	0.136	66	52	0
Current Rating/Last Rating (1st lein)												
2006	Aaa	Aa	A	Baa	Ba	B	Caa	Ca	C	Total	Down	Up
Aaa	100.00%									2,121	0	0
Aa		100.00%								1,265	0	0
A			43.90%	27.90%	17.80%	10.10%	0.20%	0.001		1,295	726	0
Baa				17.30%	18.80%	32.40%	13.50%	0.111	0.07	1,301	1,076	0
Ba					6.20%	18.40%	8.20%	0.14	0.531	450	422	0
Current Rating/Last Rating (2nd lein)												
2006	Aaa	Aa	A	Baa	Ba	B	Caa	Ca	C	Total	Down	Up
Aaa	53.80%	34.90%	7.00%	4.30%						186	0	86
Aa		23.50%	38.80%	27.90%	6.60%	1.60%	0.50%	0.011		183	0	140
A			7.00%	32.60%	35.80%	11.80%	0.50%	0.064	0.059	187	0	174
Baa				5.60%	13.60%	17.80%	6.10%	0.145	0.425	214	0	202
Ba					1.00%	6.10%		0.051	0.879	99	0	98

Source: Moodys (26 October 2007).

6. The Reliance of Investors on Credit Ratings: A Case Study

A recent New York Times Editorial (08/07/2007) writes:

> Protecting pensioners from bad investments will not be easy. A good place to start would be to make rating agencies more accountable, perhaps by asking regulators to monitor their quality. Many pension plans lack the analytical skills needed to evaluate these investments, relying on outside advisers and rating agencies. But the stellar triple-A rating assigned to many of these bonds proved to be misleading -- with the agencies now rushing to downgrade them.

In a recent Fortune article by Benner and Lachinsky (5 July 2007), Ohio Attorney General Marc Dann claims that the Ohio state pension funds have been defrauded by the rating agencies. "The ratings agencies cashed a check every time one of these subprime pools was created and an offering was made. [They] continued to rate these things AAA. [So they are] among the people who aided and abetted this continuing fraud." The authors note that Ohio has the third-largest group of public pensions in the United States, and that The Ohio Police & Fire Pension Fund has nearly 7 percent of its portfolio in mortgage- and asset-backed obligations:

> Dann and a growing legion of critics contend that the agencies dropped the ball by issuing investment-grade ratings on securities backed by subprime mortgages they should have known were shaky. To his mind, the seemingly cozy relationship between ratings agencies and investment banks like Bear Stearns only heightens the appearance of impropriety.

In this section, we review the extent to which investors rely on rating agencies, focusing on the case of this Ohio pension fund, drawing upon on public disclosures of the fund.

- Overview of the fund
- Fixed-income investment guidelines
- Conclusions

6.1. Overview of the Fund

The Ohio Police & Fire Pension Fund (http://www.op-f.org/) is a cost sharing multiple- employer public employee retirement system. The fund provides pension and disability benefits to qualified participants, survivor and death benefits as well as access to health care coverage for qualified spouses children, and dependent parents. In 2006, the fund had 912 participating employers from police and fire departments in Ohio municipalities, townships, and villages. Membership in the plan at the end of 2006 included 24,766 retired employees and 28,026 active employees. At the end of 2006, the fund had an investment portfolio of $11.2 billion. The fund's total rate of return was 16.15 percent in 2006 and 9.07 percent in 2005, each relative to an assumed actuarial rate of return of 8.25 percent.

Fund Adequacy

The current actuarial analysis performed on the pension benefits reflects an "infinite" amortization period and a funding level of 78.3 percent. While the fund believes that the current funding status is strong, Ohio law requires that a 30-year amortization period is achieved.[29] A plan was approved by the Board and submitted to ORSC that included major changes to health care funding and benefits, and a recommendation that the legislature amend the law to provide for member contribution increases and employer contribution increases. However, the legislature has not taken action on the recommended contribution increases.

Portfolio Composition

Table 33 documents the exposure of the total fund to different asset classes. At the end of 2006, about 6.7% of total assets are invested in mortgages and mortgage-backed securities.

Table 34 documents the composition of the investment-grade fixed-income portfolio in 2006 and 2005. Non-agency MBS are likely included in the first four columns of the second row, which report the amount of mortgage and MB S broken out by credit rating. At the end of 2006, it appears that the fund held $740 million in non-agency MBS which had a credit rating of A- or better. Moreover, note that the share of non-agency MBS in the total fixed-income portfolio increased from 12% (245/2022) in 2005 to 34% (740/2179) in 2006. In other words, the pension fund almost tripled its exposure to non-agency MBS. Further, note that this increase in exposure to risky MB S was at the expense of exposure to MB S backed by full faith and credit of the United States government, or an agency or instrumentality thereof, which dropped from $489.6 million to $58.9 million.

Table 33. Investment Portfolio

	2006		2005	
	($ m)	%	($ m)	%
Commercial Paper	594.6	5.03%	425.1	3.97
US Government Bonds	596.2	5.04	574.3	5.36
Corporate Bonds and Obligations	783.7	6.62	709.5	6.62
Mortgage & Asset Backed Obligations	799.4	6.76	734.6	6.85
Municipal Bonds		0.00	3.8	0.04
Domestic Stocks	2209.4	18.67	1967.7	18.36
Domestic Pooled Stocks	3181.9	26.89	2957.3	27.59
International Securities	2642.9	22.34	2328.2	21.72
Real Estate	658.	5.56	606.6	5.66
Commercial Mortgage Funds	73.3	0.62	80.4	0.75
Private Equity	291.9	2.47	230.2	2.15
Grand Total	11832.3	100.0	10717.9	100.0

Source: 2006 Comprehensive Annual Financial Report, Ohio Police & Fire Pension Fund.

Table 34. Fixed Income Investment Portfolio for 2006 [2005]

Rating of at least	A-	BBB-	B-	C-	Full Faith & Credit	Unrated	Total
Corporate Bond	$179.9	$73.9	$458.2	$69.5		$2.1	$783.7
Obligations	[$187.6]	[$67.1]	[$416.2]	[$35.8]		[$2.9]	[$709.5]
Mortgage and	$740.4				$58.9		$799.4
ABS	[$245.0]				[$489.6]		[$734.6]
Agency ABS	$37.7						$37.7
	[$3.8]						[$3.8]
Munis	--						--
	[$36.4]						[$36.4]
Treasury Strips					$62.3		$62.3
					[$29.4]		[$29.4]
Treasury Notes					$496.1		$496.1
					[$508.5]		[$508.5]
Total	$958.1	$73.9	$458.2	$69.5	$617.4	$2.1	$2179.3
	[$472.8]	[$67.1]	[$416.2]	[$35.8]	[$1027.5]	[$2.9]	[$2022.3]

Source: 2006 Comprehensive Annual Financial Report, Ohio Police & Fire Pension Fund.

29 Page ix in the 2006 Comprehensive Annual Financial Report, available at http://www.op-f.org/downloads/reports/CAFR2006.pdf.

In order to better understand the motivation for such a shift, consider Table 35, which illustrates spreads on the ABX and credit derivatives (CDS) by credit rating during 2006. While MBS backed by full faith and credit trade at close to zero credit spreads, securities secured by subprime loans pay significantly higher spreads.

Table 35. Subprime ABS vs. Corporate CDS Spreads

	June 2006		December 2006	
	ABX	CDS	ABX	CDS
AAA	18	11	11	9
AA	32	16	17	12
A	54	24	44	20
BBB	154	48	133	43

Source: ABX from Markit tranche coupon; CDS spread from Markit, average across US firms for 5-year contract with modified restructuring documentation clause.

6.2. Fixed-Income Asset Management

From the investment guidelines in the 2006 annual report:

- The fixed-income portfolio has a target allocation of 18% of total fund assets, with a range of 13% to 23%. The portfolio includes investment grade securities (target of 12%), global inflation-protected securities (target of 6%), and commercial real estate (target of 0% and maximum of 2%).
- The investment grade fixed income allocation will be managed solely on an active basis in order to exploit the perceived inefficiencies in the investment grade fixed income markets.
- The return should exceed the return on the Lehman Aggregate Index over a three-year period on an annual basis.
- The total return of each manager's portfolio should rank above the median when compared to their peer group over a three-year period on an annualized basis and should exceed their benchmark return as specified in each manager's guidelines.

Mandates (from ORC Sec 742.11)

1. The main focus of investing will be on dollar denominated fixed income securities. Non- US dollar denominated securities are prohibited.
2. The composite portfolio as well as each manager's portfolio shall have similar portfolio characteristics as that of the Lehman Aggregate Index.
3. Issues must have a minimum credit rating of BBB- or equivalent at the time of purchase.
4. Each manager's portfolio has a specified effective duration band.
5. For diversification purposes, sector exposure limits exist for each manager's portfolio. In addition, each manager's portfolio will have a minimum number of issues.

6 Each manager's portfolio has a maximum threshold for the amount of cash that may be held at any one time.
7 Each manager's portfolio must have a dollar-weighted average quality of A or above.

Note that the Lehman Aggregate Index has a weight of less than one percent on non-agency MB S.

Asset Management

In 2006, the fund's assets were 100% managed by external investment managers. The fixed- income group is comprised of eight asset managers who collectively have over $2.2 trillion in assets under management (AUM). They are (with AUM in parentheses):

- JPMorgan Investment Advisors, Inc. ($1.1 trillion, 2006)
- Lehman Brothers Asset Management ($225 billion, 2006)
- Bridgewater Associates ($165 billion, 2006)
- Loomis Sayles & Company, LP ($115 billion, 2006)
- MacKay Shields LLC ($40 billion, 2006)
- Prima Capital Advisors, LLC ($1.8 billion, 2006)
- Quadrant Real Estate Advisors LLC ($2.7 billion, 2006)
- Western Asset Management ($598 billion, 2007)

The 2005 performance audit of this fund suggested that investment managers in the core fixed income portfolio are compensated 16.3 basis points. The fund paid these investment managers approximately $1.304 million in 2006 in order to manage an $800 million portfolio of investment-grade fixed-income securities. While the 2006 financial statement reports that these managers out-performed the benchmark index by 26 basis points (= 459 - 433), this was accomplished in part through a significant reallocation of the portfolio from relatively safe to relatively risk non-agency mortgage-backed securities. One might note that after adjusting for the compensation of asset managers, this aggressive strategy netted the pension fund only 10 basis points of extra yield relative to the benchmark index, for about $2.1 million.

7. Conclusions

While this paper focuses on the securitization of subprime mortgages, many of the basic issues – intermediation and the frictions it introduces – are generic to the securitization process, regardless of the underlying pool of assets. The credit rating agencies play an important role in resolving or at least mitigating several of these frictions.

Our view is that the rating of securities secured by subprime mortgage loans by credit rating agencies has been flawed. There is no question that there will be some painful consequences, but we think that the rating process can be fixed along the lines suggested in the text above.

However, it is important to understand that repairing the securitization process does not end with the rating agencies. The incentives of investors and investment managers need to be aligned. The structured investments of investment managers should be evaluated relative to an index of structured products in order to give the manager appropriate incentives to conduct his own due diligence. Either the originator or the arranger needs to retain unhedged equity tranche exposure to every securitization deal. And finally, originators should have adequate capital so that warranties and representations can be taken seriously.

REFERENCES

Aguesse, P. (2007). "Is Rating an Efficient Response to the Challenges of the Structured Finance Markets?" Risk and Trend Mapping No.2, Autorité des Marchés Financiers; available at http://www.amf-france.org/documents/general/7693_1.pdf.

Altman, E.I. and H.A. Rijken (2004). "How Rating Agencies Achieve Rating Stability." *Journal of Banking & Finance* 28, 2679-27 14.

Amato, J.D. and E.M. Remolona (2005). "The Pricing of Unexpected Credit Losses." BIS Working Paper No. 190.

Bangia, A., F.X. Diebold, A. Kronimus, C. Schagen, and T. Schuermann (2002). "Ratings Migration and the Business Cycle, With Applications to Credit Portfolio Stress Testing." *Journal of Banking & Finance* 26: 2/3, 445-474.

Basel Committee on Banking Supervision (1996). "Amendment to the Capital Accord to Incorporate Market Risks." Basel Committee Publication No. 24. Available: www.bis.org/publ/bcbs24.pdf.

_______ (2000). "Credit Ratings and Complementary Sources of Credit Quality Information." BCBS Working Paper No. 3, available at http://www.bis.org/publ/bcbs wp3 .htm, August.

_______ (2005). "International Convergence of Capital Measurement and Capital Standards: A Revised Framework." Available at http://www.bis.org/publ/bcbs118.htm, November.

Cagan, Christopher (2007): "Mortgage Payment Reset," unpublished mimeo, May; available at http://www.facorelogic.com/landingpages/caganform.jsp?id=8037.

Cantor, R. and F. Packer (1995). "The Credit Rating Industry", *Journal of Fixed Income* 5:3 (December), 10-34.

Cantor, R. and C. Mann (2007). "Analyzing the Tradeoff between Ratings Accuracy and Stability." *Journal of Fixed Income* 16:4 (Spring), 60-68.

Committee on the Global Financial System (2005). "The Role of Ratings in Structured Finance: Issues and Implications." Available at http://www.bis.org/publ/cgfs23.htm, January.

Duffie, Darrell (2007), "Innovations in Credit Risk Transfer: Implications for Financial Stability," Stanford University GSB Working Paper, available at http://www.stanford.edu/~duffie/BIS.pdf.

The Economist (2007). "Measuring the Measurers." May 31.

________ (2007). "Securitisation: When it goes wrong..." September 20.

Federal Reserve Board (2003). "Supervisory Guidance on Internal Ratings-Based Systems for Corporate Credit," Attachment 2 in http://www.federalreserve.gov/boarddocs/meetings/2003/20030711/attachment.pdf.

Fitch Ratings (2007): "U.S. Subprime RMBS/HEL Upgrade/Downgrade Criteria," Residential Mortgage Criteria Report, 12 July 2007.

Gourse, Alexander (2007): "The Subprime Bait and Switch," In These Times, July 16.

Hagerty, James and Hudson (2006): "Town's Residents Say They Were Targets of Big Mortgage Fraud," Wall Street Journal, September 27.

Hanson, S.G. and T. Schuermann (2006). "Confidence Intervals for Probabilities of Default." *Journal of Banking & Finance* 30:8, 2281-2301.

Inside Mortgage Finance (2007): "The 2007 Mortgage Market Statistical Annual."

Knox, Noelle (2006): "Ten mistakes that I made flipping a flop," USA Today, 22 October.

Kliger, D. and O. Sarig (2000). "The Information Value of Bond Ratings." *Journal of Finance*, 55:6, 2879-2902.

Lando, D. and T. Skødeberg (2002). "Analyzing Ratings Transitions and Rating Drift with Continuous Observations." *Journal of Banking & Finance* 26: 2/3, 423-444.

Levich, R.M., G. Majnoni, and C.M. Reinhart (2002). "Introduction: Ratings, Ratings Agencies and the Global Financial System: Summary and Policy Implications." In R.M. Levich, C. Reinhart, and G. Majnoni, eds. *Ratings, Rating Agencies and the Global Financial System*, Amsterdam, NL: Kluwer. 1-15.

Lopez, J.A. and M. Saidenberg (2000). "Evaluating Credit Risk Models." *Journal of Banking & Finance* 24, 151-165.

Mason, J.R. and J. Rosner (2007). "Where Did the Risk Go? How Misapplied Bond Ratings Cause Mortgage Backed Securities and Collateralized Debt Obligation Market Disruptions." Hudson Institute Working Paper.

Moody's Investors Services (1996). "Avoiding the 'F' Word: The Risk of Fraud in Securitized Transaction," Moody's Special Report, New York,

__________ (1999). "Rating Methodology: The Evolving Meanings of Moody's Bond Ratings." Moody's Global Credit Research, New York, August.

__________ (2003). "Impact of Predatory Lending an RMBS Securitizations," Moody's Special Report, New York, May.

__________ (2004). "Introduction to Moody's Structured Finance Analysis and Modelling." Presentation given by Frederic Drevon, May 13.

__________ (2005a). "The Importance of Representations and Warranties in RMBS Transactions," Moody's Special Report, New York, January.

__________ (2005b). "Spotlight on New Century Financial Corporation," Moody's Special Report, New York, July.

__________ (2007a). "Structured Finance Rating Transitions: 1983-2006." Special Comment, Moody's Global Credit Research, New York, January.

__________ (2007b) "Early Defaults Rise in Mortgage Securitization," Moody's Special Report, New York, January.

__________ (2007c). "Corporate Default and Recovery Rates: 1920-2006." Special Comment, Moody's Global Credit Research, New York, February.

__________ (2007d). "Update on 2005 and 2006 Vintage U.S. Subprime RMBS Rating Actions: October 2007," Moodys Special Report, New York, October 26.

Morgan, Don (2007): "Defining and Detecting Predatory Lending," Staff Report #273, Federal Reserve Bank of New York.

New York Times (2007): "Pensions and the Mortgage Mess," Editorial, 7 August.

Nickell, P, W. Perraudin and S. Varotto, 2000, "Stability of Rating Transitions", *Journal of Banking & Finance*, 24, 203-227.

Scholtes, Saskia (2007). "Moody's alters its subprime rating model." *Financial Times*, September 25.

Sichelman, L. (2007). "Tighter Underwriting Stymies Refinancing of Subprime Loans." *Mortgage Servicing News*, May 1.

Smith, R.C. and I. Walter (2002). "Rating Agencies: Is there an Agency Issue?" in R.M. Levich, C. Reinhart, and G. Majnoni, eds. *Ratings, Rating Agencies and the Global Financial System*, Amsterdam, NL: Kluwer. 290-318.

Standard & Poor's (2001). "Rating Methodology: Evaluating the Issuer." Standard & Poor's Credit Ratings, New York, September.

___________ (2007). "Principles-Based Rating Methodology for Global Structured Finance Securities." Standard & Poor's RatingsDirect Research, New York, May.

Sylla, R. (2002). "An Historical Primer on the Business of Credit Rating." In R.M. Levich, C. Reinhart, and G. Majnoni, eds. *Ratings, Rating Agencies and the Global Financial System*, Amsterdam, NL: Kluwer. 19-40.

Thompson, Chris (2006): "Dirty Deeds," East Bay Express, July 23, 2007.

Tomlinson, R. and D. Evans (2007). "CDO Boom Masks Subprime Losses, Abetted by S&P, Moody's, Fitch." Bloomberg News, May 31.

Treacy, W.F. and M. Carey (2000). "Credit Risk Rating Systems at Large U.S. Banks." *Journal of Banking & Finance* 24, 167-201.

UBS Investment Research (26 June 2007): "Mortgage Strategist."

UBS Investment Research (23 October 2007): "Mortgage Strategist."

Wei, L (2007). "Subprime Lenders May Face Funding Crisis." *Wall Street Journal*, 10 January.

White, L. (2002). "The Credit Rating Industry: An Industrial Organization Analysis." in R.M. Levich, C. Reinhart, and G. Majnoni, eds. *Ratings, Rating Agencies and the Global Financial System*, Amsterdam, NL: Kluwer. 41-64.

APPENDIX 1: PREDATORY LENDING

Predatory lending is defined by Morgan (2007) as the welfare-reducing provision of credit. In other words, the borrower would have been better off without the loan. While this practice includes the willful misrepresentation of material facts about a real estate transaction by an insider without the knowledge of a borrower, it has been defined much more broadly. For example, the New Jersey Division of Banking and Insurance (2007) defines predatory lending as an activity that involves at least one, and perhaps all three, of the following elements:

- Making unaffordable loans based on the assets of the borrower rather than on the borrower's ability to repay an obligation;
- Inducing a borrower to refinance a loan repeatedly in order to charge high points and fees each time the loan is refinanced ("loan flipping"); or
- Engaging in fraud or deception to conceal the true nature of the loan obligation, or ancillary products, from an unsuspecting or unsophisticated borrower.

Loans to borrowers who do not demonstrate the capacity to repay the loan, as structured, from sources other than the collateral pledged are generally considered unsafe and unsound. Some anecdotal examples of predatory lending:

> Ira and Hazel purchased their home in 1983, shortly after getting married, financing their purchase with a loan from the Veterans' Administration. By 2002, they had nearly paid off their first mortgage. The elderly couple got a call from a lender, urging them to consolidate all of their debt into a single mortgage. The lender assured the husband who had excellent credit that the couple would receive an interest rate between 5-6% which would reduce their monthly mortgage payments. However, according to the couple, when the lender came to their house to have them sign the paperwork for their new mortgage, the lender failed to mention that the loan did not contain the low interest rate which they had been promised. Instead, it contained an interest rate of 9.9% and an annual percentage rate of 11.8%. Moreover, the loan contained 10 "discount points" ($15,289.00) which were financed into the loan, inflating the loan amount and stripping away the elderly couple's equity. Under the new loan, the monthly mortgage payments increased to $1,655.00, amounting to roughly 57% of the couple's monthly income.
>
> Moreover, the loan contained a substantial prepayment penalty, forcing them to pay approximately $7,500 to escape this predatory loan.

Source: Center for Responsible Lending (2007).

> In 2005, Betty and Tyrone, a couple living on the south side of Chicago, took out a refinance loan with a lender in order to refurnish their basement. "We just kept asking them whether we were going to remain on a fixed rate, and they just kept lying to us, telling us we'd get a fixed rate," Betty alleges in a lawsuit against lender. As they later discovered, however, the terms of the loan were not as they expected. Not only did the loan have an adjustable rate that can go as high as 13.4 percent, but the couple allege that the lender falsely told them that their home had doubled in value since they had bought it a few years earlier, thus qualifying them for a larger loan amount. As the lender didn't give them copies of their loan documents at closing, and the couple did not realize that the terms had been changed until well after the three-day period during which they could legally cancel the loan. They have since tried to refinance, but have been unable to find another lender willing to lend them the amount currently owed, as the artificially-inflated appraisal value has in effect trapped them in a loan with a rising interest rate.

Source: Gourse (2007).

> One scheme targets distressed borrowers at risk of foreclosure. The predator claims to the borrower that it is necessary to add someone else with good credit to the title, and their good credit will help secure a new loan on good terms. After the title holder uses the loan to make payments for a year, predator claims that the title would be transferred back to the original borrower. However, predator cashes most of the remaining equity out of the house with a larger loan, and leaves the distressed borrower in a worse situation.

Source: Thompson (2006).

The Center for Responsible Lending has identified seven signs of a predatory loan:

- Excessive fees, defined as points and other fees of five percent or more of the loan
- Abusive prepayment penalties, defined as a penalty for more than three years or in an amount larger than six months interest
- Kickbacks to brokers, defined as compensation to a broker for selling a loan to a borrower at a higher interest rate than the minimum rate that the lender would be willing to charge
- Loan flipping, defined as the repeated refinancing of loans in order to generate fee income without any tangible benefit to the borrower
- Unnecessary products
- Mandatory arbitration requires a borrower to waive legal remedies in the event that loan terms are later determined to be abusive
- Steering and targeting borrowers into subprime products when they would qualify for prime products. Fannie Mae has estimated that up to half of borrowers with subprime mortgages could have qualified for loans with better terms

The Role of the Rating Agencies

The rating agencies care about predatory lending to the extent that federal, state, and local laws might affect the amount of cash available to pay investors in residential mortgage-backed securitizations (RMBS) in the event of violations. Moody's analysis of RMBS transactions "includes an assessment of the likelihood that a lender might have violated predatory lending laws, and the extent to which violations by the lender would reduce the proceeds available to repay securitization investors" (Moody's, 2003).

In particular, Moody's requires that loans included in a securitization subject to predatory lending statutes satisfy certain conditions: (1) the statue must be sufficiently clear so that the lender can effectively comply; (2) the penalty to the trust for non-compliance is limited; (3) the lender demonstrates effective compliance procedures, which include a third-party review; (4) the lender represents that the loans comply with statutory requirements and agrees to repurchase loans that do not comply; (5) the lender indemnifies the trust for damages resulting from a particular statute; (6) the lender's financial resources and commitment to the business are sufficient to make these representations meaningful; and (7) concentration limits manage the risk to investors when penalties are high or statues are ambiguous.

Appendix 2: Predatory Borrowing

While mortgage fraud has been around as long as the mortgage loan, it is important to understand that fraud becomes more prevalent in an environment of high and increasing home prices. In particular, when home prices are high relative to income, borrowers unwilling to accept a low standard of living can be tempted into lying on a mortgage loan application. When prices are high and rapidly increasing, there is an even greater incentive to commit fraud given that the cost of waiting is an even lower standard of living. Rapid home price appreciation also increases the return to speculative and criminal activity. Moreover, while benefits of fraud are increasing, the costs of fraud decline as expectations of higher future prices create equity that reduces the probability of default and severity of loss in the event of default.

In support of this claim, the IRS reports that the number of real-estate fraud investigations doubled between 2001 and 2003. Recent statistics from the FBI and Financial Crimes Network (FINCEN) document that suspicious activity reports (SARs) filed by federally-regulated institutions related to mortgage fraud have increased from 3,500 in 2000 to 28,000 in 2006.

The Mortgage Asset Research Institute (2007) estimates that direct losses from mortgage fraud exceeded $1 billion in 2006, more than double the amount from 2005. The rapid slowdown in home price appreciation has made it more difficult to buy and sell houses quickly for profit, is quickly revealing the extent to which fraud permeated mortgage markets. For example,

subprime and Alt-A loans originated in 2006 have experienced historical levels of serious early payment default (EPD), defined as being 90 days delinquent only three months after origination. Moody's (2007) notes that EPDs appear to be driven by borrowers using the loan to purchase for investment purposes, as opposed to borrowers refinancing an existing loan or purchasing a home for occupancy.

Predatory borrowing is defined as the willful misrepresentation of material facts about a real estate transaction by a borrower to the ultimate purchaser of the loan. This financial fraud might also involve cooperation of other insiders – realtors, mortgage brokers, appraisers, notaries, attorneys. The victims of this fraud include the ultimate purchaser of the loan (for example a public pension), but also include honest borrowers who have to pay higher interest rates for mortgage loans and prices for residential real estate. Below, I summarize the most common forms of predatory borrowing.

Fraud for Housing

Fraud for housing constitutes illegal actions perpetrated solely by the borrower in order to acquire and maintain ownership of a home. This type of fraud is typified by a borrower who makes misrepresentations regarding income, employment, credit history, or the source of down payment. A recent example from Dollar (2006):

> A real estate agent would tell potential home buyers that they could receive substantial funds at closing under the guise of repair costs that they would be able to use for their personal benefit so long as they agreed to purchase certain "hard to sell" homes at an inflated price. Brokers would facilitate the submission of fraudulent loan applications for the potential homeowners that could not qualify for the loans. In some cases temporary loans were provided to buyers for down payments with the understanding they would be reimbursed at closing from the purported remodeling or repair costs, marketing services fees and other undisclosed disbursements. The buyers in those cases would falsely represent the sources of the down payments.

Fraud for Profit

Fraud for profit refers to illegal actions taken jointly by a borrower and insiders to inflate the price of a property with no motivation to maintain ownership. The FBI generally focuses its effort on fraud perpetrated by industry insiders, as historically it involves an estimated 80 percent of all reported fraud losses. A recent example from Hagerty and Hudson (2006):

> The borrowers, who include truck drivers, factory workers, a pastor and a hair stylist, say they were duped by acquaintances into signing stacks of documents and didn't know they were applying for loans. Instead, they thought they were joining a risk-free "investment group." Now, many of the loans are in default, the borrowers' credit ratings are in ruins, and lenders are pursuing the organizers of the purported investment group in court. Companies stuck with the defaulting loans include Countrywide Financial Corp., the nation's largest home lender, and Argent Mortgage Co., another big lender. A lawsuit filed by Countrywide accuses the organizers of acquiring homes and then fraudulently selling them for a quick profit to the Virginia borrowers. Representatives of the borrowers put the total value of loans involved at about $80 million, which would make it one of the largest mortgage-fraud cases ever.

A summary by the Federal Bureau of Investigation of some popular fraud-for-profit schemes:

- Property flipping involves repeatedly selling a property to an associate at an artificially inflated price through false appraisals.
- A silent second the non-disclosure of a loaned down-payment to a first lien lender.
- Nominee loans involve concealing the true identify of the true borrower, who use the name and credit history of the of the nominee's name to qualify for a loan. The nominee could be a fictitious or stolen identity.
- Inflated appraisals involve an appraiser acts in collusion with a borrower and provides a misleading appraisal report to the lender.
- Foreclosure schemes involve convincing homeowners who are at risk of defaulting on loans or whose houses are already in foreclosure to transfer their deed and pay up-front fees. The perpetrator profits from these schemes by re-mortgaging the property or pocketing fees paid by the homeowner.
- Equity skimming involves the purchase of a property by an investor through a nominee, who does not make any mortgage payments and rents the property until foreclosure takes place several months later.
- Air Loans involve a non-existent property loan where a broker invents borrowers and properties, establishes accounts for payments, and maintains custodial accounts for escrows.

Source: Federal Bureau of Investigation.

The Role of the Rating Agencies

(Moody's, 1996) claim that the vast majority of all securitizations are tightly structured to eliminate virtually all fraud risk. The risk of fraud is greatest when structures and technology developed for large, established issuers are mis-applied to smaller, less experienced issuers. Moreover, the lack of third-party monitors or involvement of entities with little or no track record increases the risk of fraud. The authors identify three potential types of fraud in a securitization:

- borrower fraud: the misrepresentation of key information during the application process by the borrower

- fraud in origination: misrepresentation of assets by the originator before securitization occurs, resulting in assets which do not conform with transaction's underwriting standards
- servicer fraud: the deliberate diversion, commingling, or retention of funds that are otherwise due to investors; the risk most significant among unrated, closely-held servicers that operate without third-party monitoring.

ComFed is a historical example of fraud in a mortgage securitization:

> The parties involved at ComFed exaggerated property values to increase the volume-oriented commissions that they received for originating loans. To increase underwriting volumes still more, ComFed employees granted loans to unqualified borrowers by concealing the fact that these obligors had financed down payments with second-lien mortgages.

To prevent such instances of lower-level fraud, the originator's entire underwriting process should be reviewed to ensure that marketing and underwriting capacities remain entirely separate. Personnel involved in credit decisions should report to executives who are not responsible for marketing or sales. Underwriters' compensation should not be tied to volume; rather, if an incentive program is in place, the performance of the originated loans should be factored into the level of compensation.

(Moody's, 1996) claim that exposure to fraud can be minimized by the following:

- determine the integrity and competence of the management of the seller/servicer of a transaction through due diligence and background checks
- complete a thorough review of the underwriting process, including lines of reporting and employee compensation, to eliminate interests conflicting with those of investors
- establish independent third part monitoring of closely held entities with little external accountability that originate or service assets
- consider internal and external factors that could influence a servicer's conduct during the life of a securitization

This statement makes it clear that it is largely the responsibility of investors to conduct their own due diligence in order to avoid becoming victims of fraud.

Investors do receive a small but important amount of protection against fraud from representations and warranties made by the originator. Standard provisions protect investors from misinformation regarding loan characteristics, as well as guard against risks such as fraud, previous liens, and/or regulatory noncompliance.

(Moody's, 2005a) documents that an originator's ability to honor it obligation is the crucial component in evaluating the importance of these warranties. An investment grade credit rating often suffices to meet this standard. Otherwise, the rating agency claims that it will review established practices and procedures in order to ensure compliance and adequate tangible net worth relative to the liability created by the representations and warranties.

Appendix 3: Some Estimates of PD by Rating

A credit rating at a minimum provides an ordinal risk ranking: an AAA rating is better (in the sense of lower likelihood of default and loss) than an AA rating which is better than a BBB rating, and so on. More useful, however, is a cardinal ranking which would assign a numerical value such as a PD to each rating. Roughly speaking obligor PDs increase exponentially as one descends the credit spectrum.

The three major rating agencies have seven broad rating categories as well as rating modifiers, bringing the total to 19 rating classes, plus 'D' (default, an absorbing state[30]) and 'NR' (not rated – S&P, Fitch) or 'WR' (withdrawn rating – Moody's).[31] Typically ratings below 'CCC', e.g. 'CC' and 'C', are collapsed into 'CCC', reducing the total ratings to 17.[32] Although the rating modifiers provide a finer differentiation between issuers within one letter rating category, an investor may suffer a false sense of accuracy. Empirical estimates of *PD*s using credit rating histories can be quite noisy, even with over twenty-five year years of data. Under the new Basel Capital Accord (Basel 2), U.S. regulators would require banks to have a minimum of seven non-default rating categories (FRB, 2003).

A detailed discussion of PD accuracy is given in Hanson and Schuermann (2006), but in Table 36 we provide smoothed one-year PD estimates using S&P ratings histories from 198 1-2006 for their global corporate obligor base. We present estimates at both the grade and notch level. Guided by the results Hanson and Schuermann (2006), we assign color codes to the PD estimates reflecting their estimation accuracy, with green being accurate, yellow moderately and red not accurate.[33] Hanson and Schuermann, using a shorter sample period (198 1-2002), show that 95% confidence intervals of notch-level PD estimates are highly overlapping for investment grades (AAA through BBB-) but not so for speculative grades (BB through CCC). Since the point estimates for investment grade ratings are very small, a few basis points or less, it is effectively impossible to statistically distinguish the PD for an AA-rated obligor from an A-rated one. Indeed the new Basel Capital Accord, perhaps with this in mind, has set a lower bound of 3bp for any PD estimate (BCBS 2005, §285), commensurate with about a single-A rating.

---

[30] One consequence of default being an absorbing state arises when a firm re-emerges from bankruptcy. They are classified as a new firm.

[31] The CCC (S&P) and Caa (Moody's) ratings contain all ratings below as well – except default, of course. Fitch uses the same labeling or ratings nomenclature as S&P.

[32] Sometimes a C rating constitutes a default in which case it is included in the 'D' category. For no reason other than convenience and expediency, we will make use of the S&P nomenclature for the remainder of the paper.

[33] Accurate (green) means that adjacent notch-level PDs are statistically distinguishable, moderately accurate (yellow) means that PDs two notches apart are distinguishable, and not accurate (red) means that PDs two notches apart are not distinguishable (but may be so three or more notches apart).

Table 36. S&P one-year PDs in basis points (1981 – 2006), global obligor base. Each entry is the average of two approaches: cohort based on monthly migration matrices and duration or intensity based

Rating Categories	Smoothed PD estimates (notch level)	Smoothed PD estimates (grade level)[34]
AAA	0.02	0.02
AA+	0.06	
AA	0.6	0.8
AA-	1.3	
A+	1.8	
A	1.9	2.1
A-	2.1	
BBB+	4.4	
BBB	8.0	8.5
BBB-	12.6	
BB+	22.5	
BB	40.1	51.9
BB-	71.3	
B+	145	
B	540	368
B-	964	
CCC[35]	3,633	3,633

[34] Note that grade level PD estimates for a given grade, say AA, need not be the same as the mid-point of the notch level PD estimate because a) PDs increase non-linearly (in fact approximately exponentially) as one descends the ratings spectrum, and b) the obligor distribution is uneven across (notch-level) ratings.

[35] Includes all grades below CCC.

INDEX

A

B

D

G

H

I

J

K

L

M

N

O

P

Q

R

X

Y